KU-680-427

Accounting in a Nutshell: Accounting for the Non-specialist

Third Edition

Accounting in a Nutshell: Accounting for the Non-specialist

Third Edition
Janet Walker

AMSTERDAM • BOSTON • HEIDELBERG • LONDON
NEW YORK • OXFORD • PARIS • SAN DIEGO
SAN FRANCISCO • SINGAPORE • SYDNEY • TOKYO

CIMA Publishing is an imprint of Elsevier

CIMA Publishing is an imprint of Elsevier
The Boulevard, Langford Lane, Kidlington, Oxford, OX5 1GB
30 Corporate Drive, Suite 400, Burlington, MA 01803, USA

First published 2008
Reprinted 2010

Copyright © 2009. Published by Elsevier Ltd.
All rights reserved.

No part of this publication may be reproduced, stored in a retrieval system or
transmitted in any form or by any means electronic, mechanical, photocopying,
recording or otherwise without the prior written permission of the publisher

Permissions may be sought directly from Elsevier's Science & Technology Rights
Department in Oxford, UK: phone (+44) (0) 1865 843830; fax (+44) (0) 1865 853333;
email: permissions@elsevier.com. Alternatively you can submit your request online by
visiting the Elsevier web site at http://elsevier.com/locate/permissions, and selecting
Obtaining permission to use Elsevier material

Notice
No responsibility is assumed by the publisher for any injury and/or damage to persons
or property as a matter of products liability, negligence or otherwise, or from any use
or operation of any methods, products, instructions or ideas contained in the material
herein

British Library Cataloguing in Publication Data
A catalogue record for this book is available from the British Library

ISBN: 978-0-7506-8738-6

For information on all CIMA publishing publications
visit our web site at www.elsevierdirect.com

Typeset by Charon Tec Ltd., A Macmillan Company. (www.macmillansolutions.com)

Printed and bound in Great Britain

10 11 12 13 14   8 7 6 5 4 3 2

Working together to grow
libraries in developing countries

www.elsevier.com | www.bookaid.org | www.sabre.org

ELSEVIER   BOOK AID
            International   Sabre Foundation

Contents

v

Part 1

Introduction

About this text

This is a basic text providing self-guided training for non-specialists who need an appreciation of the purposes and use of accounting information. It covers the basic principles of financial and management accounting for those who do not require detailed theoretical or technical knowledge. The text will provide grounding and outline understanding to enable the reader to contribute in the workplace or to progress to further financial studies.

The text demonstrates the subjectivity and limitations of financial information and explains the involvement of the non-financial manager in the accounting process. It has been written assuming no prior financial knowledge, and without the use of accounting jargon.

Who should use this text?

This text is designed primarily for the following groups of people:

◆ Middle and junior managers who deal with financial information without really understanding the content.
◆ Students who are studying accounting as a non-specialist subject, for example on a business studies or engineering course. The text will serve as a basic reference book to be used throughout the course. It will also be particularly helpful in providing the basic grounding which is required before moving on to the more technical and in-depth study of the subject that may be required on some courses.
◆ Students who are embarking on a course of study to become a professional accountant. The basic understanding developed in this book will serve as a valuable base on which to build future professional studies.

The content of the text

The text is suitable for those interested in the accounts of profit-making organisations or not-for-profit organisations. It also gives equal weight to manufacturing and service organisations.

The text is divided into three parts.

Part 1 explains the scope of the text, who it is for and how to use it effectively.

Part 2 begins with a review of the types of people who might use accounting statements and the sort of information that they might need.

Then, it introduces and reviews the main financial accounting statements: the income statement/profit and loss account (or income and expenditure account in not-for-profit organisations), the balance sheet and the cash flow statement. The final chapters of this part explain the basic techniques used to interpret the information contained within these financial statements.

Part 3 covers management accounting and the use of financial information to manage a business. It reviews the analysis and build-up of cost before going on to demonstrate the use of costs in short-term management decision-making. The theme of the use of financial information to manage a business is carried through the next chapter on budgetary planning and control. This part concludes with a chapter demonstrating the main techniques used in making long-term investment decisions.

The final part of the text contains a glossary of the major financial and management accounting terms used in the book, extracted from the Official Terminology of the Chartered Institute of Management Accountants.

How to use this text

The chapters are designed to be read in consecutive order. Knowledge and understanding are built in a cumulative fashion, and the material contained in each chapter builds on the material in preceding chapters.

If your attention is focused on the accounts of not-for-profit organisations, you are advised to read the earlier chapters based on the accounts of profit-making organisations. This is because the same principles apply in both sets of financial statements even though the organisations' ultimate objectives may differ. Similarly, if you are interested primarily in the financial statements of profit-making organisations, you would benefit from working the exercises in Chapter 5.

At convenient points throughout each chapter there are short exercises. You should take the time to try these exercises and think about the solutions. They will help you to test whether you have grasped the basic principles to that stage before proceeding with the subject matter.

At the end of most chapters you will find a series of review questions and self-test questions. The review questions will test your knowledge on the content of the chapter, referring you back to the relevant section of the chapter if you are unable to answer the question. The self-test questions are followed by outline answers, so that you can check your ability to apply your knowledge to a practical situation.

Thorough and diligent use of the self-testing mechanisms will be particularly useful for those readers who are not using the book as a part of a formal course of study.

Part 2

Accounting Statements

Who Needs Accounting Statements?

1.1 Introduction

In the first part of this chapter we will be reviewing the groups of people who might use financial statements and thinking about what sort of information they might need. We will also be looking at the regulatory framework within which published financial statements are prepared.

We will then obtain an overview of the three main published financial statements (the income statement/profit and loss account or income and expenditure account, the balance sheet and the cash flow statement): what they are and what general purpose they serve.

1.2 Who uses financial statements and what sort of information might they need?

The list of people who might need the information provided by financial statements seems to grow longer every day. Some of these people are directly connected with the organisation, for example its employees and managers, others are not directly connected, but they may be affected by its management of finance or by its financial stability, for example the general public.

In this part of the chapter we will look at the user groups listed below. This list is by no means exhaustive but it covers the main categories.

◆ The owners of the business
◆ Managers, employees and prospective employees
◆ Lenders and potential lenders
◆ Customers
◆ Suppliers
◆ The government
◆ Donors/sponsors
◆ The public
◆ Analysts and advisers

> *Exercise*
>
> Look at each category of the users of accounts. Think about whether you belong in that particular user group. You will probably be surprised to realise that you fit into more than just one single category.

1.2.1 The owners of the business

In many small businesses the owner or owners are likely to be those responsible for the day-to-day running of the business. These owners need information to let them know whether they are making enough profits, whether they have sufficient cash to pay their bills as they fall due, to whom they owe money, who owes money to them, etc.

As businesses begin to expand they may raise the money that they need for expansion from people who are not involved in the day-to-day running of the business. One way of doing this is to sell shares in the business and become a limited company. Shareholders are part-owners of the business. Among other things they will be concerned about the profitability of the company and how any profit is to be shared out or distributed to the shareholders. Furthermore, they will be concerned about the prospects for future returns on their investment. Potential future shareholders will also be interested in this sort of information when they are considering whether or not to purchase shares in the company.

Existing and future potential shareholders would also be interested in certain non-financial aspects of the company such as the activities it engages in and its policies, so that they can decide if this is the sort of company with which they wish to be associated.

1.2.2 Managers, employees and prospective employees

The managers of a business need financial information to help them to manage the business. They need past financial information to help them monitor the progress of the business or their part of it, current information to carry out day-to-day operational management and control, and forecast financial information to plan activities in the future.

Employees and trades unions may consult the financial statements when they are negotiating their pay and terms of employment. Current and prospective employees might be wise to use the accounts as a basis for assessing the likelihood that the company will grow and prosper, or will it (and their job!) not exist this time next year?

Exercise

Can you think of a reason why past employees might be interested in an organisation's accounts?

Solution

Will the organisation be able to meet its obligations to pay their pensions? (You may have thought of other, equally valid, reasons for past employees looking at the accounts.)

1.2.3 Lenders and potential lenders

Bankers and others who lend money to an organisation will need information concerning the organisation's ability to make interest payments in the short term and ultimately to repay the loan on its due date. They will also be concerned about the security for their loan, that is does the organisation have valuable items, or assets, that could be sold to raise the money to repay the loan if necessary?

> *Many user groups need short-term historical information (how has the business done and where is it now?) as well as longer-term future information (how well is the business likely to do in the future?).*

1.2.4 Customers

Existing and potential customers will be concerned about whether the organisation will be able to provide the goods or services concerned. Some customer relationships can be relatively long term, in which case the supplier's financial stability can be very important. For example, a potential customer of a building firm would not want the builders to go into liquidation halfway through a construction job. Alternatively, an organisation might wish to ensure that the supplier of its computer support helpline will not suddenly go out of business.

1.2.5 Suppliers

Potential suppliers will need to ensure that their customer will be capable of paying for the goods and services supplied. Furthermore, as we saw above, many customer/supplier relationships are long term and involve a considerable investment of time and money to build up the necessary close relationship. A supplier (or customer) would wish to ensure the long-term viability of the other party before embarking on the work involved.

1.2.6 The government

For example, the taxation authorities will need to consult a company's financial statements and accounts to determine whether there is any taxation liability. Another example of a government body requiring financial information from organisations is the Charity Commission, the regulator and registrar for charities in England and Wales. The Charity Commission requires registered charities to submit an annual return. Other government departments and agencies may require financial and non-financial statistics to monitor the state of the economy.

1.2.7 Donors/sponsors

This category applies particularly to charities. Those people and organisations who donate money to charities, or who otherwise sponsor their activities, might use the financial statements to monitor whether they are happy with the way that the organisation is handling the funds available to it.

1.2.8 The public

This category includes taxpayers and ratepayers. The latter might particularly be interested in studying the local authority's financial statements to see whether they consider their rates are being spent wisely. Pressure groups and other special interest groups might be interested in studying a wide range of companies' accounts.

1.2.9 Analysts and advisers

These are the people who are advising investors, lenders and the general public. They will be advising all sorts of people already considered in this list and so their information needs are likely to be similar. However, they are probably more technically competent to interpret and understand the financial statements.

Exercise

You are already aware that this is not an exhaustive list of the users of accounts. Can you think of three other users that have not been mentioned so far in this chapter?

Solution

You may have thought of some of the following users:

◆ Accountants/auditors
◆ Fund managers
◆ Club members
◆ School parents
◆ Trustees
◆ Solicitors
◆ Information providers
◆ School governors
◆ The courts
◆ Credit-rating agencies
◆ Competitors

1.3 Published accounts and financial statements for internal use

1.3.1 Financial accounts and management accounts

Given the wide range of users that we have discussed and the diversity of their information needs, it should not surprise you to discover that there is a wealth of information available in an organisation's financial statements.

In the first part of this book we will be looking at the accounting information that is usually made available to the public – the published accounts or financial accounts. These include the income statement (also known as the profit and loss account), the balance sheet and the cash flow statement.

In the second part we will look at the additional information that is necessary to help managers to run the business: the internal management accounts which are not usually made available to the public.

We will also be looking at the equivalent of the income statement for not-for-profit organisations: the income and expenditure account.

1.3.2   The regulation of financial reporting

The many users of published financial information need to be confident that it provides a true and fair view of the particular organisation's financial affairs. For this reason a system of regulation has evolved to guide and control the content and presentation of published financial information.

Some of the regulations are contained within company law; others are added by stock exchange requirements for listed companies. The largest body of guidelines and principles is provided by a series of accounting standards, which are issued by the International Accounting Standards Board (IASB). The standards are called International Financial Reporting Standards (IFRSs) and International Accounting Standards (IASs). They contain guidelines on matters ranging from the valuation of assets and accounting for leases to the content of cash flow statements and accounting for taxes.

The regulatory system is continually evolving as the business environment changes: new IFRSs are published as they are needed and existing standards are occasionally revised.

The IASB is composed of representatives with a variety of different skills from a number of different countries. Some members are professional accountants, others are preparers or users of financial statements or academics. The IASB works within a conceptual framework which provides the basis for the formulation of all accounting standards. Before issuing an IFRS the IASB will circulate draft proposals in an Exposure Draft. Comments from the public are then taken into account before the final IFRS is issued.

1.3.3 Generally Accepted Accounting Practice

Generally accepted accounting practice (GAAP) is a summary of best practice in terms of the form and content of financial statements, and acceptable alternatives in respect of accounting policies and disclosures in financial statements. The GAAP is continually reviewed and adapted in response to developments in business and economic needs. UK GAAP does not have any statutory or regulatory authority, unlike the GAAP of other countries such as the USA.

1.4 Three basic questions

Most organisations publish three financial statements, usually annually but sometimes more frequently. These are the income statement (profit and loss account), the balance sheet and the cash flow statement. In general terms these help to provide the answers to three basic questions about an organisation.

No matter which user group we are considering, it is possible to express in very general terms the questions that most users will be asking when they are reviewing an organisation's published financial statements. Basically someone who is reading accounts will be trying to find the answer to one or more of the following three questions.

Question 1: What *return* is this organisation making?
For example, the owners and potential investors will be interested in what sort of return they can earn from their investment in the business. HM Revenue and Customs will wish to calculate the amount of any taxation due. Competitors will be interested in whether the business is earning a higher or lower return than they are achieving themselves. These people will need to know:

◆ What revenue is the organisation generating?

◆ What costs are they incurring in generating that revenue, and do the costs exceed the revenue?

◆ If the organisation is making a profit, what have they decided to do with it? How much has been reinvested in the business for future growth? How much has been taken out of the business by the owners?

Questions of this sort can be answered by looking at the income statement, which will be the subject of the next chapter.

Exercise

In a not-for-profit organisation it is obviously not appropriate to ask 'what return is the organisation making?' Can you think of the sort of questions that might be asked in place of this one?

Solution

◆ What revenue is the organisation generating?
◆ What costs are they incurring in generating that revenue, and do the costs exceed the revenue?
◆ If the organisation is generating a surplus, what have they decided to do with the surplus?

Notice the similarity between these questions and those asked about a profit-making organisation. The main difference is the use of the word 'surplus' instead of 'profit'.

In a not-for-profit organisation these questions can be answered by looking at the income and expenditure account, which is the equivalent of a profit and loss account for these organisations.

We will be studying income and expenditure accounts in Chapter 5.

Question 2: What is the *risk* associated with this organisation?
For example, a potential lender will wish to know whether there is a risk that the money to be lent will not be repaid. A supplier who has been asked to send goods with payment due later will

want to know whether the bill will be paid when it falls due. These people will need to know:

◆ What does the organisation owe to other people?
◆ What valuable items (assets) does the organisation possess as security for my loan?
◆ How much of the business's capital is borrowed and how much has been invested by the owners?

> *The term used to describe the relative proportion of borrowed money and the owner's investment is 'gearing' or 'leverage'. You will be learning about this in Chapter 7.*

One of the first places to look in order to answer questions such as these is the organisation's balance sheet. We will be considering the balance sheet in detail in Chapter 3.

Question 3: Does the organisation have sufficient *cash*?

Later in this book we will see that it is not uncommon for an organisation to be generating a profit or surplus and yet still be desperately short of cash. We will be seeing the reasons for this, which include the need to spend money in advance of making sales or carrying out fund-raising activities. The ability of the organisation to generate cash from its activities and to use the cash wisely is of utmost importance to its survival.

The questions which users will be asking in respect of cash include:

◆ How much cash does the organisation generate from its activities?
◆ Is there sufficient cash to cover the organisation's investment for future growth?
◆ If there is not sufficient cash from the organisation's own activities, what sources are used to make up the cash shortfall?

The cash flow statement will help to provide the answers to these questions. We will be looking at cash flow statements in Chapter 4.

> *A mnemonic that you might find useful to remember 'the three questions' is 'the three Rs':*
>
> ◆ *Return? – income statement (profit and loss account) or income and expenditure account*
> ◆ *Risk? – balance sheet*
> ◆ *Readies? – cash flow statement.*

1.5 Summary

(1) There are many different groups of people who might need to read and understand an organisation's financial statements.

(2) The content and presentation of published financial statements is regulated by a series of accounting standards and partly by company law and, for listed companies, by additional stock exchange requirements.

(3) The three main statements published by most organisations for users external to the business are the income statement (profit and loss account), the balance sheet and the cash flow statement.

Review questions

(1) Why might an organisation's customers and suppliers need to read its financial statements? (Sections 1.2.4 and 1.2.5)

(2) What is meant by the acronym IFRS? (Section 1.3.2)

(3) What is meant by the acronym GAAP? (Section 1.3.3)

(4) What are the three general questions that can be answered by looking at an organisation's financial statements? (Section 1.4)

Self-test question

The H Company is a large supplier of specialist accounting software for businesses. Using the list of user groups given in Section 1.2 suggest one reason why the members of each group might be interested in the information provided by the H Company's financial statements.

Answer to self-test question

You might have thought of another equally valid reason for each group's interest in the information provided by the financial statements.

The owners of the business

They would wish to know whether the company is earning a sufficient profit or return on the money they have invested in the business. They might assess the return in the light of criteria such as any other opportunities they have to invest their money, the risk involved in this type of business, the profits that were earned during the previous year, etc.

Managers, employees and prospective employees

Managers would wish to know whether the company's performance, for example in terms of profitability, could be improved. They might perhaps assess the company's profitability relative to other similar companies or to the H Company's performance for the previous year.

Employees and prospective employees would be interested in information that helps them to decide whether to continue in employment with the H Company or to join them as an employee. They might review the company's profitability and cash flow to assess its ability to continue to pay their salaries and to contribute to their pension fund.

Lenders and potential lenders

Members of this group would be interested in information that will help them to assess whether the company will be able to pay the interest on any loan made to the company. They will also be concerned about the company's ability to repay the loan at the end of the agreed loan period.

Customers

The H Company probably provides after-sales service, perhaps in the form of a helpline that customers can access if they experience problems in using the software that they have purchased from the company. Customers would be interested in information that would help them to assess the H Company's ability to survive and flourish in order to be able to provide this support in the future.

Suppliers

Some suppliers might give credit to the H Company. This means that the suppliers will allow the H Company an agreed period of time in which to pay for the goods or services with which they have been supplied. These suppliers would be interested in information that will help them to assess whether the H Company will be able to pay their bills as they fall due.

The government

The government would be interested in assessing the amount of taxation to be paid by the H Company. They will review the income and the various items of expenditure and will often consult with the company's managers before reaching their decision as to the amount of taxation payable.

Donors/sponsors

This category is not really relevant to the H Company. It applies more to organisations such as charities who receive donations in order to pursue their objectives.

The public

Members of the local community would be interested in assessing whether the H Company will continue to provide employment for the community. They would be interested in information that would help them to assess the H Company's ability to survive and grow in order to be able to provide employment and thus generate wealth for the local community.

Analysts and advisers

An analyst might be interested in assessing the H Company's financial statements in order to advise a client whether or not to invest in the company. The analyst would assess the return and future prospects of the company in the light of criteria such as the risk involved in a business that supplies specialist accounting software and the return offered by other similar businesses.

The Income Statement
(Profit and Loss Account)

2.1 Introduction

In this chapter we will be looking at the income statement (also called the profit and loss account): what it is and what is its purpose. Even if your attention is focused on the accounts of not-for-profit organisations you should read this chapter because the principles that will be discussed apply in the preparation of the income and expenditure account. Throughout the chapter we will be using the following typical example as a basis for our discussion.

Example plc

Income statement for the year ended 31 December Year 7

	£'000	£'000
Revenue		5,590
Cost of sales		4,100
Gross profit		1,490
Distribution costs	340	
Administrative expenses	405	
Other expenses	95	
Total operating expenses		840
Operating profit		650
Net finance costs		50
Profit before tax		600
Taxation		135
Profit for the period		465

2.2 The title of the statement

2.2.1 Public limited company

The statement above is the income statement for Example plc. The acronym 'plc' stands for 'public limited company'. A limited company is one which has sold shares to investors as a way of raising the capital to fund its growth. If you buy a share in a company then you literally do buy for yourself a share in that company's fortunes. If, say, a company sells in total 1 million shares and you buy one share, then you own a millionth share in the company. A millionth of all the valuable items that it possesses, its assets, belong to you and a millionth of all of its profits belong to you. Luckily you will not have to shoulder a millionth of its losses because of the concept of limited liability.

Limited liability means that the people who have purchased shares in the company (the shareholders) have limited their liability to the amount they have paid for their share. If the company goes into liquidation all they will lose will be the amount they have paid or agreed to pay for their share, hence the term 'limited' in 'public limited company'.

The term 'public' means that our company, Example, is free to offer its shares for sale to the public if it wishes. This contrasts with a private company which may not offer its shares to the public. If our company was a private company then its title would be Example Limited.

Exercise

Have a look at the titles of some of the companies that you come across during the next few days. Are they public limited companies (e.g. ABC plc), private limited companies (e.g. XYZ Limited) or are they not limited companies at all (e.g. Bill Jones and Company – without the word 'Limited')?

2.2.2 Income statement for the year

The income statement is a financial statement which shows the profit or loss earned by the business in a particular accounting period. In our case the accounting period is one year but income statements are sometimes published for shorter periods of, say, six months.

An important point to grasp is that the title clearly states that the statement is for Year 7. This means that every item shown in this statement belongs as a cost or revenue in Year 7. For example as regards costs, the statement will not show items that have been paid in advance for Year 8, neither will it show items for Year 6 that were paid late, during Year 7.

Later in this chapter we will see how these cost items – known as prepayments and accruals – are dealt with in the income statement and we will work through a numerical example.

This is the application of the *accruals concept*, which is the principle that revenues and costs are recognised as they are earned or incurred and are matched with one another in the income statement of the period to which they relate, irrespective of when the cash is actually received or paid out.

2.3 Calculating the gross profit

2.3.1 Revenue

The first item shown on the income statement is the revenue. This is the amount to be received from customers in return for the provision of Example's goods or services. As soon as a sale is made it is shown in the income statement, even if the money has not yet been received from the customer. Other terms used instead of 'revenue' include 'sales turnover' or 'sales income'.

You may be starting to appreciate how a company can be showing a profit in its income statement but still have no cash.

The issue of revenue recognition refers to the point in time at which a particular item of revenue can be shown in an income statement. If you think for a moment about the question in the following exercise you will begin to see why this might be an important issue.

Exercise

The J Company manufactures precision measuring equipment to individual customers' specifications. Certain details relating to an order from customer C are as follows:

Enquiry received from customer	11 March
Quotation supplied to customer	17 March
Quotation accepted and order confirmed	27 March
Manufacturing of equipment completed	30 March

Equipment despatched to customer	2 April
Invoice sent to customer	10 April
Customer pays first of three instalments	10 May
Customer pays final instalment	10 July

At what date should the J Company recognise (i.e. show in the income statement) the revenue earned on this order?

Solution

It has taken almost four months for all transactions to be completed in respect of this particular order and we have potentially at least eight different dates on which we could recognise the revenue earned.

The general rule is that revenue is recognised when all of the following criteria have been fulfilled:

◆ The J Company has transferred to the customer the ownership and control of the equipment
◆ The revenue from the order can be measured reliably
◆ The customer has recognised its liability and indicated its willingness to pay for the equipment.

The date on which these criteria are all fulfilled is 2 April.

In this exercise the revenue was recognised in the income statement before the cash was actually received from the customer. Sometimes the issue of revenue recognition works the other way round. The revenue might have been already received from the customer, but it cannot yet be recognised in the income statement.

For example a company that provides mobile phone services might require its customers to pay in advance for phone calls that the customer will make during the following period (prepaid phone calls). If the prepaid phone calls are not used by the end of the period then the prepayment expires and the customer's right to make the calls is lost.

The revenue received for the prepaid calls will be deferred, that is not shown in the income statement, until the customer actually makes the call. Thus the revenue earned will be correctly matched with the costs of providing the calls, in the income statement of a future period when the service is actually used. If the customer does not use the service, that is the credit expires, there will be no future costs against which to match the revenue and it can therefore be recognised as revenue at that point.

By now you should appreciate that the £5,590,000 shown as revenue on Example plc's income statement is almost certainly not the amount of cash that has been received from customers during Year 7. Rather, it is the amount of revenue that has been recognised in respect of the goods sold or services supplied to customers during the year.

2.3.2 Cost of sales

The cost of sales is deducted from the revenue recognised. This is the cost of the goods or services that have been sold to generate the revenue for the period.

An alternative term used to describe cost of sales might be 'cost of goods sold'.

The cost of goods sold is most easily derived for a manufacturing company. For example, in a company which manufactures washing machines it is the actual cost of producing the machines for sale: the materials used, the wages paid to manufacturing labour, the overhead cost of running the factory, etc.

Another term which may be used to describe this type of cost is 'direct cost'. We will return to consider direct costs in a later chapter.

The cost of goods sold would not include 'support costs' such as advertising and head office secretarial costs. These would be included later in the income statement.

It is also fairly easy to derive the cost of sales or cost of goods sold for a retailing organisation such as a supermarket. In this case it would probably be the amount paid to the supplier for the goods to be sold to the supermarket's customers, plus distribution costs and store operating costs.

It is not so easy to derive the cost of sales for a service organisation. For example, for a haulage company the cost of sales might be the actual costs of providing the haulage service to the customer, including fuel costs and drivers' wages. It would not include support costs such as those mentioned earlier.

> *Exercise*
>
> Have a think about the company you work for or a company with which you are familiar. Which costs would you say they should include as a part of cost of sales and which costs should be treated as 'other costs'? You can probably appreciate that the decision as to whether to treat a particular cost as a part of cost of sales or as an 'other cost' calls for some subjective judgement.

2.3.3 Gross profit

This is the first measure of a company's profit which is calculated by deducting the cost of sales from the revenue. It shows whether the company sold its goods and services for more than they cost to provide. You can see that if a company does not make a gross profit then it is really in trouble! It is the gross profit that is used to pay all the other expenses of running the business.

Another term used to describe gross profit is 'gross margin'.

2.4 Calculating the profit for the period

2.4.1 Expenses

These include all the costs which have not been included as a part of cost of sales. The costs in Example plc's income statement have been classified according to function; that is, cost of sales, distribution costs, administrative expenses, etc.

An alternative way in which costs might be classified in an income statement is according to the nature of the cost. If Example plc chose to classify its costs in this way it would show separately the cost of raw materials, the cost of employee benefits, the depreciation cost, etc. regardless of the function that has incurred the cost. The total of the costs would be the same but different cost headings would be shown.

The form of presentation used by Example plc (the functional analysis of costs) probably provides information that is more relevant to the users of the accounts. It enables them to monitor the efficiency of the various functions of the company.

However, the allocation of expenses to individual functions requires the use of some judgement because many resources are shared by more than one function. Therefore the final figure for the total cost incurred by each function can be rather arbitrary. Consequently when this classification is used companies often disclose additional information in the notes accompanying the income statement. This additional information provides detail about staff costs, depreciation expense, etc.

In the next chapter we will discuss the depreciation expense in more detail and look at how it is calculated.

2.4.2   Accruals and prepayments

Whichever way the expenses are classified, it is not simply a case of picking up the expenditure balances from the accounts and showing them as the costs for the year. We have seen that the cost shown in the income statement must be only the cost that relates to the year. Therefore we have to adjust for any items paid in advance (prepayments) or for any bills that are still unpaid or owing (accruals).

For instance, if Example has paid its insurance bill for the period up to the end of March Year 8 then it would not be fair to charge all of that insurance cost as a cost of running the business in Year 7. This would overstate the cost for Year 7 and understate the cost for Year 8. The amount of the insurance that relates to January, February and March Year 8 is deducted from the insurance balance and only the remainder is shown as the insurance cost for Year 7.

Furthermore, Example may have paid its latest head office telephone bill on 30 November Year 7. To be able to include a fair telephone cost for the period it will be necessary to estimate the telephone cost for December and add this on to the amount paid so far. Can you imagine how difficult it is to produce an accurate estimate? It is hard enough to estimate what your own telephone bill will be for the next quarter, but when you are estimating for dozens or even hundreds of telephones and data processing lines, the task is extremely difficult.

In the next chapter we will see what happens to the part of the insurance bill that has been deducted (the prepayment) and to the extra that has been added to the telephone bill (the accrual).

For other types of accrual such as a newspaper advertisement that is still to be invoiced, the accountant often needs to rely on the relevant manager informing the accounts department when invoices are still expected. Those readers who are or who work for budget managers might now appreciate why the accounts department asks them for their accruals at the end of each period.

The amount of £840,000 shown in Example plc's income statement is therefore not simply the total of the balances shown on the company's accounting records. The amounts paid during the year will have been adjusted (albeit often subjectively) to arrive at the best possible estimate of a true and fair cost for the year.

Another subjective item included within the various cost classifications is depreciation. We shall see what this is and how it is calculated in the next chapter.

Attempt the following exercise to adjust for accruals and prepayments. Do not worry if you get it wrong or if you are not quite sure how to begin. The main thing is to ensure that you understand the solution and the reason for the adjustments before reading on.

Exercise

A company rents its office photocopier. The basic rental payments are made in advance and in addition, at the end of each quarter the company pays 2 pence per copy made during the last quarter. The latest invoice for photocopier expenses was paid on 31 March. Relevant information is as follows:

◆ Latest rental payment made on 31 March: £90 for the quarter ended 30 June

- ◆ Number of photocopies taken, 1–30 April = 9,800
- ◆ Photocopier charges account balance as at 30 April = £2,700

What is the correct cost for photocopier charges to be included in the company's income statement for the period ended 30 April?

Solution

	£
Account balance	2,700
Less rental paid in advance for May and June (2/3 × £90)	(60)
	2,640
Plus amount owing for copy charges for April (9,800 × £0.02)	196
Amount to be shown in the income statement	2,836

2.4.3 Operating profit

The profit before interest and taxation is known as the operating profit. Later in this book we will see that this is a very important profit measure because it is the profit over which operational managers can exercise day-to-day control. It is the profit measure which they can most easily influence because it is not affected by factors such as taxation and interest which are largely outside their control.

2.4.4 Net finance costs

The net finance cost is the interest payable on bank loans and other borrowings, minus the interest receivable on any bank deposits and other investments. The company will show the separate figures for interest receivable and interest payable as well as the net figure. This information will be provided either on the face of the income statement or as a separate note accompanying the income statement.

2.4.5 Taxation

Companies pay corporation tax, also referred to as income tax, on their profits. It is outside the scope of this book to examine the taxation charge in any detail but basically companies pay taxation at a very similar percentage rate to that paid by individuals.

However, there are many adjustments which must be made to the profit figure in order to calculate the company's taxable profit. These adjustments will be discussed with HM Revenue and Customs before the final taxation charge is agreed.

2.5 Dividends and retained profits

2.5.1 The profit attributable to the shareholders

Once the taxation charge has been deducted the remainder of the profit belongs to the shareholders: the accounting jargon for this is 'the profit attributable to the shareholders'. All other costs and charges have been paid and the company directors can now distribute or pay out this profit to the shareholders in the form of cash dividends if they wish.

In practice, the directors are unlikely to pay out all the profits in the form of dividends. One reason is that the shareholders may have to pay income tax on the dividends and they may not be too keen on this! However, the main reason for not paying out all the profits is that the profits provide a ready source of finance to help the company to grow. If the company wants to take on more customers and provide more products or services, it will need capital to do this. One of the best places to obtain this extra capital is to use the profits that the business is generating.

Think about the following situation. A company's profit after taxation for the period is £600,000. The directors decide to distribute all of this profit in the form of a cash dividend to the shareholders. At a board meeting a few weeks later the directors are considering a proposal to update some of the company's manufacturing equipment at a cost of £250,000. The update is necessary in order to comply with new legislation.

Since the directors distributed all of the £600,000 profit as dividends a few weeks earlier they will now have to invest unnecessary time and expense in arranging the finance required to update the equipment.

If the directors had planned ahead and thought about the fact that they would need to finance the equipment update they could have retained at least £250,000 of the profit to reinvest in the business.

In practice the decision about how much of the profit should be distributed as dividend is much more complicated than this. However, you should now appreciate the fact that retained profit is an important source of finance for a company. This profit is taken to reserves, which will be discussed in more detail in the next chapter when we look at the contents of the balance sheet.

So how will the shareholders react if they do not receive all of the profit in the form of a dividend? They probably will not mind, for the following reason.

If the value of the company increases as it expands then it follows that the value of a share in the company is also likely to increase. Therefore the shareholders will probably make a capital gain and so will be quite happy not to have received all of the profits in the form of dividends from the company.

Companies usually make two dividend payments each year. An interim dividend payment is made to shareholders part way through the year. This is followed by the payment of a final dividend after the end of the year, once the full year's profit attributable to the shareholders has been determined. The total annual dividend payable to the shareholders in respect of a particular year is therefore the sum of the interim and final payments.

Exercise

Look again at the income statement for Example plc. What would you say is the answer to the question 'what profit did Example plc make in year 7?'

Solution

This is really a bit of a trick question. Any of the following answers would be correct.

◆ Gross profit = £1,490,000
◆ Operating profit = £650,000
◆ Profit before taxation = £600,000
◆ Profit for the period = £465,000

You could even add taxable profit to the list, if we had the figure available. The figure for taxable profit is not shown on a company's income statement. It is derived after various adjustments have been made to the accounting profit for the period, usually in consultation with HM Revenue and Customs.

The problem with the question set in the last exercise was that it was imprecise. You should never refer to profit without specifying to which particular profit measure you are referring.

2.6 Summary

(1) The income statement is also known as the profit and loss account. It is a financial statement which shows the profit or loss earned by the organisation in a particular accounting period.

(2) Every item in a period's income statement is a revenue or cost that relates specifically to that period, irrespective of when the cash is actually received or paid out. Many of the items are estimated amounts which involve subjective judgements.

(3) The costs in an income statement can be classified according to function (cost of sales, distribution expenses, administrative expenses, etc.) or according to the nature of the cost (raw materials cost, employee benefits, depreciation cost, etc.).

(4) There are several different profit measures which can be used to monitor the performance of a business.

(5) Not all the profits attributable to shareholders are paid out as dividends. It is usual for some profits to be retained in reserves to finance the company's plans for growth.

We will look at the interpretation of income statements in a later chapter

---

Review questions

(1) What is meant by 'limited liability'? (Section 2.2.1)
(2) What is the main practical difference between a public limited company and a private limited company? (Section 2.2.1)

(3) What is the accruals concept? (Section 2.2.2)
(4) What is cost of sales? (Section 2.3.2)
(5) How is gross profit calculated? (Section 2.3.3)
(6) What term is used to describe the profit before interest and taxation? (Section 2.4.3)
(7) What is meant by the term 'interim dividend'? (Section 2.5.1)

Self-test questions

(1) Comment critically on the following statement.

'The income statement shows the cash that has been received from customers for sales made during the period. From this is subtracted the money spent on costs in order to calculate the profit or loss for the period.'

(2) The JS Company has just completed its first year of trading, the year ending 30 September Year 3.

Information concerning advertising costs and rent is as follows.

Advertising

Adverts were placed in a trade journal published on 1 March and 1 September. One month's credit is available on all invoices.

Advert placed	Cost	Invoice date	Invoice paid
1 March Year 3	£2,890	6 March Year 3	4 April Year 3
1 Sept Year 3	£3,220	5 Sept Year 3	(not yet paid)

Rent

Rent = £18,000 per annum, payable quarterly in advance.

Payments made during the first year:

4 October	Year 2	£4,500
28 December	Year 2	£4,500
29 March	Year 3	£4,500
29 June	Year 3	£4,500
28 September	Year 3	£4,500

Required

What is the correct charge in the income statement for the year ending 30 September Year 3 in respect of

(a) advertising
(b) rent.

(3) Company S sold goods to Company C for £3,400. The goods were delivered by Company S on 25 September and Company C paid £1,700 in cash. The remaining £1,700 was paid by Company C on 20 October.

In respect of these goods, what amount should be included as revenue in Company S's income statement for the year ending 30 September?

(4) Company R began renting office space from Company L on 1 April Year 5. The annual rent payable is £9,500. During the year ended 31 March Year 6 Company R paid a total of £10,800 rent to Company L.

In respect of this rental contract, what amount should be included as rental income in Company L's income statement for the year ending 31 March Year 6?

(5) Company E supplies web hosting services. A two-year contract was sold to a customer for £1,200 on 1 July Year 7. The customer paid the full amount due on 1 August Year 7. The contract covers the period from 1 July Year 7 to 30 June Year 9.

In respect of this contract, what amount should be included as revenue in Company E's income statement for the year ending 30 June Year 8?

(6) Company G's vehicle rental agreement has remained unchanged for two years. It requires the payment of £5,000 per month for hire costs plus £0.04 per mile travelled, payable at the end of each three month period. The latest vehicle rental invoice was paid on 14 December, relating to the period ending 30 November. The number of miles travelled during December was 8,200.

The balance on the vehicle rental account as at 31 December was £62,200, made up of £55,000 paid for vehicle hire costs and £7,200 for mileage charges.

What is the correct charge for total vehicle rental costs to be included in Company G's income statement for the year ended 31 December?

Answers to self-test questions

(1) The statement is incorrect, because it assumes that the profit for a period is calculated on the basis of the actual cash received from customers and the actual cash paid out to suppliers. In fact the accruals principle is applied. This means that the revenues and costs are recognised as they are earned or incurred and are matched against each other in the income statement of the period to which they relate, regardless of when the cash actually moves into or out of the business.

(2) (a) *Advertising*
The advert placed on 1 September represents a valid cost to be included in the income statement for the year ending 30 September Year 3, even though the invoice has not yet been paid. The correct charge in the income statement for the year is:

£2,890 paid + £3,220 accrued = £6,110

(b) *Rent*
The correct charge for the year is the annual rent figure of £18,000. The income statement will be charged with £18,000 and the extra £4,500 paid in advance is a prepayment.

(3) Company S has transferred the ownership and control of the goods to Company C before the year end. The revenue from the sale can be measured reliably and the customer will pay the amount due at the end of the agreed period of credit. Therefore the whole of the £3,400 revenue from the sale can be included in Company S's income statement for the year ending 30 September.

(4) The period from when the rental contract began on 1 April Year 5 to Company L's year end of 31 March Year 6 is a full year. The amount to be included in Company L's income statement is therefore a full year's rental, that is £9,500. The extra amount of £1,300 paid in advance by Company R will

be deferred to be included as rental income in Company L's income statement for the following year.

(5) The actual date that the customer paid the amount due is not relevant to the revenue recognition decision. The obligation to provide the service and the obligation to pay for it both commenced on 1 July Year 7. The contract is for two years but at the date of Company E's year end of 30 June Year 8 only one year of service has been provided. Therefore only one year of revenue from the contract should be included in Company E's income statement for the year ending 30 June Year 8. The amount to be included as revenue is £600. The amount of £600 paid in advance by the customer will be deferred to be included as revenue in Company E's income statement for the year ending 30 June Year 9.

(6) The correct charge is calculated as follows.

	£
Hire costs for a year (12 months × £5,000)	60,000
Payment for miles travelled (£7,200 to end of November + (8,200 × £0.04) for December)	7,528
Total vehicle rental costs to be included in the income statement for the year	67,528

At the end of the next chapter we will review the effect on the balance sheet of each of the transactions discussed in self-test questions 2–6.

The Balance Sheet

3.1 Introduction

In this chapter we will be looking at the balance sheet: what it is and what is its purpose; what it does and does not show. We will be using a profit-making public limited company as the basis for our discussion. However, the same basic principles apply to the preparation of balance sheets for all types of organisation, ranging from the smallest not-for-profit tennis club to the largest public limited company. Throughout this chapter we will be using the following illustration of a typical company's balance sheet:

Example plc: Balance sheet as at 31 December Year 7

	£'000	£'000
Non-current (fixed) assets		
Intangible assets		250
Tangible assets: property, plant and equipment		2,400
Investments		35
		2,685
Current assets		
Inventories (stocks)	328	
Trade receivables (debtors)	502	
Other current assets	31	
Cash and cash equivalents	120	
	981	
Current liabilities		
Trade and other payables (creditors)	(550)	
Short-term borrowings	(50)	
	(600)	
Working capital		381
Total assets less current liabilities		**3,066**
Share capital		2,200
Reserves – retained profits		350
Other reserves		230
Shareholders' equity		2,780
Non-current liabilities		286
Capital employed		**3,066**

3.2 What is a balance sheet?

3.2.1 The balance sheet must balance

A balance sheet is a statement which shows the things of value that an organisation owns (the assets), as well as the sources of finance used to buy them. The statement is divided into two parts. The top part of Example plc's balance sheet provides details of the assets and the bottom part lists the sources of finance. Logically the total of the two parts must be equal, that is the total value of the assets must be equal to the total amount of finance raised to buy them. In other words, the balance sheet must balance.

If you look at the lower part of the balance sheet of Example plc you will see that the total capital invested in the business (the capital employed) is £3,066,000. This is the total of one part of this balance sheet. The top part shows where this money is invested and in this chapter we will be looking separately at each of these items.

> *Balance sheets are occasionally presented the 'other way up', that is capital is listed in the top part and the assets in the bottom part. You may also see balance sheets presented 'side by side' with the capital on the left-hand side and the assets on the right. In practice you will come across a number of different balance sheet layouts but they all follow the same basic principles. We will return to look at different balance sheet presentations once we have reviewed the individual items within the balance sheet.*

The order in which an organisation chooses to present its balance sheet items makes no difference to the fundamental information that the balance sheet portrays: the assets that the organisation owns and the sources of finance used to purchase these assets.

3.2.2 The balance sheet date

Look carefully at the title of the balance sheet. Then turn back and look at the title of the income statement at the beginning of Chapter 2. Can you see the difference? The title of the income statement clearly indicates that it shows the results for the whole year, whereas the balance sheet states *as at* 31 December Year 7. The balance sheet is like a photograph of the business taken on the last day of the company's financial year.

Many asset balances are constantly changing, and the balances shown on the balance sheet for some assets, for example inventory (stock) and cash, may be nothing like the balances that were in the business at the end of, say, November. Furthermore they are highly likely to be different again by the end of January Year 8.

All the balances shown on the statement are simply the balances that existed on the last day of the company's financial year. This will be an important point to bear in mind when you come to learn about the interpretation of financial statements.

The values of some of the items on the balance sheet are more likely to change than others. You will appreciate which are likely to change once you have finished studying this chapter.

3.2.3 The use of columns in the balance sheet

People are often confused by the use of columns in the balance sheet. Before going on to the detail of the balance sheet, and to learn the meaning of each of the terms, look carefully at Example plc's balance sheet and check that you can see which figures have been added together to derive each total and subtotal.

The columns in the balance sheet are used to calculate any required subtotals. For example, a separate column is used to calculate the current asset total of £981,000 and then the current liabilities of £600,000 are deducted from this. The net balance of £381,000 is called the 'working capital' (also referred to as the net current assets). This final total is brought out into the end column to be added to the total of non-current (fixed) assets.

The columns have no particular meaning: they are simply providing space to do separate subtotal calculations, so that the right-hand column does not become too cluttered.

3.3 Capital expenditure and revenue expenditure

When money is put into a business there are basically two areas in which it can be invested. It can either be used to purchase items that are going to be kept in the business for several years or it can be invested in or used to pay for items that will be used relatively rapidly in the day-to-day running of the business.

Items which are going to be kept for several years and which are not bought with the intention of resale are called fixed assets. Another term used to describe fixed assets is non-current assets.

Examples are buildings, machinery, office equipment and vehicles. Money spent on fixed or non-current assets is called capital expenditure and it will benefit the business for several years.

You might sometimes hear accountants use the term 'capex' when they are referring to capital expenditure.

Money spent on day-to-day running costs where the benefit will be rapidly used up is called 'revenue expenditure'. Examples are salaries, telephone bills and the purchase of inventory items for resale.

Revenue expenditure is sometimes called operating expenditure, a term which you might hear abbreviated to 'opex'.

It is easy to see that the first two items in this list (salaries and telephone bills) are items of a short-term nature and that the benefit from the expenditure will be rapidly used up. The purchase of inventory is slightly different. The inventory is an asset of the business (it has value) but because the intention is to use it relatively quickly for resale, it is classified as a current asset. You can see that Example plc has some inventory included under current assets in the balance sheet. As a general rule, current assets are those which are going to be used up within a year.

Now that you have a general idea of the different types of expenditure in a business, we will look in detail at each of the items on Example plc's balance sheet.

3.4 Non-current (fixed) assets

3.4.1 Tangible and intangible non-current assets

We have already seen that non-current assets are those assets which are going to be kept and used in the business for several years. If you look at Example plc's balance sheet you will see that the first two types of non-current asset shown are intangible non-current assets and tangible non-current assets. Tangible non-current assets are those which have a physical identity, for example office equipment and delivery vehicles. Intangible non-current assets are those which do not have a physical identity, but which have some value to the business, for example patents and trademarks.

Another intangible non-current asset that you might come across is goodwill. We will return to discuss goodwill later in the chapter.

3.4.2 Depreciation

You should recall that the income statement for the year shows the fair cost of running the business for the year. Think about what happens when a non-current asset, for example a delivery van costing £22,000, is purchased.

The £22,000 is paid out to the supplier, but it would not really be fair to charge the whole of that £22,000 in the income statement for the year. Otherwise the profit for that year would be relatively low and then in later years the business would be using the vehicle without suffering any charge in the income statement for the year. Profits would be distorted, and managers and others who are using the accounts would not find it easy to monitor the business's performance.

This problem is resolved by sharing out the original cost of the asset over the years that will benefit from its use. Suppose in our example of the delivery van we assumed that it would last the business for four years, after which time it would be sold for £2,000. This means that over the years we are using it we will have used up £20,000 of the van's value (£22,000 cost less £2,000 final sales value). A fair share of the loss of value for each year could therefore be £5,000.

$$\frac{£22,000 - £2,000}{4 \text{ years}} = £5,000 \text{ per year}$$

This £5,000 is known as the depreciation charge for the year.

This method of calculating depreciation is called straight-line depreciation. Other methods commonly used charge greater amounts in the earlier years and less in the later years of the asset's life.

The depreciation charge is applied as follows:

Year 1   In the first year of the van's life, £5,000 depreciation will be charged to the income statement, as the fair cost of using the van for the year. The remaining £17,000 (£22,000 less £5,000) will be shown in the balance sheet at the end of Year 1 under tangible non-current assets. This £17,000 is known as the *net book value* of the non-current asset. Other terms that might be used instead of net book value are *carrying value, net book amount* or *written down value.*

Year 2 In the second year, another £5,000 depreciation will be charged in the income statement for Year 2. The remaining £12,000 will be shown in the balance sheet at the end of Year 2 under tangible non-current assets.

The value of the delivery van used up by the business will thus be shared out over the years that receive the benefit.

48

	Charge to income statement	Net book value shown in balance sheet at end of year
	£	£
Year 1	5,000	17,000
Year 2	5,000	12,000
Year 3	5,000	7,000
Year 4	5,000	2,000
	20,000	

Notice that the final value shown in the balance sheet at the end of the van's useful life is £2,000, that is the amount we expect to sell it for.

Exercise

A landscape gardening company has purchased a new fleet of lawnmowers for £5,000. They expect to use the lawnmowers for three years, after which time they will be sold for a total of £500. Using straight-line depreciation (equal depreciation charges for each year) produce a table which shows, for each of the three years, the depreciation charge in the income statement and the net book value of the lawnmowers to be shown in the balance sheet.

Solution

Annual depreciation charge $= \dfrac{£5,000 - £500}{3} = £1,500$ per annum

	Depreciation charge to income statement	Net book value shown in balance sheet at end of year
	£	£
Year 1	1,500	3,500
Year 2	1,500	2,000
Year 3	1,500	500
	4,500	

3.4.3 Cost sharing, not valuation

It is important for you to appreciate that the aim of the depreciation charge is simply to share out the cost of the asset over the years that it is used. In the example of the delivery van, the £17,000 shown in the balance sheet for Year 1 is simply the amount of the delivery van's cost left in the accounts which has not yet been shared out or charged to the income statement. It is not a valuation of the asset, therefore the term 'net book value' can be rather misleading.

We could just as easily, and quite defensibly, have stated that the van would last for five years instead of four years. The annual depreciation charge would then be £4,000 [(£22,000 − £2,000)/5] and the net book value at the end of Year 1 would be £18,000 (£22,000 less £4,000 depreciation). The same asset, in the same business, is apparently 'worth' £1,000 more and the profit for the year is £1,000 more.

In this example the figures involved are relatively small, but imagine what a difference a change in depreciation policy could make in companies with a very large investment in non-current assets, for example aircraft and expensive manufacturing machinery. For this reason companies are required to state their depreciation policy in their published accounts.

To give you an idea of what this statement might say, here is the statement of depreciation policy from the 2007 Annual Report of

Thorntons plc, the manufacturer, retailer and distributor of high quality confectionery. The statement is included in the section headed 'Accounting policies'.

> All property, plant and equipment, other than land and assets in the course of construction, are depreciated to write their cost down to residual value over their remaining useful lives by equal annual instalments, as follows:

> ***In equal annual instalments:***
>
> | | |
> |---|---|
> | Freehold premises | 50 years |
> | Short leasehold land and buildings | Period of the lease |
> | Retail fixtures and fittings | Up to 5 years |
> | Retail equipment | 4 to 5 years |
> | Retail store improvements | Up to 10 years |
> | Other equipment and vehicles | 3 to 7 years |
> | Manufacturing plant and machinery | 10 to 15 years |
> | Computer software and licences | 3 to 5 years |

The statement uses the term 'residual value' to refer to the forecast value of the asset at the end of its estimated useful life. This is the amount for which it is expected the asset will be sold after three years or after ten years, or after whatever period the company expects to keep the asset for its own use.

Notice also that the policy involves charging depreciation in equal annual instalments. This means that Thorntons are using the straight line method of depreciation that you learned about in the last section.

3.4.4 Amortisation

Amortisation is similar to depreciation but the term is usually used to describe the 'depreciation' of intangible non-current assets. For example, J Sainsbury plc, a leading UK food retailer, includes in its accounting policy statement for 2007 the following in the section headed 'Intangible assets'. The extract is reproduced by kind permission of Sainsbury's Supermarkets Ltd.

> Pharmacy licenses are carried at cost less accumulated amortisation and any impairment loss and amortised on a straight-line basis over their useful economic life of 15 years.

You can see that the effect of the amortisation charge is the same as that of a depreciation charge. The cost of acquiring a pharmacy licence is spread over the income statements of the 15 years that benefit from the acquisition of the licence. At the end of each year the balance sheet will show the amount of the original cost that has not yet been 'shared out' to any of the income statements, that is the licences are stated ('carried') in the balance sheet at their original cost less the accumulated amortisation to date.

In addition to this systematic amortisation charge, as stated by Sainsbury's in the above extract, there may be a further charge for an impairment loss. This means that Sainsbury's reviews the carrying amounts (the balance sheet values) of its pharmacy licences every year, to check that the true value is not below the balance sheet value. If there is a reduction in value this is called an *impairment loss*. The net book value of the asset is reduced immediately and the loss is recognised in the income statement for the year. This will be in addition to the systematic amortisation charge that is made every year.

3.4.5 Revaluing non-current (fixed) assets

Some non-current assets may increase in value; for example, property values tend to increase over time. In this situation the company may revalue the property, based on the advice of a suitably qualified professional. Depreciation of the property must then be based on the new, higher revalued figure in the balance sheet, using the same principles that you learned about earlier. For this reason you might see the statement 'tangible non-current assets are shown at cost or valuation, less accumulated depreciation'.

You might think that it is strange to depreciate properties, but they do not last forever! Most types of property are depreciated over a long time period of, say, 50 years.

> The statement of Thorntons plc's depreciation policy in Section 3.4.3 indicates that the company depreciates its properties over 50 years.

Of course a revaluation will not always reveal a significant increase in value. If a company chooses to revalue its non-current assets it must do so on a regular basis. The frequency of the valuation depends on the volatility of the values of the particular assets. When an item of property, plant and equipment is revalued, the whole of the class of assets to which it belongs must be revalued at the same time. These rules prevent a company from picking out for revaluation only those assets whose updated values might present more favourable results in the financial statements.

3.4.6 Investments

A company may decide to buy shares in another company and hold them on a long-term basis. These shares would be shown under non-current assets as investments. If you look at Example plc's balance sheet you will see that they are holding £35,000 of non-current asset investments. There are many reasons why one company might decide to buy shares in another, including the following:

◆ To gain some control over the supply of an important material or component.
◆ To spread or reduce their business risk. To give a simplified example of this, a manufacturer of sun hats might purchase shares in a company which manufactures raincoats. Then, come rain or shine, the company should be able to earn a profit!
◆ To engage in a joint venture which is beneficial to both companies.

   Sometimes you might see investments listed under current assets. These are shares which the company has bought as a short-term investment and they are usually held for less than one year.

3.5 Working capital

3.5.1 The flow of money round the working capital cycle

The remainder of an organisation's money that is not invested in non-current assets will be invested in its working capital. Figure 3.1 shows how money flows around the working capital cycle.

Imagine that you are starting a new business. Let us assume that the business is going to produce decorated plant pots to sell in garden centres. Once you have raised some money or capital,

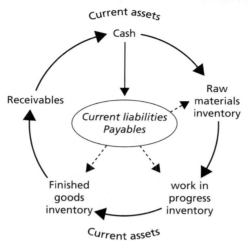

Current assets

Cash

Receivables

Current liabilities
Payables

Raw
materials
inventory

Finished
goods
inventory

work in
progress
inventory

Current assets

Figure 3.1 The Working Capital cycle

you might purchase the non-current assets that you need for your operations (for example, a kiln, office equipment, delivery vehicles, and so on). The remainder of the money will initially be held as a current asset in the form of cash.

Remember that current assets are generally those that are going to be used up within a year.

Now the business will need to start using that cash to produce plant pots that can be sold at a profit. First you must buy some raw materials inventory (stock): clay, paint and so on. Some of the current asset of cash has now been converted into a different form of current asset: raw materials inventory. Now you will need to start converting the raw materials into saleable plant pots. Cash will be spent on wages, power, telephone bills, etc. as the business carries on its operations and converts some of the materials into pots. A point will be reached where the material is no longer basic untouched raw material, but neither is it in a state to sell to the customer. This is known as work-in-progress inventory, another form of current asset.

Finally, after more cash has been spent on day-to-day running costs (remember this is called 'revenue expenditure' or 'operating expenditure') the work in progress is converted into finished goods inventory: another type of current asset.

You should be able to trace the movement of cash in the flower pot business round the working capital cycle in Figure 3.1.

Now it is time to deliver the pots to the garden centre to sell them. The cash from the sale can then be used to buy more raw materials, convert this into work in progress, etc. round the cycle again. Unfortunately it is not that simple!

Most businesses work on credit. The customer (in this case the garden centre) will usually expect to be given time to pay. This means that the current asset of finished goods inventory, once sold, is converted into a different form of current asset: trade receivables or debtors. You can see this in Figure 3.1. Receivables or debtors are customers who are taking time to pay for the goods or services that they have received.

Another term often used instead of debtors or trade receivables is 'accounts receivable'.

Eventually the customers should pay what is owed, and the cash can then be sent off again round the working capital cycle.

Contrast the circulating nature of the investment in working capital with the more permanent nature of the investment in non-current assets.

You should be able to appreciate that in some businesses it may take quite a long time for cash to move round the cycle described so far. Meanwhile, cash is being continually pumped into the cycle every day. If no cash comes out 'the other end' then the business will very soon grind to a halt because it is starved of cash. Therefore it is vital to control the working capital cycle, to keep the cash moving round as quickly as possible, rather like the blood in a human body. If the blood stops pumping, the body will die!

A slight buffer is provided by trade payables or creditors. A credit-worthy business should be able to obtain credit for many of the items and services that it purchases. Trade payables or creditors are people who are giving the business time to pay. Therefore it is possible, for example, to start some raw materials moving round the cycle before the cash has to be found to pay for them.

Another term often used instead of creditors or trade payables is 'accounts payable'.

Eventually the business will have to find the cash to pay the creditors and it is vital that it is there when it is needed. In the next chapter we will see that cash flow forecasting helps to ensure that cash is available when it is needed.

Exercise

Can you think of one type of business that would have a relatively short working capital cycle, that is where cash would not take long to travel round the cycle to be converted into cash once more? And can you think of a type of business that would have a relatively long working capital cycle?

Solution

A retailing organisation such as a supermarket chain would have a relatively short working capital cycle. Inventories are not held for long because they may be perishable, and trade receivables may be non-existent because the majority of customers pay for their goods in cash.

A heavy manufacturing organisation such as a shipbuilder would have a relatively long working capital cycle. It takes a long time to convert the raw materials into finished goods, etc.

3.5.2 Valuing the working capital

The layout of Example plc's balance sheet shows the amount of money invested in the company's working capital on the date that the balance sheet was prepared. Looking at Example plc's balance sheet you will see that the total value of the working capital is £381,000.

Extract from Example plc's balance sheet as at 31 December Year 7

	£'000	£'000
Current assets		
Inventories (stocks)	328	
Trade receivables (debtors)	502	
Other current assets	31	
Cash and cash equivalents	120	
	981	
Current liabilities		
Trade and other payables (creditors)	(550)	
Short-term borrowings	(50)	
	(600)	
Working capital		381

The current assets are listed together and a subtotal is given for their value (£981,000). From this the value of the current liabilities is deducted (the payables and the borrowings: £600,000) to arrive at the total value for working capital.

> *Just to remind you what the second column in the balance sheet is for! This is simply a 'working column' so that the value of the working capital can be calculated without cluttering the end column. The 'answer' to the calculation, that is the value of the working capital (£981,000 − £600,000 = £381,000), is brought out into the end column.*

Many balance sheets do not use the term 'working capital' to describe this balance (£381,000). Instead they use the term 'net current assets'. What does this mean?

In accounting, 'net' means 'after something has been deducted'. Hence your salary slip might show first the gross salary, then the deductions for tax, pension, etc. to arrive at the *net* salary. Therefore, if you see the word 'net' in an accounting statement you simply have to look further up the statement to see what has been deducted. In this case the current liabilities have been deducted from the current assets to deduce the net value remaining, that is the net current assets.

In some organisations the current liabilities exceed the current assets. In this situation the balance sheet would show 'net current liabilities' instead of 'net current assets'. This does not necessarily mean that they are in financial trouble! Many organisations thrive with net current liabilities, or negative working capital.

For example, the balance sheets in the 2007 annual reports of Tesco plc and of J Sainsbury plc, both major supermarket retailers, show figures for net current liabilities of £3,576 m and £781 m as at 24 February 2007 and 24 March 2007, respectively.

A supermarket retailer's inventories are very liquid, which means they can be converted very quickly into cash. New supplies are received every day and the majority of customers do not receive credit on their purchases. Therefore the speed of rotation of the working capital cycle is very rapid and a supermarket does not necessarily need a large positive figure for the investment in working capital in order to be able to generate the cash to pay its way on a daily basis.

Exercise

Before going on to consider each item of working capital in detail, check your understanding by calculating the value of this company's working capital.

Balances at 31 December Year 6: Cash £130, Trade payables (creditors) £760, Trade receivables (debtors) £980, Inventory (stock) £840, Bank overdraft £320.

Solution

Current assets = £130 + £980 + £840 = £1,950
Current liabilities = £760 + £320 = £1,080
Working capital = net current assets = £1,950 − £1,080 = £870.

Remember that this is the working capital balance only at the balance sheet date. It might have been totally different one day before and will almost certainly be different in one month's time.

3.5.3 Current assets: Inventory (stock)

In Figure 3.1 there were three types of inventory: raw materials, work in progress and finished goods. Valuing these inventories for the balance sheet involves some subjective judgement. This will become obvious as we now discuss each type of inventory in turn.

Raw materials inventory

For example, consider the case of the raw materials purchased by your plant pot business. Suppose that, at the year end, the business was holding a number of containers of paint in inventory which need to be valued. A logical way to value them might be to look up the invoices and find out how much was paid for them. This is in fact the accounting practice recommended in the international accounting standard: 'inventories should be measured at the lower of cost and net realisable value'.

> Net realisable value is the amount that the items can be sold for, less any amount that has to be spent to complete the sale.

But what if several batches of paint are muddled together, some of which cost £5 each, some cost £6 each, and some cost, say, £7 each. Which price should be used?

The answer is that there are two possible prices that could be used for the published accounts. Inventories can be valued either at the price of the latest items received (this is the 'first in, first out' or FIFO valuation method) or at a weighted average price of all the items held in inventory. Management is free to select the method that they feel is most appropriate, but once an inventory valuation method is selected it must be applied consistently. It is not acceptable to continually change the inventory valuation method in use.

> For internal management accounting purposes any inventory valuation method may be used, as long as it provides information that is useful to managers.

The following extract from the 2006/2007 annual report for Whitbread plc, a leading UK hospitality company, will demonstrate how a company might explain its inventory valuation policy:

> Inventories are stated at the lower of cost and net realisable value. Cost is calculated on the basis of first in, first out and net realisable value is the estimated selling price less any costs of disposal.

Work in progress inventory

Valuing work in progress can be even more problematic. Imagine that your business has some plant pots that have been painted, but which are awaiting finishing and packing. Following the 'lower of cost and net realisable value' rule we could value them by working out the cost incurred so far.

We can determine the value of the raw materials that have gone into them, and we should be able to work out the wages incurred in making and painting them, although of course there would be some subjective judgement involved in this. We should also be able to calculate a reasonable charge for the overhead cost incurred so far (the power to run the kiln, etc.) and add this on to the total value.

In a later chapter you will be looking at how the overhead cost is determined for each item produced.

An item of work in progress would therefore have a higher value than the basic raw material, because wages and overhead costs have been incurred in beginning to convert it into a finished product.

However, if you tried to sell a part-finished plant pot it would probably be very difficult. You would almost certainly have more trouble selling it than you would if you tried to sell the untouched basic raw material. Therefore in practice the work in progress has very little value, certainly a lower value than we are placing on it. Are we overstating its value?

The point is that the business will not be trying to sell a part-finished plant pot. The intention is to incur further cost in finishing and packing the pot ready for sale. Therefore the part-finished pot has a greater *value to the business as a going concern* than the untouched raw materials.

The going concern concept assumes that the business will continue in operation for the foreseeable future. Therefore the assets should be valued on this basis and not on the basis of what they could be sold for if the business was broken up.

Finished goods inventory

Finished goods inventory is also valued at the lower of cost and net realisable value and of course its unit value will be higher than the work in progress. This is because yet more costs will have been incurred in bringing each item to its finished condition.

The policy statement in Thorntons plc's 2007 annual report is even more detailed. It demonstrates the practical application of many of the principles we have discussed so far concerning the valuation of inventory.

> Inventories are stated at the lower of cost and net realisable value. Cost includes materials, direct labour and an attributable proportion of manufacturing overheads, based on normal operating capacity, according to the stage of production reached. Net realisable value is the estimated value which would be realised after deducting all costs of completion, marketing and selling. Provision is made to reduce the cost to net realisable value having regard to the age and condition of inventory, as well as its anticipated saleability.

3.5.4 Current assets: Receivables (debtors)

Current assets are usually arranged on a balance sheet in reverse order of liquidity, that is in the order of how difficult they are to turn into money. Inventory is the least liquid current asset because it is necessary to find a customer for it, and then give the customer credit, before the cash is finally received. Inventories therefore appear first in the list of current assets. Next in order of liquidity comes receivables, which are shown below inventories on Example plc's balance sheet.

Exercise

You have seen that the valuation of inventory is subjective. Can you think of a reason why the valuation of receivables for the balance sheet might also be subjective?

Solution

Some of the customers might not pay their bills!

Although it is fairly straightforward to work out how much money is owed to the business by its customers, some subjective judgement is involved in determining how much of this is actually likely to be received. The business may know of certain customers who are in difficulties and will not pay. These debts can be written off as bad debts and they are not shown as a valuable asset on the balance sheet. The trade receivables balance on the balance sheet is reduced by the amount of the bad debt, and the amount of the debt written off is charged as an additional expense in the income statement.

However, the managers may know from past experience that other customers are also unlikely to pay, but they may not be able to pinpoint which specific customers these are. Therefore it is common practice to make a provision for doubtful debts in addition to writing off the definite bad debts.

Exercise

X Limited has trade receivables balances of £345,000 at the year end. Included in these balances is a customer who owes £5,000 but who has gone into liquidation, informing X Limited that he is unlikely to be able to settle any of the outstanding debt. After writing off this debt, X Limited wishes to make a general provision for doubtful debts equal to one per cent of the remaining balances.

What amount should be shown as trade receivables on X Limited's balance sheet?

Solution

General provision for doubtful debts = 1% × (£345,000 − £5,000)
= £3,400

Trade receivables balance for balance sheet

= £345,000 − £5,000 − £3,400
= £336,600

It should be clear to you that a degree of subjectivity is involved in identifying bad debts and in making an appropriate provision for doubtful debts.

For example, in the last exercise the directors of X Limited might have decided that a one per cent general provision for doubtful debts was sufficient based on very accurate historical records of customer payment patterns. However, no matter how accurate the records are, the past is never a completely reliable guide to what will happen in the future.

Perhaps X Limited has recently begun trading with a completely new set of customers. These customers might be more likely or less likely to default on their debts. In either case the one per cent provision will not be the correct amount. These customers might be more likely to be bad payers and thus the provision should be, say, two per cent instead of one per cent. An additional £3,400 provision is required.

The important point to grasp is that the amount shown on a company's balance sheet for trade receivables is likely to have undergone some subjective adjustments before the final figure is settled on. The BT Group plc, a leading provider of communications solutions and services, explains in detail to the readers of its 2007 annual report how bad and doubtful debts have been provided for as follows.

> BT provide services to around 18 million individuals and businesses, mainly on credit terms. We know that certain debts due to us will not be paid through the default of a small number of our customers. Estimates, based on our historical experience are used in determining the level of debts that we believe will not be collected. These estimates include such factors as the current state of the economy and particular industry issues.

BT is obviously very careful to ensure that the provision for doubtful debts is as accurate as possible. But there is no escaping the fact that the final result will always be an estimate based on past experience. The provision might be too high or it might be too low; it is unlikely to be exactly correct.

3.5.5 Current assets: Prepayments

In Chapter 2 we saw how the charge to the income statement for some expenses was adjusted if payments had been made in advance. For example, if insurance has been paid in advance for the next quarter then the amount paid in advance (the prepayment) is deducted from the total paid and only the remainder is charged as an expense in the income statement.

The amount of the prepayment is another form of current asset which represents value to the business: the right to continue for three months without needing to pay any more insurance costs. Prepayments are usually shown within the figure for 'other current assets' in the balance sheet.

3.5.6   Current assets: Cash and cash equivalents

Cash

Cash comprises the company's cash in hand and deposits which can be withdrawn on demand.

You are probably thinking, at last, surely cash is an asset which is not subjectively valued! In many cases you would be correct. But what if Example plc is holding balances of foreign currency to finance its international trading activities? At what rate should these be converted to sterling for the balance sheet?

If you have ever returned from a foreign holiday with a few bank notes to exchange you will know that the amount they are worth in sterling can vary dramatically on a daily basis. You will therefore appreciate the difficulty in valuing what could be fairly substantial holdings of foreign currency. Guidelines exist in the accounting standards to help accountants with this task but there is still plenty of scope for management judgement.

Sadly, even the cash figure in the balance sheet might be the subject of subjective judgement and estimation!

Cash equivalents

Accounting standards define cash equivalents as short-term, highly liquid investments that are readily convertible to a known amount of cash and that are subject to an insignificant risk of changes in value. Cash equivalents are not held for investment purposes but are held to meet short-term cash requirements.

To be classified as a cash equivalent, an investment's maturity date should be less than three months from its acquisition date.

Exercise

Using this definition of a cash equivalent, decide whether each of the following two items can be classified on the balance sheet as a cash equivalent. Both of the balances are held to meet short-term cash requirements. Managers have made both the investments in order to utilise a temporary balance of surplus cash.

(1) Shares in a listed public company.
(2) Money held in a deposit account for which one month's notice is required to withdraw any cash.

Solution

(1) This is not a cash equivalent. Although the shares are held to meet short-term cash requirements and are readily convertible to cash, the value of listed shares fluctuates on a daily basis. Therefore the shares are subject to significant risk of changes in value and for this reason do not fulfil the criteria for the definition of a cash equivalent.
(2) This is a cash equivalent. The deposit is held to meet short-term cash requirements and is readily convertible to a known amount of cash in less than three months.

3.5.7 Current liabilities

A liability is an amount of money owed by the organisation. A *current* liability is one which is due to be paid within a year. There are many different types of creditor or current liability since, as we have already stated, a business may be able to obtain credit for almost everything. If you are an employee you may be a creditor of your organisation at the moment because they may owe you up to one month's salary, assuming that you are paid monthly and depending on the payment date. Therefore if you go into work tomorrow and your boss tells you that you are a liability, this is hopefully stated in the context that you are a current liability on your organisation's balance sheet!

Before leaving our discussion of current liabilities we will have a look at some common types of current liability that you may come across.

Trade payables

Also known as trade creditors, these are the people to whom money is owed for supplies of the goods and services used in day-to-day operations.

Bank loans and overdrafts

Many bank loans are for more than one year and will be shown elsewhere on the balance sheet, as you will see later. However, if, say, a ten-year loan was taken out nine years ago, it is now due for repayment within one year and should be shown as a current liability within short-term borrowings.

Many overdrafts are in practical terms a permanent source of finance and are effectively like a long-term loan. However, an overdraft is in reality liable to be recalled at any time. The bank manager may request that it should be repaid at quite short notice. Hence it should also be classified within short-term borrowings as a current liability.

Accruals

In Chapter 2 we saw how the charge to the income statement for some expenses was adjusted if payments were still outstanding. For example, if the telephone bill for the latest quarter has not yet been paid then an estimate of the amount owing (the accrual) is added to the total paid to arrive at the amount to be charged as an expense in the income statement.

The amount of the accrual is another form of current liability to be included within the figure for 'trade and other payables' in the balance sheet.

3.5.8 The working capital cycle in non-manufacturing organisations

Non-manufacturing organisations also have a working capital cycle, but it will be slightly different from the one described above. For example, retail organisations who purchase finished goods ready for sale to the customer will not have any inventories of raw materials and work in progress. But they will still have inventories of finished goods, cash, prepayments, current liabilities and some receivables.

Other types of service organisation such as a haulage company or contract cleaning service would not hold any inventories at all for sale to the customer (although they may have inventories of spare parts or cleaning materials). Most of these organisations' working capital cash goes into overheads which are incurred to provide the service for the customer. This overhead expenditure does not immediately produce a tangible asset such as inventory which can be shown on the balance sheet. Instead the expenditure creates the service for the customer, who can then be shown as a receivable (debtor) under current assets on the balance sheet, until they have paid the amount owed for the service provided.

3.6 Goodwill

Now that we have finished looking at all the items on one side of Example plc's balance sheet you should stop to think for a minute. Can you see that the total of the top part of this balance sheet shows the total amount of money tied up in Example's non-current assets and working capital? In very simple terms you might say that this shows the value of the business. But it does not. The business is likely to be worth far more than £3,066,000.

Exercise

Can you think of valuable assets that Example plc might possess that do not seem to be shown on the balance sheet?

Solution

Items that you might have thought of include skilled employees, customer and supplier relationships, databases and information technology systems.

If another company wanted to acquire or take over Example plc it is likely that they would have to pay a lot more than £3,066,000 to acquire the business. The extra amount that they would have to pay is called goodwill, an intangible asset.

If there is goodwill in a business it means that its value as a going concern is higher than the sum of the value of all of the separately identifiable assets.

The problem with goodwill is that it is very difficult to say how much it is worth. Its valuation is very subjective and the value of goodwill tends to fluctuate all the time.

For example, the value of the tables and chairs in a restaurant is relatively easy to establish for balance sheet purposes. However, it might be argued that a restaurant is only as good as its chef. An excellent chef who keeps the customers coming back again and again is a valuable asset to a restaurant business but the chef's 'value' would not be shown on the balance sheet along with the value of the tables and chairs.

This does not seem right but think for a minute about the value of the goodwill in the restaurant business, a substantial part of which is probably represented by the chef's skill and perhaps by the personality of the waiters.

The value of the goodwill changes on a daily basis. Just one customer who has a bad experience in the restaurant can damage the value of the goodwill and conversely one enjoyable experience can substantially increase the value of the goodwill. An excellent chef might leave at any time to find employment elsewhere and be replaced by a chef without the same degree of experience and skill. A pleasant waiter might increase the value of the goodwill but if the waiter is in a bad mood or leaves the business, the value of the goodwill can be impaired again.

Internally generated goodwill that has been created by the organisation's own efforts is inherent in any business but it does not have an objective historical cost value that can be stated with any certainty. We intuitively know that goodwill exists but we have no objective way of placing a value on it.

For these reasons internally generated or non-purchased goodwill is not shown on an organisation's balance sheet.

However, when a business is sold a price is agreed between the buyer and the seller. This price will include an element for the goodwill of the acquired business. The value of the purchased goodwill is a matter of agreement between the buyer and the seller.

Purchased goodwill is shown at cost on the acquiring company's balance sheet as an intangible non-current (fixed) asset. This historical cost value is then retained on successive balance sheets but the value must be reviewed annually for impairment.

In subsequent years the purchased goodwill is shown in the balance sheet (as an intangible non-current asset) at its original historical cost less any accumulated impairment losses.

3.7   Capitalisation of costs

When expenditure is capitalised this means that it is treated as non-current asset expenditure (capital expenditure) and is held in the balance sheet to be spread over the income statements of several years. A cost may be treated in this way if it can be demonstrated that the expenditure incurred will provide benefit for future years.

This has the effect of increasing profits, but perhaps only in the short term since the capitalised non-current asset will usually have to be depreciated in future.

A common example is the *capitalisation of interest*. Sometimes the interest charges incurred on money borrowed to finance the construction of a non-current asset are not charged against the profit for the year in which they are incurred. Instead the interest is added to the value of the non-current asset in the balance sheet, and the total amount will be depreciated over the estimated useful life of the relevant asset.

For example, J Sainsbury plc's annual report for 2007 details the following accounting policy. The extract is reproduced by kind permission of Sainsbury's Supermarkets Ltd.

> **Capitalisation of interest**. Interest costs that are directly attributable to the acquisition or construction of qualifying assets are capitalised to the cost of the asset ...

The notes to J Sainsbury's accounts reveal that £10m out of the total interest payable of £117m was capitalised into the value of non-current assets, that is added to the non-current asset value in the balance sheet instead of being charged against the profit for the year.

Other costs which some companies may capitalise and amortise over several years include the costs of developing software or an Internet site. Some companies charge these expenses to the income statement in the year in which they are incurred, but in some circumstances they can be capitalised and depreciated or amortised over several years.

The following accounting policy statement from the Walt Disney Company in its 2007 annual report demonstrates the principles that are applied when determining whether or not a cost should be capitalised.

> The Company expenses costs incurred in the preliminary project stage of developing or acquiring internal use software, such as research and feasibility studies, as well as costs incurred in the post-implementation/operational stage, such as maintenance and training. Capitalisation of software development costs occurs only after the preliminary project stage is complete, management authorises the project, and it is probable that the project will be completed and the software will be used for the function intended. As of September 29, 2007 and September 30, 2006, capitalised software costs, net of accumulated depreciation, totaled $555 million and $491 million, respectively. The capitalised costs are amortised on a straight-line basis over the estimated useful life of the software, ranging from 3–10 years.

This statement indicates that the Walt Disney Company 'expenses costs' incurred in the early stages of development, that is charges them to the income statement of the period they are incurred. This occurs until a project has been authorised and it is likely that the software will be used in the future for the purpose intended.

Once this preliminary stage is completed, the Company is assured that future benefits will arise from the costs incurred. Any further costs of developing the software are capitalised as an intangible non-current asset in the balance sheet. These capitalised costs are held as an asset on the balance sheet and are shared out (amortised) in equal instalments over the income statements of all the periods that benefit from the use of the software.

3.8   Capital and reserves

Now we can move on to the bottom part of Example plc's balance sheet. The part that shows where the money has come from to invest in the non-current assets and working capital.

So that you can refer to it easily, the relevant part of the balance sheet from the beginning of the chapter is repeated below.

Extract from Example plc's balance sheet as at 31 December Year 7

	£'000
Share capital	2,200
Reserves – retained profits	350
Other reserves	230
Shareholders' equity	2,780
Non-current liabilities	286
Capital employed	3,066

3.8.1   Share capital

We have already discussed at the beginning of Chapter 2 that the shareholders are the owners of the business – they each have a share in its fortunes.

The most common types of share are preference shares and ordinary shares. Preference shares are so called because they have preference over the payment of dividends and the repayment of capital. Each year the preference shareholders will receive their dividend payment first, and the whole of any profits left will usually belong to the ordinary shareholders. This may be a large or small (or non-existent!) amount of money, depending on how well the company has performed during the year.

However, preference shares will receive only a fixed rate of dividend. For example, if a company has issued 5,000 8% preference shares of £1 each the preference shareholders would receive their dividend of £400 first. The potential dividends for ordinary shareholders after payment of the preference dividend are, in theory, unlimited.

In most cases, even the preference shareholders' dividends are not guaranteed. Dividend payments depend on the company making profits. Furthermore, remember that the company will not necessarily pay out as dividend all of the remaining profit available for the ordinary shareholders. Some of the profit will be kept as reserves to fund future growth.

Another difference between the two types of share is that in the event of the company winding up, the preference shareholders' capital would be repaid before the ordinary shareholders receive any repayment.

It is the ordinary shareholders that are the true owners of the business. They have voting rights which give them control over the business, for example, through their ability to vote for the appointment of individual directors or for the removal of directors from office. Preference shareholders do not usually have any voting rights.

3.8.2   Retained profit reserve

We saw in Chapter 2 that retained profit is an important source of finance for a company. Retained profit is one of the most common reserves that you will see in company balance sheets. The retained profit reserve balance is merely a statement of how much profit has been retained over the years to fund the company's growth.

Do not make the very common mistake of thinking that the retained profit reserve balance represents hoards of cash which the company has access to. Reserves are not cash. They are merely a source of finance that has been used to buy, say, more non-current assets or inventory to expand the company's oper-ations. The retained profit reserve figure shows where the money originally came from. It is a sort of historical listing or balance that usually grows larger each year as more profits are retained in the business.

If you want to know whether the company has any cash then look at the other side of the balance sheet, under current assets!

The retained profit reserve might be referred to as the retained earnings reserve. Confusingly, some companies might label the retained profit reserve balance on their balance sheet as 'profit and loss account'!

There will usually be other reserves on a balance sheet in addition to the retained profit reserve. We will look now at the two reserves you are most likely to come across: the revaluation reserve and the share premium.

3.8.3 Revaluation reserve

In Section 3.4.5 we saw how companies can revalue their non-current assets on a regular basis. For example, if a property has increased in value the new, higher value can be shown within non-current assets on the balance sheet.

However, this will mean that the total of the top part of the balance sheet has increased. It will now be 'out of balance' with the total of the lower part. The sum of the values of the non-current assets and the working capital will be higher than the sum of the finance sources shown on the lower part of the balance sheet.

Accounting in a Nutshell

72

Exercise

Consider that the increased value of the non-current asset is rather like a profit that the business has made but which the directors cannot afford to distribute to the shareholders as dividends. The value of the property could just as easily fall in the future and the gain has not actually been realised yet in cash.

How do you think this gain should be recorded in the lower part of the balance sheet in order to make the balance sheet balance again?

Solution

The gain is shown in the lower part of the balance sheet as a reserve.

This specially created reserve is called a 'revaluation reserve'.

For example, if the valuer or surveyor certifies that the property has increased in value by £100,000 the balance sheet value of the property within non-current assets will be increased by £100,000 and a revaluation reserve of £100,000 will be shown in the lower part of the balance sheet.

Therefore the valuation gain is effectively treated in just the same way as a retained profit. It is shown as a reserve in the balance sheet. The difference is that the revaluation reserve cannot be used for dividends in the future whereas a retained profit reserve can be used for dividends if the directors so desire.

The revaluation reserve is a capital reserve, which contrasts it with the retained profit reserve which is a revenue reserve. Revenue reserves are created out of profits and can be distributed to shareholders as dividends. Capital reserves cannot be distributed as dividends.

3.8.4 Share premium

The nominal value of a share is the face value that is shown on the share certificate. For example, a £1 ordinary share has a nominal value of £1 that will be printed on the share certificate. Ordinary shares with nominal values of 50 pence and 25 pence are also common.

The nominal or face value of a share might also be referred to as its par value.

The nominal value remains constant whereas the market value or price of the share will fluctuate depending on the company's performance and on factors such as investors' opinions of the company's future prospects.

When a company's £1 shares are already trading in the market the directors might decide to issue or sell some more shares. Even though these shares will still have a nominal value of £1 each the company should be able to sell them at the current market price.

The share premium is the excess which the company receives for the sale of the shares, above the nominal value of the shares sold. For example, if 1,000 shares with a nominal value of £1 each are sold by the company at the market value of, say, £3,000 the amount of share premium received is £2,000.

This transaction will be reflected in the balance sheet as follows:

Top part of the balance sheet

Increase cash by £3,000.

- -

Lower part of the balance sheet

Increase share capital by £1,000 (the nominal value of the shares issued/sold)

Increase share premium by £2,000 (the share premium reserve)

- -

The share premium is thus another special reserve which is shown in the lower part of the balance sheet. It is a capital reserve which means that the directors cannot use it to pay dividends to the shareholders.

3.8.5   Shareholders' equity

The shareholders' equity is the total of the share capital and all of the reserves. It might also be referred to as the shareholders' funds. The total of the shareholders' funds represents their total investment in the company. The reserves belong to the shareholders just as much as their original capital does.

For example in the case of retained profits the shareholders have effectively agreed that the company should reinvest the profits on their behalf. The profits still belong to the shareholders, but the profits are now tied up in the company's assets.

3.9   Longer-term liabilities

The last item on Example plc's balance sheet is 'non-current liabilities'. These are all the liabilities, apart from share capital, that are not current liabilities and are due to be paid more than a year after the balance sheet date.

The most common item within this category is loan capital. For example, money may be borrowed from a bank on a 20-year loan. There will be a legally binding agreement to repay the loan after 20 years and to pay regular amounts of interest at agreed rates throughout the duration of the loan.

Mortgages are another form of loan that would be shown under this category, if they are due to be repaid after more than one year.

Exercise

The following balances have been extracted from The List Company's accounts on 31 December:

	£
Office premises (at valuation less accumulated depreciation)	381,000
Inventory of goods for resale	87,000
Bank loan (due for repayment in ten years)	72,000
Bank overdraft	6,500
Fixtures and fittings at cost	118,000
Amount owed by customers	68,000
Share capital	390,000
Retained profit reserve	68,500
Insurance prepaid	750
Accumulated depreciation on fixtures and fittings	35,000
Wages and salaries owing	1,250
Cash in tills	200
Amount owed to suppliers	81,700

Reorganise this data to produce The List Company's balance sheet as at 31 December.

Solution

Notice how the second and third columns are used to carry out the calculations of any required subtotals.

The List Company Balance Sheet as at 31 December

	£	£	£
Non-current assets			
Office premises (at valuation less accumulated depreciation)			381,000
Fixtures and fittings at cost		118,000	
less accumulated depreciation		(35,000)	
			83,000
			464,000
Current assets			
Inventories	87,000		
Receivables	68,000		
Prepayments	750		
Cash	200		
		155,950	
Current liabilities			
Payables	(81,700)		
Accrued expenses	(1,250)		
Bank overdraft	(6,500)		
		(89,450)	
Net current assets			66,500
Total assets less current liabilities			530,500
Share capital			390,000
Retained profit			68,500
Shareholders' equity			458,500
Non-current liabilities			72,000
Capital employed			530,500

3.10   Alternative balance sheet layouts

3.10.1   Highlighting the working capital balance

So far in this chapter we have been looking at balance sheets that are arranged so that the top part shows where the organisation's money was invested at the date of the balance sheet; how much was invested in non-current assets and how much in working capital.

An equation to represent this arrangement of the balance sheet would look like this.

$$\text{USES OF FINANCE} = \text{SOURCES OF FINANCE}$$
$$\text{(non-current assets} + \text{working capital)} = \text{(share capital} + \text{reserves}$$
$$+ \text{long-term liabilities)}$$

The current liabilities are netted off against the current assets within working capital so that the reader can easily see how much the organisation has invested in the more liquid area of its business: the working capital.

Sometimes a balance sheet will be arranged in a different way and we will now look at three other common arrangements that you might come across.

3.10.2   Including current liabilities within the sources of finance

An alternative balance sheet arrangement in common use is to include the current liabilities as a source of finance rather than net them off against the current assets to derive a figure for working capital. Instead of showing the current liabilities as a subtraction from the top part of the balance sheet they are shown as an addition to the lower part. The balance sheet still balances; it is simply presented in a different way.

An equation to represent this arrangement of the balance sheet would look like this.

$$\text{USES OF FINANCE} = \text{SOURCES OF FINANCE}$$
$$\text{(non-current assets} + \text{current assets)} = \text{(share capital} + \text{reserves}$$
$$+ \text{long-term liabilities}$$
$$+ \text{current liabilities)}$$

This arrangement serves to highlight a total for the amount invested in the organisation's assets, both current and non-current.

The organisation's funds are invested in two types of asset: non-current (fixed) assets and current assets. The funds to make these investments have come from a number of sources, both short term (current liabilities) and longer term (share capital, reserves and non-current liabilities).

If we arrange Example plc's balance sheet according to this form of presentation it would look like this.

Example plc: Balance sheet as at 31 December Year 7

	£'000	£'000	£'000
Non-current assets			
Intangible assets		250	
Tangible assets: property, plant and equipment		2,400	
Investments		35	
			2,685
Current assets			
Inventories		328	
Trade receivables		502	
Other current assets		31	
Cash and cash equivalents		120	
			981
Total assets			**3,666**
Share capital		2,200	
Reserves – retained profits		350	
Other reserves		230	
Shareholders' equity			2,780
Non-current liabilities		286	
Current liabilities			
Trade and other payables (creditors)	550		
Short-term borrowings	50		
Total current liabilities		600	
Total liabilities			886
Total equity and liabilities			**3,666**

The logic and principles of the balance sheet have not altered. The information is simply rearranged and presented in a different way. The working capital figure is not shown on the balance sheet but the reader can see a clear figure for the organisation's total assets and total liabilities.

> *If readers of the balance sheet wish to know the organisation's working capital balance the figures required to deduce it are still available on the balance sheet. However it will be necessary for readers to do their own separate calculation of the current assets minus the current liabilities.*

3.10.3 Highlighting the shareholders' investment in the company

You may come across balance sheets where the working capital is shown but the longer-term (non-current) liabilities are shown as a deduction from the 'other side' of the balance sheet.

An equation to represent this arrangement of the balance sheet would look like this.

$$\text{Non-current assets} + \text{working capital} - \text{long-term liabilities}$$
$$= \text{Share capital} + \text{reserves}$$

The equation has been rearranged yet again so that the shareholders' equity is highlighted and presented in isolation as one side of the balance sheet. This arrangement focuses the reader's attention on the amount of the shareholders' equity.

Exercise

Rearrange Example plc's balance sheet according to this form of presentation to show the shareholders' equity separately as one side of the balance sheet.

Solution

Example plc: Balance sheet as at 31 December Year 7

	£'000	£'000	£'000
Non-current assets			
Intangible assets			250
Tangible assets: property, plant and equipment			2,400
Investments			35
			2,685
Current assets			
Inventories		328	
Trade receivables		502	
Other current assets		31	
Cash and cash equivalents		120	
		981	
Current liabilities			
Trade and other payables	(550)		
Short-term borrowings	(50)		
		(600)	
Working capital			381
Total assets less current liabilities			3,066
Non-current liabilities			(286)
Net assets			**2,780**
Share capital			2,200
Reserves – retained profits			350
Other reserves			230
Total shareholders' equity			**2,780**

Note that the total of the top part of the balance sheet is labelled as *net assets*.

The principles of the balance sheet have still not altered. This alternative presentation merely serves to highlight the shareholders' investment in the company.

3.10.4 Highlighting the total assets and the net assets

One more arrangement of the equation produces yet another common balance sheet layout. This form of presentation does not show a clear figure for the working capital balance but it does highlight figures for the total assets and the net assets at the balance sheet date.

An equation to represent this arrangement of the balance sheet would look like this.

(Non-current assets + current assets) − (current liabilities + long-term liabilities) = Share capital + reserves

or

Total assets − total liabilities = Share capital + reserves

Exercise

Rearrange Example plc's balance sheet according to this form of presentation to show a separate figure for total assets and net assets.

Accounting in a Nutshell

Solution

Example plc: Balance sheet as at 31 December Year 7

	£'000	£'000	£'000
Non-current assets			
Intangible assets			250
Tangible assets: property, plant and equipment			2,400
Investments			35
			2,685
Current assets			
Inventories		328	
Trade receivables		502	
Other current assets		31	
Cash and cash equivalents		120	981
Total assets			3,666
Current liabilities			
Trade and other payables		(550)	
Short-term borrowings		(50)	
		(600)	
Non-current liabilities		(286)	
Total liabilities			(886)
Net assets			**2,780**
Share capital			2,200
Reserves – retained profits			350
Other reserves			230
Total shareholders' equity			**2,780**

3.11 Consolidated balance sheet

Many large businesses operate as a group of several separate companies, rather than as one large, single company. The controlling company, called the 'parent company' or the 'holding company', holds some or all of the shares in all of the other companies, which are called the 'subsidiaries' of the parent company.

Each subsidiary company will produce its own set of financial statements and in addition the parent company produces the consolidated or group accounts. The consolidated accounts combine the results of all the individual companies in the group into one consolidated income statement, one consolidated balance sheet, etc.

The group accounts are prepared by adding together on a line-by-line basis each type of revenue and expense and each type of asset and liability in order to produce a total consolidated income statement, a total consolidated balance sheet, etc. for the group.

3.11.1 Minority interests

The group or consolidated results will show 100 per cent of the revenues, expenses, assets and liabilities of the subsidiaries even if the parent company does not actually own 100 per cent of the shares in every subsidiary company.

This is because the parent company's large shareholding in each subsidiary enables it to exercise control over the activities of the subsidiary. Therefore even though the group does not own 100 per cent of the assets it does control them. If we are to obtain an overall picture of how well the group is being controlled and managed, the consolidated accounts must show 100 per cent of all of the subsid-iaries' assets and liabilities.

This means that a proportion of the assets shown on the group balance sheet actually belongs to shareholders from outside the group. These outside shareholders are called 'minority interests'.

In a group or consolidated balance sheet the minority interest is shown as an additional line within the figures for shareholders' equity. It represents the proportion of the net assets that is financed by or attributable to other shareholders from outside the group.

3.12 Statement of recognised income and expense

The statement of recognised income and expense is a financial statement that is provided by companies in addition to the income statement and the balance sheet. This statement shows all the gains and losses that have been recognised during the period, both those that have passed through the income statement and those that have been recognised only on the balance sheet and have not passed through the income statement. You should recall an example of the latter that we saw earlier in this chapter in the context of upwards property revaluations. We saw that the gain on revaluation of properties does not pass through the income statement but it is recognised by showing an increased asset value on the balance sheet. This is because the gain has not actually been realised because the asset is still owned by the company.

Other key gains and losses that are recognised on the balance sheet but do not pass through the income statement are certain gains or losses on the company's pension schemes and exchange differences that arise when the results of overseas subsidiaries are translated into sterling for the consolidated/group accounts.

The statement of recognised income and expense enables the users of the financial statements to see all of the gains and losses that have been recognised during the period in a single statement.

3.13 Summary

(1) A balance sheet is a statement that shows the things of value that an organisation owns (the assets), as well as the sources of finance used to buy them.

(2) Expenditure on non-current (fixed) assets is called capital expenditure and it benefits the organisation for several years.

(3) Expenditure on running costs is called revenue expenditure or operating expenditure.

(4) The depreciation charge in the income statement is used to share out capital expenditure over the years that gain benefit from it.

(5) Working capital is the capital that is circulating round the business. The balance of working capital is calculated as current assets minus current liabilities.

(6) Another term used to describe working capital is 'net current assets'.

(7) Inventories are valued at the lower of cost and net realisable value.

(8) Current liabilities are those that are due for payment within a year of the balance sheet date.

(9) Goodwill is the difference between the value of the business as a whole and the value of the net assets. Only purchased goodwill may be shown on the balance sheet.

(10) Retained profit reserves are shown within shareholders' funds. They indicate the original source of finance when

profits have been re-invested in the business rather than distributed to the shareholders as dividends.

(11) A number of alternative layouts can be used to present a balance sheet but the basic principles underlying its preparation do not change.

(12) A consolidated or group balance sheet combines the individual balance sheets of all the subsidiary companies within the group on a line-by-line basis.

(13) When the parent company does not own 100 per cent of the shares in a subsidiary, a minority interest is shown in the consolidated balance sheet.

(14) The statement of recognised income and expense brings together in a single statement all of the gains and losses that have been recognised during the period.

Review questions

(1) What is the difference between capital expenditure and revenue expenditure? (Section 3.3)

(2) State another term that is used to describe non-current assets. (Section 3.3)

(3) What are intangible non-current assets? (Section 3.4.1)

(4) What is meant by the term 'net book value'? (Section 3.4.2)

(5) What is the purpose of the depreciation charge in the income statement? (Section 3.4.3)

(6) What is the connection between depreciation and amortisation? (Section 3.4.4)

(7) What are the constituent parts of net current assets? (Section 3.5.2)

(8) What accounting term is used to describe negative working capital? (Section 3.5.2)

(9) State another term that is used to describe the current asset of inventory. (Section 3.5.3)

(10) What is the going concern concept and what is its significance in terms of the valuation of inventory? (Section 3.5.3)

(11) State another term that is used to describe the current asset of receivables. (Section 3.5.4)

(12) What is a cash equivalent? (Section 3.5.6)

(13) What distinguishes a current liability from a non-current liability? (Section 3.5.7)

(14) State another term that is used to describe the current liability of trade payables. (Section 3.5.7)

(15) How is the value of goodwill calculated? (Section 3.6)

(16) What does the term 'capitalisation' mean? (Section 3.7)

(17) What is share premium? (Section 3.8.4)

(18) Why is a minority interest often shown in a consolidated or group balance sheet? (Section 3.11.1)

Self-test questions

(1) The following items are to be included on the balance sheet of a company that manufactures office furniture. State whether each of the items would be classified as a non-current (fixed) asset, a current asset, a current liability or a non-current liability.

◆ amount owed to the company by its customers

◆ office premises

◆ amount borrowed on a 15-year loan

◆ last month's telephone bill which has not yet been paid

◆ amount owing to a supplier of wood, due to be paid next month

◆ new manufacturing equipment that was purchased and received from the supplier last week

◆ goodwill purchased on acquiring the business of a competitor last year

◆ pine desks awaiting finishing and polishing.

(2) Look back at self-test question 2 at the end of Chapter 2. State the effect of each of the transactions on the JS Company's balance sheet dated 30 September Year 3.

(3) Look back at self-test question 3 at the end of Chapter 2. State the effect of the transaction described on the balance sheet of Company S as at 30 September.

(4) Look back at self-test question 4 at the end of Chapter 2. State the effect of the transaction described on the balance sheet of Company L as at 31 March Year 6.

(5) Look back at self-test question 5 at the end of Chapter 2. State the effect of the transaction described on the balance sheet of Company E as at 30 June Year 8.

(6) Look back at self-test question 6 at the end of Chapter 2. State the effect of the transaction described on the balance sheet of Company G as at 31 December.

(7) The information below relates to a company as at 31 December. Present this information as a balance sheet using each of the following presentations.
   (i) Non-current assets + working capital = shareholders' equity + non-current liabilities
   (ii) Non-current assets + current assets = shareholders' equity + non-current liabilities + current liabilities
   (iii) Non-current assets + working capital – non-current liabilities = shareholders' equity
   (iv) Total assets – total liabilities = shareholders' equity.

Balances as at 31 December

	£
Accounts payable	29,700
Ordinary share capital	68,000
Delivery vehicle at cost	17,100
Accrued expenses	1,700
Inventory	70,000
Accounts receivable, before provision for doubtful debts	26,667
Cash	1,100
Share premium	6,400
Other payables	1,800
Office equipment at net book value	8,400
Prepaid expenses	7,200
Retained profit reserve	8,300
Loan (repayable in seven years)	10,000
Accumulated depreciation on delivery vehicle	4,300
Provision for doubtful debts	267

(8) Comment critically on the following statements.
   (a) 'Charging a depreciation provision in the income statement ensures we will have funds to replace the relevant non-current asset.'

(b) 'The balance sheet measures the value of a business because it lists the values of all the assets and then deducts the liabilities to deduce the net business value.'

(c) 'An accrued expense is one that should be charged in next year's income statement.'

(9) A retail company is valuing damaged inventories of two items for balance sheet purposes: Item X and Item Y.

Details concerning damaged inventory of the two items on 31 March are as follows:

Item	Number of damaged items held in inventory	Original cost £ per item	Final selling price anticipated £ per item	Cost to be incurred to repair items before sale £ per item
X	1,805	14	23	5
Y	1,789	11	19	9

What value should be placed on the inventory of Item X and Item Y for the balance sheet as at 31 March? (*Hint: Inventory must be valued at the lower of cost and net realisable value.*)

(10) A company purchases a packing machine for £39,000 on over 1 January Year 1. The company expects to use the machine for three years after which it will be sold for an estimated £3,000. The company uses the straight-line method of depreciation.

Calculate the annual depreciation charge that will be shown in the income statement and the net book value that will be shown on the balance sheet as at 31 December at the end of each of the three years. Assume that the machine is still shown on the balance sheet as at 31 December Year 3, before it is finally sold early in Year 4.

Answers to self-test questions

(1)

◆ Amount owed to the company by its customers. These are trade debtors or trade receivables and are a current asset.

- ◆ Office premises. Assuming that the premises are owned by the company they would be classified as a fixed or non-current asset.

- ◆ Amount borrowed on a 15-year loan. This is a non-current or long-term liability. After 14 years, when the loan is due for repayment within a year, it will be reclassified as a current liability.

- ◆ Last month's telephone bill which has not yet been paid. This is a current liability.

- ◆ Amount owing to a supplier of wood, due to be paid next month. This is a trade creditor or trade payable and is a current liability.

- ◆ New manufacturing equipment that was purchased and received from the supplier last week. This is a non-current or fixed asset. The fact that the equipment has probably not yet been paid for does not alter its classification. The company intends to keep the equipment and use it for several years therefore it is classified as a non-current asset as soon as it is purchased. (If the equipment has not yet been paid for, the amount owing will also be shown on the balance sheet as a current liability.)

- ◆ Goodwill purchased on acquiring the business of a competitor last year. This is a fixed or non-current asset. It will be shown on the balance sheet as an intangible non-current asset.

- ◆ Pine desks awaiting finishing and polishing. This is a work-in-progress inventory item and is a current asset.

(2) The invoice for the advert placed on 1 September Year 3 will be shown as a current liability (an accrual) of £3,220 on the balance sheet as at 30 September Year 3.

The rent of £4,500 paid in advance will be shown as a current asset (a prepayment) on the balance sheet as at 30 September Year 3.

(3) Company S's balance sheet as at 30 September would show a trade receivable (debtor) of £1,700.

(4) The balance sheet of Company L as at 31 March Year 6 will show a current liability (deferred income) of £1,300. Company R has paid this amount in advance therefore

Company L has a liability either to provide the rental service paid for or potentially to repay the £1,300 to Company R.

(5) The balance sheet of Company E as at 30 June Year 8 will show a current liability (deferred income) of £600. The customer has paid this amount in advance, therefore Company E has a liability either to provide the web service paid for or potentially to repay the £600 to the customer.

(6) The balance sheet of Company G as at 31 December will show a current liability (an accrual) of £5,328, consisting of £5,000 owing for the December hire costs plus £328 (8,200 × £0.04) for December mileage costs.

(7)

(i) Non-current assets + working capital = shareholders' equity + non-current liabilities

Balance sheet as at 31 December

	£	£	£
Non-current assets at net book value			
Office equipment			8,400
Delivery vehicle (17,100 − 4,300)			12,800
			21,200
Current assets			
Inventory		70,000	
Accounts receivable (26,667 − 267)		26,400	
Prepaid expenses		7,200	
Cash		1,100	
		104,700	
Current liabilities			
Accounts payable	(29,700)		
Other payables	(1,800)		
Accrued expenses	(1,700)		
		(33,200)	
Net current assets (working capital)			71,500
Total assets less current liabilities			**92,700**
Share capital			68,000
Retained profit reserve			8,300
Share premium			6,400
Shareholders' equity			82,700
Non-current liabilities			10,000
			92,700

(ii) Non-current assets + current assets = shareholders' equity + non-current liabilities + current liabilities

Balance sheet as at 31 December

	£	£	£
Non-current assets at net book value			
Office equipment			8,400
Delivery vehicle (17,100 − 4,300)			12,800
			21,200
Current assets			
Inventory		70,000	
Accounts receivable (26,667 − 267)		26,400	
Prepaid expenses		7,200	
Cash		1,100	
			104,700
Total assets			**125,900**
Share capital			68,000
Retained profit reserve			8,300
Share premium			6,400
Shareholders' equity			82,700
Non-current liabilities		10,000	
Current liabilities			
Accounts payable	29,700		
Other payables	1,800		
Accrued expenses	1,700		
Total current liabilities		33,200	
Total liabilities			43,200
Total equity and liabilities			**125,900**

(iii) Non-current assets + working capital – non-current liabilities = shareholders' equity

Balance sheet as at 31 December

	£	£	£
Non-current assets at net book value			
Office equipment			8,400
Delivery vehicle (17,100 – 4,300)			12,800
			21,200
Current assets			
Inventory		70,000	
Accounts receivable (26,667 – 267)		26,400	
Prepaid expenses		7,200	
Cash		1,100	
		104,700	
Current liabilities			
Accounts payable	(29,700)		
Other payables	(1,800)		
Accrued expenses	(1,700)		
		(33,200)	
Net current assets (working capital)			71,500
Total assets less current liabilities			92,700
Non-current liabilities			(10,000)
			82,700
Share capital			68,000
Retained profit reserve			8,300
Share premium			6,400
Shareholders' equity			**82,700**

(iv)   Total assets – total liabilities = shareholders' equity

Balance sheet as at 31 December

	£	£	£
Non-current assets at net book value			
Office equipment			8,400
Delivery vehicle (17,100 – 4,300)			12,800
			21,200
Current assets			
Inventory		70,000	
Accounts receivable (26,667 – 267)		26,400	
Prepaid expenses		7,200	
Cash		1,100	
		104,700	
Total assets			**125,900**
Current liabilities			
Accounts payable		(29,700)	
Other payables		(1,800)	
Accrued expenses		(1,700)	
		(33,200)	
Non-current liabilities		(10,000)	
Total liabilities			(43,200)
Net assets			**82,700**
Share capital			68,000
Retained profit reserve			8,300
Share premium			6,400
Shareholders' equity			**82,700**

(8)

(a)   The depreciation provision is a mechanism to allocate, as fairly as possible, the cost of the asset (less any residual value) over its useful life. The depreciation provision is charged as a cost in the income statement for each year, but this does not involve actually putting aside any cash for the non-current asset's replacement. Even if an amount of cash equal to the depreciation provision was set aside each year, this would still not ensure the availability of adequate funds for replacement of the asset. Inflation and technological change may mean that the replacement asset will cost more (or might not even be available at all!).

(b) The balance sheet does not measure the value of a business.

  (i) It does not necessarily include all the business assets. For example, only purchased goodwill may be shown on the balance sheet. Internally generated or non-purchased goodwill may not be shown on the balance sheet.

  (ii) Those assets which are shown are not necessarily included at their market value. For example:

  ◆ Non-current assets are shown at their net book value. This is merely the part of the original cost that has not yet been depreciated through the income statement. It is not necessarily an indication of the market value of the non-current assets.

  ◆ Inventories are valued at the lower of cost and net realisable value. The cost includes subjective elements such as an amount of allocated overhead.

  ◆ Receivables are stated net of a provision for doubtful debts, which may be too high or too low.

  (iii) Some of the liabilities which are included may be estimates, for example the accrued expenses.

(c) This statement is incorrect. An accrued expense is charged in the current year's income statement. It is an expense which should be matched with the current year's revenue, but which has not yet been paid. It will appear as a current liability in the balance sheet.

(9) Inventory must be valued at the lower of cost and net realisable value. Therefore we need to determine the net realisable value of each of items X and Y and compare this with the original cost.

Item X

The net realisable value per item is £23 − £5 = £18 per item. The original cost of £14 is lower than this, therefore Item X will be valued at £14 per item.

Value of inventory of Item X = £14 × 1,805 items = £25,270

Item Y

The net realisable value per item is £19 − £9 = £10 per item. This is lower than the original cost of £11, therefore Item Y will be valued at £10 per item.

Value of inventory of Item Y = £10 × 1,789 items = £17,890

(10) Annual depreciation charge in income statement = £(39,000 − 3,000)/3 years = £12,000

As at 31 December Year		Net book value £
1	£(39,000 − 12,000)	27,000
2	£(27,000 − 12,000)	15,000
3	£(15,000 − 12,000)	3,000

Cash Flow Reporting

4.1   Introduction

In this chapter you will find out about the importance of cash flow. We will be looking at the published cash flow statement and the internal document which is used to monitor cash flow: the cash flow forecast.

4.2   The importance of cash flow

Suppose that one morning you wake up with the most brilliant idea for a business. You cannot believe your luck in that nobody else has thought of it and it is obviously an absolute winner! There is no doubt that if you embark on this venture then you will be a millionaire by Christmas. The only problem is that you will need plenty of capital, and your savings will not be sufficient.

Undaunted, you ring your bank manager to arrange an appointment to negotiate a loan. You are told that the manager will be leaving for an extended holiday that afternoon, but that you can be seen this morning. Otherwise you will have to wait for two weeks and that will be too late – somebody else will get into the market before you!

So you jump into the car and drive towards the bank in plenty of time for your appointment. Then you notice that you do not have enough petrol to reach town so you stop at the petrol station. A big notice states 'Please do not put petrol into your vehicle if you do not have the means to pay.' At this point you realise that in your rush to leave the house you did not pick up any money or your credit cards. So what can you do?

You do not have enough petrol to go back home, you cannot reach the bank on foot and you have no money for a bus or a taxi. You could try negotiating with the petrol station cashier, offering vast sums of money for a tank of petrol, with the promise that you will pay this afternoon, once you have seen the bank manager. You could try approaching the other people in the queue.

But these people are unlikely to help you. They do not know who you are, they have only your word for it that you are on your way to being a millionaire. Therefore you are stuck and your business is stopped before it has even started. A potentially profitable venture has failed because of a lack of cash planning. If you had stopped and thought ahead about the fact that you would need cash part way through your journey you could have made plans to cover the cash deficit – you would have picked up some cash before you left!

This may seem like an oversimplification, but it is what is happening to businesses every day. An otherwise sound, potentially profitable business can fail due to what might be a temporary cash problem, because nobody is willing to take the risk and advance them the cash that they need to continue.

Cash planning and cash management are therefore vital to the success and survival of every business.

4.3 Comparing profits and cash flows

In addition to an income statement and balance sheet, companies are required to include in their annual report a cash flow statement. This enables the users of accounts to assess the amounts, timing and uncertainty of the organisation's cash flows. Where does the organisation get cash from? What large cash movements have there been during the year? The income statement shows how much profit has been earned, but this does not necessarily mean that the organisation will have any cash.

Exercise

Can you think of a few reasons why an organisation might be making profits, but still be very short of cash?

Solution

There are many varied reasons that you might have suggested, including:

(1) Profits may have been reinvested into building up inventories in anticipation of a sales drive.

(2) Although sales have been made and are included in the income statement as revenue (and therefore a profit on the sale is shown), the customers may not yet have paid. Therefore the cash is tied up in receivables.

(3) Cash may have been invested in non-current assets. This represents a drain on cash, but the cost is not charged immediately to the income statement. Only a proportion of the cost is charged as depreciation. Therefore, profits can be relatively high when cash balances are low.

4.4 The presentation of cash flows

Cash flows are presented under a number of main headings as shown in the following simplified cash flow statement for Example plc.

Example plc: Simplified cash flow statement for the year ended 31 December Year 7

	£'000
Cash flows from operating activities	
Cash received from customers	5,440
Cash paid to suppliers and employees	(4,850)
Interest paid	(40)
Taxation paid	(125)
Net cash flow from operating activities	425
Cash flows from investing activities	(180)
Cash flows from financing activities	(220)
Net increase in cash and cash equivalents	25
Cash and cash equivalents at beginning of year	95
Cash and cash equivalents at end of year	120

Notice that cash flows are presented under three main headings: from operating activities, from investing activities and from financing activities. In a full cash flow statement more detail would be provided to show the cash flow from individual activities within investing and within financing. However, for our initial discussion we have excluded the detail from this simplified statement.

Now we will look at each of the main headings in turn.

4.4.1 Net cash flow from operating activities

This is the cash generated by Example plc's everyday activities, which you will by now appreciate is not the same as the profit earned during the year. If you look at the detail in the statement you will see that the largest cash flows in this category are the cash received from customers during the year (which is not the same as the sales made) and the cash paid to suppliers and employees.

> *Because of a possible build-up of inventories, and the delays caused by credit payments, the cash paid to suppliers will not be the same as the amount charged in the income statement.*

Also deducted are the amounts of cash paid for interest and taxation. Remember again that the focus is on cash flow during the year. For example, the amount of £125,000 is the actual cash paid to the tax authorities during the year. This is not the same as the taxation charge in the income statement because of the timing of tax payments.

The final total of £425,000 within this sub-heading is important because it highlights the cash flow generated by Example plc from its operating activities, after taking account of the cost of the money (interest) used to finance these activities.

> *Instead of being shown as an operating cash flow the interest paid might alternatively be included in the sub-heading of cash flows from financing activities. Also it is permissible to show the payment of dividends in this section as an operating cash flow, rather than as a cash flow from financing activities, later in the cash flow statement.*

4.4.2 Cash flows from investing activities

This section shows how much cash was invested during the year in assets which will generate profits and cash flows in the future.

Cash flows arising from the purchase and sale of non-current assets such as property, plant and equipment will be shown under this heading. As you have already seen, the purchase of this type of non-current asset can lead to some very large cash outflows.

Also included here would be the cash flows associated with the purchase and sale of shares in other companies and the cash received in respect of dividends and in respect of interest on loans made by the company to other organisations.

4.4.3 Cash flows from financing activities

These are the cash flows arising from the providers of capital. Items under this heading would include cash inflows from the sale of shares and the issue of loans. Cash outflows shown would be from the repayment of long-term loans and share capital, as well as from the payment of dividends to shareholders (if the latter have not already been shown as an operating cash flow). If interest paid has not already been shown as a part of the net cash flow from operating activities, then it will be included here as a financing cash flow.

4.4.4 Net increase/decrease in cash and cash equivalents

The summation of the three main cash flow headings results in the net increase or decrease in cash and cash equivalents for the year.

If you have forgotten what is meant by a cash equivalent refer back to the previous chapter to refresh your memory.

Companies will usually then show a reconciliation of the balance of cash and cash equivalents at the beginning of the year with the balance at the end of the year.

You will learn how to interpret cash flow statements in Chapter 7 but to give you a sound basis from which to do this we will now move on to learn how to prepare cash flow statements from some basic data.

4.5 Preparing a simple cash flow statement

We will begin with a simple example to give you some practice at analysing the cash flows into the appropriate headings.

Example

The CF Company began trading on 1 January Year 3. Shares were issued for £120,000 cash and a £54,000 long-term loan was raised. The following transactions occurred during Year 3:

◆ Non-current assets were purchased for £185,000 cash.
◆ Sales to customers amounted to £156,000; the receivables balance at 31 December was £7,200.

- Purchases from suppliers amounted to £64,900; the payables balance at 31 December was £5,600.
- Salaries and wages paid during the year were £61,100.
- Interest paid on the loan was £6,500; no interest payments were outstanding at the end of the year.
- £4,000 of the long-term loan was repaid during the year.
- Taxation paid during the year amounted to £620.

The cash flow statement for the year ended 31 December Year 3 will look like this. The notes at the end of the statement will help you to understand the derivation of some of the figures.

The CF Company

Cash flow statement for the year ended 31 December Year 3

	£	£
Cash flows from operating activities		
Cash received from customers[1]		148,800
Cash paid to suppliers and employees[2]		(120,400)
Interest paid		(6,500)
Taxation paid		(620)
Net cash flow from operating activities		21,280
Cash flows from investing activities		
Purchase of non-current assets		(185,000)
Cash flows from financing activities		
Issue of shares[3]	120,000	
Cash received from long-term loan	54,000	
Repayment of long-term loan[4]	(4,000)	
Net cash flows from financing activities		170,000
Net increase in cash and cash equivalents		6,280

Notes

(1) Cash received from customers = £156,000 − £7,200 not yet received = £148,800

(2) Cash paid to suppliers = £64,900 − £5,600 not yet paid = £59,300
Total paid to suppliers and employees = £59,300 + £61,100 salaries and wages = £120,400

(3) The second column is being used simply to deduce a sub-total of the net cash flows from financing activities.

(4) Cash received and cash paid back in respect of the loan must be shown separately and not netted off against each other.

4.6 Determining the cash flows from operating activities

There are two different methods which can be used to determine the first subtotal in the cash flow statement, that is the cash flows from operating activities: the direct method and the indirect method.

The direct method shows the major types of operating cash receipts and operating cash payments. This is the method we have used so far in the cash flow statements in this chapter.

The indirect method is more common in practice but at first it can seem more complicated. The indirect method begins by adjusting the profit or loss for the period for any non-cash transactions. An example will help to demonstrate how the indirect method works.

Example

Extracts from the accounting records of the F Company are as follows:

	£'000
Operating profit for the year (profit before interest and taxation)	436
Depreciation charge included in the calculation of operating profit	87
Cash payments made during the year	
Interest paid	12
Taxation paid	102

	Balance at the beginning of the year £'000	Balance at the end of the year £'000
Inventories	28	22
Trade and other receivables	31	39
Trade payables	26	24

The calculation of the cash flows from operating activities begins by adjusting the profit figure for non-cash items. Use the notes below the calculations to help you to understand the adjustments being made.

Cash flows from operating activities	£'000	£'000
Operating profit for the year		436
Add back:		
Depreciation[1]		87
		523
Decrease in inventories[2]	6	
Increase in trade and other receivables[3]	(8)	
Decrease in trade payables[4]	(2)	
		(4)
Cash generated from operations		519
Interest paid[5,6]		(12)
Taxation paid[5]		(102)
Net cash from operating activities		405

Notes

(1) Depreciation is not a cash flow. It is the sharing out of the original amount paid for the non-current asset when it was first purchased. Since we are trying to derive the potential cash flow from profit the amount of depreciation that has been charged must be added back into profit.

(2) A decrease in inventories will increase the cash balance because less cash is tied up in the investment in inventory.

(3) An increase in receivables will decrease the cash balance because less cash has been received from customers.

(4) A decrease in payables will decrease the cash balance because more cash has been used to pay suppliers and others.

(5) Note this is the actual cash paid for interest and tax, not the amount of interest or tax expense shown in the income statement for the year. The difference is due to the timing of payments for interest and tax.

(6) Alternatively the interest paid might be shown later in the cash flow statement, as a cash flow from financing activities. In this case the interest paid would not be deducted here and the net cash from operating activities would be higher.

4.7 Preparing a cash flow statement from the income statement and balance sheets

Now that you understand the indirect method of determining the cash flow from operating activities we will look at a more advanced example of cash flow statement preparation. This example will demonstrate how a cash flow statement can be derived from an income statement and the balance sheets for two consecutive years. It should help you to appreciate the relationship between the income statement, the balance sheet and the cash flow statement.

Example

The income statement for Year 6 and the balance sheets as at 31 December Years 5 and 6 for the B Company are as follows.

The B Company: Income statement for the year ended 31 December Year 6

	£'000	£'000
Revenue		3,075
Cost of sales		2,255
Gross profit		820
Distribution costs	190	
Administrative expenses	225	
Other expenses	52	
Total operating expenses		467
Operating profit		353
Interest payable		28
Profit before tax		325
Taxation		73
Profit for the period		252

The B Company: Balance sheets as at 31 December

	Year 5 £'000	Year 6 £'000
Non-current assets		
Intangible assets	154	154
Tangible assets: property, plant and equipment	1,180	1,300
	1,334	1,454
Current assets		
Inventories	122	178
Trade receivables	207	272
Cash and cash equivalents	78	82
	407	532
Current liabilities		
Trade payables	(276)	(288)
Taxation owing	(26)	(37)
	(302)	(325)
Working capital (net current assets)	105	207
Total assets less current liabilities	**1,439**	**1,661**
Share capital	1,020	1,190
Reserves – retained profits	39	190
Share premium	95	127
Shareholders' equity	1,154	1,507
Non-current liabilities: long-term loans	285	154
Capital employed	**1,439**	**1,661**

The following information also relates to Year 6:

◆ The company paid £250,000 for new equipment.
◆ No non-current assets were disposed of during the year.
◆ The dividend paid during the year to shareholders was £101,000.
◆ No new long-term loans were arranged during the year.

Work carefully through the cash flow statement for Year 6 which follows. Use the notes below the statement to help you to understand the content.

The B Company: Cash flow statement for the year ended 31 December Year 6

	£'000	£'000
Cash flow from operating activities		
Operating profit for the year		353
Add back: Depreciation[1]		130
		483
Increase in inventories[2]	(56)	
Increase in trade receivables[3]	(65)	
Increase in trade payables[4]	12	
		(109)
Cash generated from operations		374
Interest paid[5]		(28)
Taxation paid[6]		(62)
Net cash from operating activities		284
Cash flows from investing activities		
Purchase of non-current assets		(250)
Cash flows from financing activities		
Payment of dividends [7]	(101)	
Issue of ordinary shares[8]	202	
Repayment of long-term loan [9]	(131)	
Net cash flow from financing activities		(30)
Net increase in cash and cash equivalents		4
Cash and cash equivalents at the beginning of the period[10]		78
Cash and cash equivalents at the end of the period[10]		82

Notes

(1) The addition of the new equipment would have increased the net book value of property, plant and equipment to £1,430,000 (£1,180,000 + £250,000). The balance sheet for Year 6 shows a net book value of £1,300,000. Therefore the charge for depreciation during Year 6 must have been £1,430,000 − £1,300,000 = £130,000.

(2) Inventories have increased from £122,000 in Year 5 to £178,000 in Year 6. Investing an additional £56,000 in inventories would reduce the cash balance.

(3) Trade receivables have increased from £207,000 in Year 5 to £272,000 in Year 6. Allowing credit to more customers would reduce the cash balance.

(4) Trade payables have increased from £276,000 in Year 5 to £288,000 in Year 6. Taking more credit from suppliers would increase the cash balance.

(5) All of the interest for the year must have been paid in cash. Otherwise we would see an amount for interest owing listed as a current liability on the balance sheet.

(6) The balance that was owed for taxation at the end of Year 5 is shown by the taxation owing of £26,000 on the balance sheet. The income statement shows that an additional amount of £73,000 must be paid for Year 6 tax. However, not all of this has been paid because the balance sheet shows that £37,000 is still owed at the end of Year 6. Therefore we can deduce the amount of tax that must have been paid as cash during Year 6 as follows:

	£'000
Amount owed at end of Year 5	26
Additional tax payable for Year 6	73
Total tax to be paid	99
Amount still owing at end of Year 6	(37)
Cash paid for tax during Year 6	62

(7) You should recall that the dividend paid might alternatively be shown earlier in the cash flow statement as a cash flow from operating activities.

(8) The share premium balance has increased in Year 6 and so has the share capital account. Therefore shares must have been sold at a premium and the total cash received is calculated as follows:

	£'000	£'000
Share capital balance Year 6	1,190	
Share capital balance Year 5	1,020	
Nominal/face value of shares sold		170
Share premium balance Year 6	127	
Share premium balance Year 5	95	
Premium received on sale of shares		32
Total cash received for shares		202

(9) The balance on the long-term loan has reduced by £285,000 − £154,000 = £131,000

(10) These are the balance sheet figures for Year 5 and Year 6.

4.8 Cash forecasts

The cash flow statement in the annual accounts helps people outside the company to monitor the cash-generating ability of the organisation. However, this statement will be of little assistance to managers internal to the business when they are trying to ensure that the business does not run into cash problems in the future, that is when they are trying to ensure that they do not get stuck at the petrol pumps!

For planning cash requirements in the future an internal planning document is used which is called the 'cash forecast'. This is one of the most important financial planning documents in a business. It will show the cash effect of all the decisions taken in the planning process: management decisions are taken every day concerning factors such as the level of inventories to be held and the amount of credit to be given to customers. As you have seen, these decisions will all affect cash flow.

These decisions may be designed to maximise the profitability of the organisation, but if there are insufficient cash resources to finance the plans they may need to be modified, or action might be needed to alleviate the cash restraint.

> *The cash forecast is referred to as an internal planning document because it is not usually made available to people outside the business.*

A cash forecast can give forewarning of potential cash problems so that managers can be prepared for the situation and not be caught unawares.

There are four possible cash positions that could arise:

Cash position	Possible management action
Short-term deficit	Arrange a bank overdraft, reduce receivables and inventories, increase payables.
Long-term deficit	Raise long-term finance, such as a loan or share capital.
Short-term surplus	Invest for a short term, increase receivables and inventories to boost sales, pay suppliers early to obtain a cash discount.
Long-term surplus	Expand or diversify operations, replace or update non-current assets.

A business that is permanently short of cash is not necessarily doomed. It may be that it simply needs more long-term capital to finance an increased level of activity.

You can see that the type of action taken by management will depend not only on whether a surplus or deficit is expected but also on how long the situation is expected to last. For instance, there would be little point in raising a long-term loan to cover a deficit which is expected to last for only three months.

The efficient manager must ensure that there is ample warning of both factors:

◆ Will there be cash surpluses or deficits?
◆ For how long will the surpluses or deficits last?

The cash forecast can provide the necessary warning. It is a statement which shows for each period in the near future (this could be months, weeks or even days) the forecast cash receipts and payments and the resulting forecast cash balances.

For example, a cash forecast might look like this.

	January £'000	February £'000	March £'000	April £'000	May £'000	June £'000
Receipts						
Sales	100	120	180	165	140	150
Other	10	10	10	10	10	10
Total receipts	110	130	190	175	150	160
Payments						
Material	65	90	80	55	60	55
Labour	50	50	50	50	50	50
Overheads	40	40	40	40	40	40
Purchase of office equipment	–	80	–	–	–	–
Total payments	155	260	170	145	150	145
Net cash flow	(45)	(130)	20	30	–	15
Opening cash balance	115	70	(60)	(40)	(10)	(10)
Closing cash balance	70	(60)	(40)	(10)	(10)	5

For each type of receipt and payment the cash flow is forecast to give the forecast net cash flow for the month. Looking at the January column, the forecast cash inflow is £110,000. The forecast cash outflow is £155,000 which results in a net cash outflow for January of £45,000 (£155,000 − £110,000). Based on the estimated cash flows between the date that the forecast is prepared and the beginning of January, the forecast opening cash balance in January is £115,000. This means that the forecast closing cash balance for January is £70,000 (£115,000 − £45,000). This becomes the opening balance for February, and so on to the end of June.

Managers using this cash forecast will be able to see that they will need short-term overdraft facilities from February until May. Alternatively, they could revise some of the planning decisions that they have taken; for example they could alter their proposed inventory or credit policy. However, if you look within the figures in the cash forecast, you can see that the main item causing the short-term deficit is the purchase of office equipment in February. If this item was removed from the forecast then no deficit would arise at all.

◆ Perhaps the purchase of the equipment could be delayed until June, when sufficient cash will be available?
◆ Could credit facilities be negotiated?
◆ Could the equipment be leased instead of purchased outright? This would improve the cash flow situation.

The important point is that the cash forecast has forewarned managers that a cash deficit will arise if they proceed as planned. They can take action in plenty of time to cover the deficit, or to avoid it arising.

Exercise

Based on the above cash forecast, what level of overdraft facility would you recommend?

Solution

The answer is not simply to look along the bottom line of closing cash balances and assume that the overdraft requirement is £60,000, that is the highest month-end overdrawn balance. It is important to consider the possible timing of cash flows within each month. For example, in March the opening balance is forecast to be £60,000 negative. If all the payments in March happen before any receipts come in, then the possible overdrawn balance could be as high as £60,000 + £170,000, or £230,000 negative.

This extreme situation is unlikely to arise, but it is possible that the timing of cash flows during the month could result in an overdraft greater than £60,000. Therefore it is important to look within the figures when interpreting the information provided by a cash forecast.

4.9 Income statement, cash flow and balance sheet: An example

To conclude this chapter there now follows a worked example which will draw on everything you have learned so far. Work through the example carefully and ensure that you understand where each figure in the solution has come from.

S and P Catering Limited

Sheila and Paul have recently been made redundant from their jobs in the company which employed them both. They have decided to use their redundancy money to set up a catering business. Since they intend to expand the business and seek investment from their friends and family in the future, they have decided to create a limited company, S and P Catering Limited.

Their business will offer a mobile catering service to offices, shops, pubs and factory premises in the local area. Hot meals, salads and sandwiches will be prepared in the business premises and then delivered to customers in insulated containers.

Sheila and Paul have already identified a ready market for their service and the business will commence trading on 1 July. They have approached their bank to negotiate overdraft facilities for the company and the bank manager has asked them to produce for the first six months of trading a forecast income statement, a cash forecast and a forecast balance sheet.

This is the sort of information that would be required to present to the bank manager when you go to discuss a loan for your brilliant business idea.

They have spent a lot of time in preparing the forecasts below, but they have no idea how to produce the statements which their bank manager has requested.

They have asked you to help them by preparing the required statements. Sheila and Paul have provided you with the following forecasts:

(1) **Capital**

The initial share capital will consist of Sheila and Paul's redundancy money of £8,000 each.

(2) **Forecast sales**

	£
July	7,500
August	8,750
September	10,750
October	11,000
November	11,500
December	11,500
	61,000

Eighty per cent of the sales will be paid for immediately in cash. The remainder will be made on credit, payable one month later.

(3) **Non-current assets**

(a) Equipment will be purchased on 1 July for £4,000 cash. The equipment is expected to have a ten-year life with no residual value after ten years.

(b) Two second-hand delivery vehicles will also be purchased for cash on 1 July for £6,000 each. They are expected to last for three years, after which time they will have no value.

(4) **Ingredients**

All ingredients will be purchased as they are required and no inventories will be held. Although Sheila hopes to negotiate a credit agreement once the business has got going, initially they will have to pay cash for all ingredients.

Ingredients will be purchased as follows:

	£
July	2,525
August	2,775
September	2,685
October	2,745
November	3,335
December	3,335
	17,400

(5) *Packing materials*

Packing materials will be purchased as follows:

	£
July	3,300
August	1,060
September	1,305
October	1,335
November	1,395
December	1,405
	9,800

Credit arrangements have been negotiated and the suppliers will require payment one month after the purchases are made.

Inventories of packing materials are expected to amount to £2,400 at the end of December.

(6) Salaries

Paul and Sheila will each be paid salaries of £1,500 per month. A part-time driver will be paid £400 per month.

(7) Overheads

(a) The business premises will be rented for £600 per month, payable quarterly in advance.

(b) Rates will amount to £1,200 per annum. This will be paid in two equal instalments on 1 July and 31 December.

(c) Expenses for telephones, gas and electricity will amount to £350 for the quarter ending 30 September. This will be paid in cash in October. These expenses for the quarter ending 31 December will be £600, which will be paid in cash next January.

(d) £180 per month is to be allowed for sundry cash expenses.

(e) Insurance of £800 will be paid on 1 July to cover the 12-month period ending 30 June of the following year.

(f) Advertising expenses of £440 will be incurred in cash in July. From August onwards, a continuous advertisement will be placed in a number of local newspapers for a monthly cost of £150, to be paid in cash.

(8) Dividend

Sheila and Paul intend to authorise an interim dividend of £2,000 on 31 December, to be paid in cash on 31 March of the following year.

(9) Taxation and interest

Ignore taxation, VAT and PAYE, and the interest cost of any overdraft.

Solution

The superscript numbers refer to the notes at the end of the solution.

Notice that the third column is used to perform a separate calculation for packing materials.

S and P Catering Limited: Forecast income statement for the six months ending 31 December

	£	£	£
Sales revenue[1]			61,000
Less			
Ingredients cost		17,400	
Packing materials purchases[2]	9,800		
less closing inventory[3]	(2,400)		
		7,400	
Salaries[4]		20,400	
Rent[5]		3,600	
Rates[6]		600	
Telephone, etc.[7]		950	
Sundry[8]		1,080	
Insurance[9]		400	
Advertising[10]		1,190	
Depreciation:			
equipment[11]		200	
vehicles[12]		2,000	
			55,220
Profit for the period			5,780
Dividend[13]			2,000
Retained profit to reserves			3,780

S and P Catering Limited: Cash forecast for the six months ending 31 December

	July £	August £	September £	October £	November £	December £
Receipts						
Share capital	16,000					
Cash sales[14]	6,000	7,000	8,600	8,800	9,200	9,200
Credit sales[15]		1,500	1,750	2,150	2,200	2,300
Total receipts	22,000	8,500	10,350	10,950	11,400	11,500
Payments						
Equipment[16]	4,000					
Vehicles	12,000					
Ingredients	2,525	2,775	2,685	2,745	3,335	3,335
Packing[17]		3,300	1,060	1,305	1,335	1,395
Salaries	3,400	3,400	3,400	3,400	3,400	3,400
Rent	1,800			1,800		
Rates	600					600
Telephone, etc.[18]				350		
Sundry	180	180	180	180	180	180
Insurance	800					
Advertising	440	150	150	150	150	150
Total payments	25,745	9,805	7,475	9,930	8,400	9,060
Net cash flow[19]	(3,745)	(1,305)	2,875	1,020	3,000	2,440
Opening balance[20]		(3,745)	(5,050)	(2,175)	(1,155)	1,845
Closing balance	(3,745)	(5,050)	(2,175)	(1,155)	1,845	4,285

S and P Catering Limited: Forecast balance sheet as at 31 December

	£	£	£
Non-current assets			
Equipment at cost	4,000		
less depreciation	(200)		
		3,800	
Vehicles at cost	12,000		
less depreciation	(2,000)		
		10,000	
Total non-current assets			13,800
Current assets			
Inventories		2,400	
Receivables[21]		2,300	
Prepaid expenses:			
rates[22]		600	
Insurance[23]		400	
Bank[24]		4,285	
		9,985	
Current liabilities			
Payables[25]	(1,405)		
Accrued expenses:			
Telephone, etc.[26]	(600)		
Dividend payable[27]	(2,000)		
		(4,005)	
Net current assets			5,980
			19,780
Capital and reserves			
Share capital			16,000
Reserves – retained profit[28]			3,780
			19,780

Note that the company is forecast to make profits over the six months, but that in the short term they will have a cash deficit for which arrangements must be made.

Notes

(1) Even though some of the sales are made on credit, all the sales revenue for the period is shown in the income statement.

(2) Similarly, all the packing material purchases are shown, even though some of the purchases will not yet have been paid for.

(3) It would not be fair to charge against sales the cost of all purchases made in the period, because some of the packing materials will still be in inventory. Therefore the cost of inventory is deducted to arrive at the true cost of the packing materials actually used up in the period.

(4) Salaries $= [(£1,500 \times 2) + £400] \times 6$ months $= £20,400$

(5) Rent $= £600 \times 6$ months $= £3,600$

(6) Rates for six months $= £1,200/2 = £600$

(7) Telephone, etc. $= £350 + £600 = £950$

(8) Sundry expenses $= £180 \times 6 = £1,080$

(9) Insurance for six months $= £800/2 = £400$

(10) Advertising $= £440 + (£150 \times 5) = £1,190$

(11) Depreciation for one year $= £4,000/10 = £400$. Therefore depreciation for six months $= £200$

(12) Depreciation for one year $= £12,000/3 = £4,000$. Therefore depreciation for six months $= £2,000$

(13) Interim dividend is paid part-way through the year, pending a final dividend payment at the end of the year (not known in this case).

(14) Cash sales receipts in July $= £7,500 \times 80\% = £6,000$, etc. for the remaining months.

(15) Credit sales receipts in July $=$ Nil, because these customers take one month to pay. They will pay in August, that is £7,500 $\times 20\% = £1,500$, and so on for the remaining months.

(16) All the non-current assets are purchased on 1 July, representing an immediate cash flow.

(17) No payments will be made for packing materials in July because purchases are on one month's credit. July's packing materials will be paid for in August, etc.

(18) The £600 to be paid next January for telephone, etc. does not feature in the cash forecast, because it is not a cash flow that will arise in this six-month period.

(19) The forecast net cash flow for July is £22,000 inflow less £25,745 outflow, that is £3,745 net outflow, and so on for the remaining months.

(20) The opening cash balance for July is zero because this is a new business. The closing balance from July becomes the opening balance for August, etc.

(21) Receivables will consist of December's credit customers who will not yet have paid, that is £11,500 $\times 20\% = £2,300$

(22)   The rates for the second half year will have been paid by 31 December. These will represent a payment in advance or prepayment.

(23)   The insurance for the full year will have been paid but only half has been charged to the income statement for six months. The remaining half is a prepayment.

(24)   The forecast bank balance is the closing balance for December taken from the cash forecast.

(25)   The packing material purchased in December will not have been paid for since it will be supplied on one month's credit.

(26)   The £600 expenses for the quarter ending 31 December have been charged as a valid cost in the income statement for the six months. However, they will not yet have been paid by the end of December therefore they must be shown as a current liability.

(27)   The dividend will have been authorised but not yet paid by the end of December, thus creating a liability of the company to the shareholders.

(28)   This is the retained profit figure shown in the income statement.

It might be a good idea to return in a day or two and attempt this example without looking at the solution. Good luck!

4.10 Summary

(1) A business can be making profits but still experience problems with cash flow because of the timing of receipts and payments.

(2) A cash flow statement enables people outside the business to make judgements about its ability to generate and manage cash.

(3) A cash flow statement presents cash flows under three main headings: from operating activities, from investing activities and from financing activities.

(4) A cash forecast is an internal planning document. It forewarns management of the cash effect of the decisions that they have taken in the planning process.

Review questions

(1) In a cash flow statement, which items are included under the heading 'Cash flows from investing activities'? (Section 4.4.2)

(2) Name two items that would be included in a cash flow statement under the heading 'Cash flows from financing activities'. (Section 4.4.3)

(3) Explain how the cash flow from operating activities is determined using the indirect method. (Section 4.6)

(4) What four possible cash positions could be signalled by a cash forecast? (Section 4.8)

Self-test questions

(1) Your friend has recently commented to you, 'I can't understand it. My accountant tells me I have made a £60,000 profit this year, but my cash balance has actually fallen by £10,000. How can this happen?'
Prepare an explanation for your friend.

(2) For each of the events below, state whether it will have:
  ◆ a positive impact on cash flow
  ◆ a negative impact on cash flow, or
  ◆ no impact on cash flow
    (a) An increase in receivables
    (b) Depreciation of a non-current asset
    (c) A reduction in payables
    (d) Write-off of a bad debt
    (e) An issue of ordinary shares

(3) The income statement for the year ended 30 June Year 3 and the balance sheets as at 30 June Years 2 and 3 for the Z Company are as follows:

The Z Company: Income statement for the year ended 30 June Year 3

	£'000	£'000
Revenue		675
Cost of sales		490
Gross profit		185
Distribution costs	52	
Administrative expenses	61	
Other expenses	12	
Total operating expenses		125
Operating profit		60
Interest payable		(6)
Interest receivable		3
Profit before tax		57
Taxation		12
Profit for the period		45

The Z Company: Balance sheets as at 30 June

	Year 2 £'000	Year 3 £'000
Non-current assets		
Intangible asset: purchased goodwill	42	20
Tangible assets: property, plant and equipment	256	259
	298	279
Current assets		
Inventories	27	61
Trade receivables	46	72
Cash and cash equivalents	15	12
	88	145
Current liabilities		
Trade payables	60	57
Taxation owing	4	7
Interest payments owing	–	2
	64	66
Working capital (net current assets)	24	79
Total assets less current liabilities	**322**	**358**
Share capital	250	255
Reserves – retained profits	9	33
Share premium	23	27
Shareholders' equity	282	315
Non-current liabilities: long-term loans	40	43
Capital employed	**322**	**358**

The following information also relates to the year ended 30 June Year 3:

◆ The company paid £47,000 for new office equipment.
◆ Non-current assets with a net book value of £5,000 were disposed of during the year for £7,000. The profit on the sale is included within administrative expenses in the income statement.
◆ The impairment of the purchased goodwill is included within administrative expenses in the income statement.
◆ No long-term loans were repaid during the period.
◆ The dividend paid during the year to shareholders was £21,000.

Required

Prepare a cash flow statement for the Z Company for the year ended 30 June Year 3.

(4) On 1 January, AB Limited will be formed with a share capital of £150,000. You are asked to use the following information to produce:

◆ A forecast income statement for the first six months.
◆ A cash forecast for each of the first six months.
◆ A forecast balance sheet as at 30 June Year 1.
   (a) £95,000 will be invested immediately in non-current assets.
   (b) Sales will be generated as follows:

	£
January	120,000
February	130,000
March	135,000
April	180,000
May	200,000
June	200,000
	965,000

   (c) All sales will be made on one month's credit.
   (d) Purchases of materials for which one month's credit will be allowed:

	£
January	80,000
February	75,000
March	60,000
April	70,000
May	70,000
June	70,000
	425,000

   (e) It is expected that £75,000 of this material will still be in inventory at the end of June, but that there will be no work-in-progress or finished goods inventory.
   (f) Labour costs will be paid as incurred, amounting to £270,000 incurred in even amounts over the six-month period.
   (g) Cash will be paid for overhead costs as follows:

	£
January	65,000
February	33,000
March	32,000
April	48,000
May	31,000
June	31,000
	240,000

Included in the January payment is an insurance bill for £20,000 which will provide cover for the whole of the year ending 31 December. Furthermore the rent bill of £8,000 for the period 1 April to 30 June will be outstanding at the end of June and is not included in the above figures.

(h) Depreciation on the non-current assets will be £3,000 for the six months.

Answers to self-test questions

(1) A number of factors such as the following could have caused the cash balance to fall, despite a profit being earned:

- ◆ Non-current assets may have been purchased. This would reduce the cash balance but only a proportion of the cost would be charged against profit, in the form of a depreciation provision.
- ◆ Inventories may have increased. This would reduce cash but if the inventory is unused it would not yet have been charged as an expense in the income statement.
- ◆ Sales may have been made on credit. The profit would have been increased by the sale, but no cash inflow would yet have resulted.
- ◆ A loan may have been repaid. This would reduce the cash balance but would not be shown as an expense in the income statement.
- ◆ Certain expenses may have been paid in advance for the next accounting period. The cash balance would have reduced but the expense would have been carried forward as a prepayment to be matched against the revenue for the forthcoming period.

(2)

(a) An increase in receivables would have a negative impact on cash flow.

(b) Depreciation provisions have no impact on cash flow. The cash is paid out when the non-current asset is originally purchased.

(c) A reduction in payables would have a negative impact on cash flow.

(d) Writing off a bad debt has no impact on cash flow.

(e) An issue of ordinary shares will have a positive impact on cash flow.

(3) The Z Company:

Cash flow statement for the year ended 30 June Year 3

	£'000	£'000
Cash flow from operating activities		
Operating profit for the year		60
Add back:		
Depreciation[1]		39
Impairment charge[2]		22
Less: Profit on disposal of non-current assets[3]		(2)
		119
Increase in inventories[4]	(34)	
Increase in trade receivables[5]	(26)	
Decrease in trade payables[6]	(3)	
		(63)
Cash generated from operations		56
Interest paid[7]		(4)
Taxation paid[8]		(9)
Net cash from operating activities		43
Cash flows from investing activities		
Purchase of non-current assets	(47)	
Proceeds from the sale of non-current assets	7	
Interest received	3	
Net cash flows from investing activities		(37)
Cash flows from financing activities		
Payment of dividend[9]	(21)	
Issue of ordinary shares[10]	9	
Proceeds from long-term loan[11]	3	
Net cash flows from financing activities		(9)
Net decrease in cash and cash equivalents		(3)
Cash and cash equivalents at beginning of period		15
Cash and cash equivalents at end of period		12

Notes

(1) The addition of the new office equipment would have increased the net book value of property, plant and equipment to £303,000 (£256,000 + £47,000). The disposal of non-current assets would then have reduced the net book value to £298,000 (£303,000 − £5,000). The balance sheet for Year 3 shows a net book value of £259,000. Therefore the charge for depreciation during Year 3 must have been £298,000 − £259,000 = £39,000.

(2) The impairment charge is the reduction in the balance sheet value of the purchased goodwill (£42,000 − £20,000). This is simply an accounting adjustment which does not involve the movement of cash. Like depreciation it is a non-cash item which has been charged in the calculation of profit. Therefore it must also be added back to the profit figure.

(3) The sale of non-current assets does not represent an operating cash flow. The cash proceeds from the sale of these assets will be shown later as a cash flow from investing activities. However, the profit on the sale of the assets has been included in the profit for the year, therefore we must deduct it to exclude it from the operating figures.

(4) Investing an additional £34,000 (£61,000 − £27,000) in inventories would reduce the cash balance.

(5) Allowing £26,000 additional credit to customers would reduce the cash balance (£72,000 − £46,000).

(6) Reducing the amount payable to suppliers (£60,000 − £57,000) would reduce the cash balance.

(7) We can deduce that not all of the interest payable for the year has actually been paid out in cash because a current liability is shown for interest payments still owing at the end of Year 3. Therefore the amount which has actually been paid in cash during the year is £4,000 (£6,000 payable (from income statement) less £2,000 still owing (from balance sheet)). Remember that the interest paid might alternatively be shown later in the statement as a cash flow from financing activities.

(8) The balance that was owed for taxation at the end of June Year 2 is shown as £4,000 within current liabilities on the balance sheet. The income statement shows that an additional amount of £12,000 must be paid for the latest year's tax. However, not all of this has been paid because the balance sheet shows that £7,000 is still owed at the end of June Year 3. Therefore we can deduce the

amount of tax that must have been paid as cash during the latest year as follows:

	£'000
Amount owed at end of June Year 2	4
Additional tax payable for latest year	12
Total tax to be paid	16
Amount still owing at end of June Year 3	(7)
Cash paid for tax during latest year	9

(9) The dividend paid might alternatively be shown earlier in the cash flow statement as a part of cash flow from operating activities.

(10) The share premium balance has increased in the latest year and so has the share capital account. Therefore shares must have been sold at a premium and the total cash received is calculated as follows:

	£'000	£'000
Share capital balance Year 3	255	
Share capital balance Year 2	250	
Nominal/face value of shares sold		5
Share premium balance Year 3	27	
Share premium balance Year 2	23	
Premium received on sale of shares		4
Total cash received for shares		9

(11) The balance on the long-term loan has increased from £40,000 to £43,000. This represents an additional inflow of cash.

(4) **AB Limited**
Forecast income statement for the six months ended 30 June Year 1

	£'000	£'000
Sales revenue		965
Less: Materials	425	
Less inventory[1]	(75)	
	350	
Labour	270	
Overhead[2]	238	
Depreciation	3	
		861
Profit to reserves[3]		104

AB Limited
Cash forecast for the six months ended 30 June Year 1

	January £'000	February £'000	March £'000	April £'000	May £'000	June £'000
Receipts						
Share capital	150	–	–	–	–	–
Sales receipts[4]	–	120	130	135	180	200
Total receipts	150	120	130	135	180	200
Payments						
Non-current assets	95					
Materials[5]	–	80	75	60	70	70
Labour	45	45	45	45	45	45
Overhead[6]	65	33	32	48	31	31
Total payments	205	158	152	153	146	146
Net cash flow	(55)	(38)	(22)	(18)	34	54
Opening cash balance[7]	–	(55)	(93)	(115)	(133)	(99)
Closing cash balance	(55)	(93)	(115)	(133)	(99)	(45)

AB Limited
Forecast balance sheet as at 30 June Year 1

	£'000	£'000	£'000
Non-current assets at cost			95
Less depreciation			(3)
			92
Current assets			
Material inventory	75		
Receivables[8]	200		
Prepaid expenses[9]	10	285	
Less current liabilities			
Payables[10]	(70)		
Accrued expenses[11]	(8)		
Bank overdraft[12]	(45)	(123)	
Working capital (net current assets)			162
			254
Financed by:			
Share capital			150
Reserves – retained profit[13]			104
			254

Notes

(1) The inventory will not have been sold, therefore it should not be charged as a cost against the revenue for the period.

(2)

	£'000
Expenditure incurred	240
Less insurance paid in advance (£20,000 × 6/12)	(10)
Plus rent accrued, from 1 April to 30 June	8
	238

(3) There will probably be some interest and tax to be paid or provided for and possibly a dividend will be declared. However, there is no mention of this in the example data, so for now the balance of profit will be taken to reserves.

(4) All sales will be made on one month's credit, therefore the sales for January will be received in cash in February, etc.

(5) One month's credit is allowed on material purchases, therefore the material received in January will be paid for in cash in February, etc.

(6) Overhead cash payments are detailed in the example data. The £8,000 owing for rent will not be paid in cash during this period.

(7) The opening cash balance for January is zero because this is a new business.

(8) The customers for June will not have paid by the end of June and they represent the receivables balance at the balance sheet date.

(9) The prepaid insurance is an unused asset at the end of June.

(10) As at 30 June, AB Limited will not have paid for the materials purchased in June. Therefore these suppliers represent the payables balance at the balance sheet date.

(11) The £8,000 rent owing is a current liability at the end of June.

(12) The bank overdraft is the closing balance for June as shown on the cash forecast.

(13) The reserve balance is the profit transferred at the end of June as shown on the forecast income statement.

The Accounts of Not-for-Profit Organisations

5.1 Introduction

In this chapter we will be looking at the accounts of organisations that are not set up to make a profit, for example clubs, societies and charities. We will be assuming that you have already studied the preceding chapters on income statements, balance sheets and cash flow statements. You will see that most of the principles in the accounts of not-for-profit organisations are exactly the same as the principles covered in these earlier chapters.

Even if your interest is focused on the accounts of profit-making organisations this chapter will provide some useful revision of the basic concepts underlying financial statements. The exercise in the chapter will also give you further practice in their application.

5.2 The differences in the accounts of not-for-profit organisations

The accounts for not-for-profit organisations are prepared in the same way as those for profit-making organisations. For example, the accruals principle is followed. You should recall that this means that expenses are only charged against revenue (or income/turnover) if they represent a fair cost for the period, and only the revenue that relates to the period is shown in that period's accounts.

For example Nominet, the not-for-profit registry for .uk domain names, includes the following statement in the Accounting Policies section of its 2006 annual report.

> Turnover
>
> Turnover represents fees for domain name registration and related services and membership subscriptions, excluding value added tax. Only subscriptions and fees relating to this accounting period are included as income of this accounting period. That part of subscriptions and fees which relates to future accounting periods is included in creditors as deferred income.

Thus Nominet accounts for its revenue/turnover received in advance in exactly the same way as the profit-making mobile phone companies that we discussed in Chapter 2. Subscriptions and fees received in advance are shown as a current liability of deferred income in the balance sheet until the service has actually been provided to the customer.

Another important similarity between the accounts of profit-making organisations and those of not-for-profit organisations is that expenditure in the accounts of not-for-profit organisations is divided between capital expenditure and revenue (or operating) expenditure. The capital expenditure is apportioned over the accounts of several accounting periods, using the depreciation methods that were demonstrated in Chapter 3. The following extract from the Accounting Policies section of the charity Oxfam's accounts for 2006–2007 provides an example of this.

Oxfam is a development, relief and campaigning organisation that works with others to overcome poverty and suffering around the world.

Tangible fixed assets and depreciation
Tangible fixed assets costing more than £1,000 are capitalised and included at cost, including any incidental expenses of acquisition.

Depreciation is provided on tangible fixed assets at rates calculated to write off the cost by equal annual instalments over their expected useful economic lives as follows:

Freehold land	Nil
Freehold buildings	50 years
Warehouse fittings and equipment	10 years
Computer infrastructure	10 years
Leasehold assets	5 years
Furniture, fixtures and equipment in GB	5 years
Motor vehicles	4 years
Computer equipment	3 years
Furniture, fixtures and equipment overseas	3 years

Just to refresh your memory of some of the principles covered in Chapter 3, it will be useful to have a look at the wording of parts of this statement.

◆ 'Tangible fixed assets costing more than £1,000 are capitalised . . .'
   The cost of these assets is not charged in full as expenditure in the year in which they are purchased. Instead the cost is *capitalised*, that is taken to the balance sheet, and is charged more gradually as depreciation over the asset's useful life. A depreciation charge is made in each year's income and expenditure account (often

used as the not-for-profit organisation's equivalent of an income statement).

♦ 'Depreciation is provided . . . at rates calculated to write off the cost . . .' Write off in this context means to share out the ori-ginal cost of the assets over the years that benefit from their use, that is over the fixed assets' 'expected useful economic lives'.

♦ '. . . by equal annual instalments . . .' means that Oxfam is using the straight-line method of depreciation, which we demonstrated in Chapter 3.

Exercise

Find the annual report of a company or organisation with which you are familiar. Annual reports are usually easy to locate on the organisation's website, if it has one. Turn to the section headed 'Accounting Policies' and look at the way that the organisation presents its depreciation policy. The information will not usually be as detailed as that provided by Oxfam but the type of information provided will be the same.

Hopefully you are beginning to appreciate that the same principles that you learned about in earlier chapters do indeed apply to not-for-profit organisations. However, there are some differences in the financial statements which are prepared for not-for-profit organisations:

(a) A not-for-profit organisation's version of the income statement will often be titled the *income and expenditure account*. This account is prepared following the same principles as an income statement. It lists separately all the items of income and expenditure, showing the net difference between the totals.

(b) The difference between income and expenditure for the period is referred to as a surplus or deficit, rather than a profit or loss.

(c) Not-for-profit organisations produce a balance sheet which usually shows on one side the fixed (non-current) assets, current assets and current liabilities. However, because these organisations are funded differently, they will not show 'capital' or 'shareholders' equity' on the other side of the balance sheet. The capital account is replaced by 'accumulated funds' or 'reserves'.

The fixed (non-current) assets will be shown at net book value and the current assets will be valued in the same way as for profit-making organisations. For example, any stock (inventory) is valued at the lower of cost and net realisable value, and a provision will be made for any doubtful debts.

(d) The accumulated funds or reserves are carried forward in the accounts to finance the activities of future periods. Sometimes part of the fund is earmarked for specific uses, and transfers may be made to separate reserves or funds, such as the maintenance reserve to provide for maintenance work to be carried out over a number of years.

You will see from the following example that there are many similarities between the accounts of not-for-profit organisations and those of profit-making organisations.

The Managers Club: Income and expenditure account for Year 5

	£	£
Income		
Fees and subscriptions[1]		40,800
Investment income		460
Income from magazine – advertising and sales		5,750
		47,010
Expenditure[2]		
Salaries	9,760	
Magazine costs	27,870	
Depreciation of fixed (non-current) assets	1,500	
Other expenses	950	
		40,080
Surplus for the year transferred to accumulated fund		6,930
Retained surplus brought forward[3]		5,650
Retained surplus carried forward		12,580

The Managers Club: Balance sheet as at the end of Year 5

	£	£	£
Fixed (non-current) assets			
Office equipment (at cost less depreciation)			7,500
Investments			5,000
			12,500
Current assets			
Stock (inventory)		320	
Debtors (receivables)		400	
Cash at bank		900	
		1,620	
Current liabilities			
Creditors (payables)	(1,020)		
Salaries owing[4]	(520)		
		(1,540)	
Net current assets[5]			80
Net assets			12,580
Accumulated fund/reserves			12,580

The balance sheet shows that the assets held by the Managers Club have been financed by accumulated surpluses of £12,580.

These assets comprise fixed (non-current) assets held at a net book value of £12,500 and net current assets (or working capital) of £80.

Notes

(1) All the income for the year is shown whether or not it has actually been received. Any income received in advance (e.g. advance subscriptions) is not shown in this year's income and expenditure account: it is instead carried forward on the balance sheet as a current liability.

(2) The expenses are adjusted for accruals and prepayments, in the same way as for a profit-making organisation.

(3) This is the balance on the accumulated fund/reserve account brought forward from Year 4. This balance would have been shown on the balance sheet at the end of Year 4.

(4) This is an accrual for salaries owing. This amount owed to staff at the end of Year 5 would have been added to the

amount paid for salaries during the year. The final total would have been charged as an expense in the income and expenditure account.

(5) Notice that not-for-profit organisations need working capital in the same way that profit-making organisations need it to keep their operations moving. As with the balance sheets for profit-making organisations, different arrangements of the balance sheet exist and a figure for the net current assets might not actually be shown. However the figures for total current assets and total current liabilities will be available from the balance sheet so that it is possible to calculate the value of the organisation's working capital.

Exercise

Using the Managers Club's income and expenditure account as a guide to the type of activities that they undertake, can you think of examples of the items that might be included in the following figures in this organisation's balance sheet?

  (i) Stock (inventory)
 (ii) Debtors (receivables)
(iii) Creditors (payables)

Solution

You might have thought of the following:

  (i) Inventory: inventory of magazines, and advertising and recruitment literature
 (ii) Receivables: credit customers for sales of the magazines; amounts owed to the club by organisations that have placed advertisements in the magazine but have not yet paid the amount due; members' subscriptions for Year 5 still outstanding at the end of the year
(iii) Payables: an outstanding bill for magazine printing costs that the club has not yet paid; members' subscriptions for Year 6 received in advance (this is deferred income)

You might have thought of many other items to include under these headings, following the principles that you have learned in this and earlier chapters.

You should now be in a position to prepare a set of accounts for a not-for-profit organisation. This exercise will also provide useful practice at applying the fundamental concepts underlying the preparation of financial statements for all types of organisation.

Exercise

The following balances have been extracted from the books of the Sporting Tennis Club as at the end of Year 7. Use these balances, and the notes which follow, to prepare an income and expenditure account for Year 7 and a balance sheet as at the end of Year 7.

	£
Subscriptions received	1,600
Utilities (gas, electricity, etc.)	375
Insurance	280
Maintenance	322
Equipment at cost	2,500
Depreciation of equipment to end of Year 6	1,000
Other expenses	108
Profit from Christmas dance	380
Cash at bank	125
Fund/reserves at end of Year 6	730

Notes

(1) A further £350 of subscriptions is in arrears, that is these members have not yet paid their subscriptions for Year 7. All are expected to pay early in Year 8. There were no arrears at the end of Year 6.

(2) A gas bill of £145 has been received but not yet paid. No other utility bills are outstanding.

(3) Insurance of £75 has been paid in advance for Year 8.

(4) Equipment is depreciated on a straight-line basis over five years, assuming that it will have no residual value at the end of five years.

Solution

The Sporting Tennis Club:
Income and expenditure account for Year 7

	£	£
Income		
Subscriptions[1]		1,950
Profit from Christmas dance		380
		2,330
Expenditure		
Utilities[2]	520	
Insurance[3]	205	
Maintenance	322	
Depreciation on equipment[4]	500	
Other expenses	108	
		1,655
Surplus for the year to reserves		675

The Sporting Tennis Club:
Balance sheet as at the end of Year 7

	£	£
Fixed (non-current) assets		
Equipment (at cost less depn.)[4]		1,000
Current assets		
Debtors/receivables[1]	350	
Prepaid expenses[3]	75	
Cash at bank	125	
	550	
Current liabilities		
Accrued expenses[2]	(145)	
Net current assets		405
		1,405
Accumulated fund[5]		**1,405**

Notes

(1) The subscriptions for the year on an accruals basis are £1,600 received plus £350 still to be received in respect of Year 7. The £350 outstanding is shown as a debtor (receivable) under current assets on the balance sheet.

(2) Utilities expense = £375 paid plus £145 accrued = £520. The £145 accrual is shown under current liabilities on the balance sheet.

(3) Insurance expenses = £280 paid less £75 paid in advance = £205. The £75 relates to Year 8 and should not be charged in this year's income and expenditure account. It is shown under current assets in the balance sheet.

(4) The equipment cost should not be charged in the income and expenditure account because it is to be capitalised and apportioned over a number of years using the depreciation charge. Annual depreciation = £2,500/5 = £500. The net book value to be shown in the balance sheet is calculated as follows.

	£
Equipment at cost	2,500
Less: depreciation to end of Year 6	(1,000)
depreciation for Year 7	(500)
Net book value at the end of Year 7	1,000

(5) Balance on accumulated fund at end of Year 7:

	£
Balance at the end of Year 6	730
Surplus added for Year 7	675
	1,405

How did you get on? That was quite a tough exercise and if you were able to follow its logic then you are now in a good position to move on and learn the basics of the interpretation of financial statements.

5.3 Summary

(1) In a not-for-profit organisation an income and expenditure account usually replaces the income statement that would be prepared in a profit-making organisation.

(2) The main difference that arises in the balance sheet is in depicting the way in which the organisation is financed.

Review questions

(1) How is capital expenditure treated in the accounts of not-for-profit organisations? (Section 5.2)

(2) If expenditure exceeds income for a period in a not-for-profit organisation this is not referred to as a loss. What term is used instead? (Section 5.2)

Self-test questions

(1) The Mother and Toddler Club received £780 in subscriptions from members during Year 4, which included £90 in arrears for Year 3. At the end of Year 4 the members' subscriptions outstanding were £60, all of which were received early in Year 5.

What are the correct entries in respect of members' subscriptions in the:

(a) income and expenditure account for Year 4?
(b) balance sheet as at the end of Year 4?

(2) In its statement of accounting policies, Oxfam describes its policies concerning vehicles and equipment depreciation and stocks (inventories) as follows.

Vehicles and equipment used in programmes overseas are considered to have a useful economic life of one year or less. They are not capitalised but are charged in full to charitable expenditure when purchased.

Unsold donated items are not included in closing stock since their cost is nil and their value is uncertain until sold.

Required

(a) Explain what is meant by the statement about vehicles and equipment and why Oxfam may have decided not to capitalise these items.

(b) Explain why Oxfam have placed no value on the stock (inventory) of unsold donated items in their shops.

(3) The following balances have been extracted from the books of the Shaldon Amateur Dramatic Society as at the end of Year 8. Use these balances, and the notes which follow, to prepare an income and expenditure account for Year 8 and a balance sheet as at the end of Year 8.

	£
Subscriptions received	1,280
Secretary and treasurer's expenses	292
Insurance	280
Hire of village hall for meetings	100
Equipment at net book value at end of year 7	891
Payment for equipment repairs	156
Other expenses	94
Profit from Christmas pantomime	548
Cash at bank	77
Fund/reserves at end of Year 7	1,674
Equipment purchased during Year 8	224
Donation received	150
Entertainment expenses	52
Interest received	27
Bank deposit account	1,489
Inventory of programmes for forthcoming Spring show	24

Notes

(1) Subscriptions received include £30 which has been received from members in advance for Year 9. There were no arrears or payments in advance at the end of Year 7.
(2) Hire of the village hall costs £10 per meeting. The society holds one meeting every month.
(3) Insurance of £40 has been paid in advance for Year 9.
(4) The equipment depreciation charge for Year 8 is £358.

Answers to self-test questions

(1) (a) The income and expenditure account for Year 4 will show, in the income section, members' subscriptions of £750 for the year. This is calculated as follows.

	£
Received during Year 4	780
Less amount relating to Year 3	(90)
Plus Year 4 subscriptions outstanding	60
	750

(b) The balance sheet as at the end of Year 4 will include a current asset of £60 in respect of members' subscriptions receivable.

(2) (a) If an asset is capitalised it is classified as a fixed (non-current) asset and its cost is not charged in full against the income of the period when it is purchased. Instead it is held on the balance sheet and its cost is depreciated over the years of its useful life.

In this case Oxfam has taken a more prudent approach and has charged the full cost of the assets in the income and expenditure account for the year of purchase.

An asset should only be capitalised if future accounting periods will benefit from its use. Oxfam considers that this is not the case with vehicles and equipment used in overseas programmes. These items are considered to have a useful economic life of one year or less, therefore their cost is charged in full as revenue expenditure in the year of purchase.

(b) An organisation's inventories should be valued at the lower of cost and net realisable value. Oxfam does not pay a supplier for donated items, therefore as far as Oxfam's records are concerned these items have no cost value. Accordingly they are valued at the lower of their cost and resale value, which is zero. Therefore no value is shown on Oxfam's balance sheet in respect of these donated items.

(3) **Shaldon Amateur Dramatic Society: Income and expenditure account for Year 8**

	£	£
Income		
Subscriptions[1]		1,250
Profit from Christmas pantomime		548
Donation received		150
Interest received		27
		1,975
Expenditure		
Secretary and treasurer's expenses	292	
Insurance[2]	240	
Hire of village hall[3]	120	
Equipment repairs[4]	156	
Entertainment expenses	52	
Equipment depreciation	358	
Other expenses	94	
		1,312
Surplus for the year to reserves		663

Shaldon Amateur Dramatic Society: Balance sheet as at the end of Year 8

	£	£
Fixed (non-current) assets		
Equipment (at cost less depn.)[5]		757
Current assets		
Inventory of programmes	24	
Prepaid expenses[2]	40	
Bank deposit account	1,489	
Cash at bank	77	
	1,630	
Current liabilities		
Deferred income[1]	(30)	
Accrued expenses[3]	(20)	
	(50)	
Net current assets		1,580
		2,337
Accumulated fund[6]		**2,337**

Notes

(1) Subscriptions receivable for Year 8 = £1,280 − £30 received in advance = £1,250. The amount of £30 received in advance is shown as a liability of deferred income in the balance sheet as at the end of Year 8.

(2) Insurance for Year 8 = £280 − £40 paid in advance = £240. The amount of £40 paid in advance is shown as an unused current asset in the balance sheet.

(3) Hall hire cost for 1 year = 12 months × £10 = £120. Since only £100 has actually been paid an accrual for £20 of hire cost owing is shown in the balance sheet under current liabilities.

(4) Equipment repairs cannot be capitalised, that is added to the net book value of the equipment. Only expenditure which enhances the value of a fixed (non-current) asset can be capitalised. Therefore this expenditure must be charged in full to the income and expenditure account for the year.

(5)

	£
Equipment net book value for Year 7	891
Additions during Year 8	224
	1,115
Less depreciation for Year 8	(358)
Equipment net book value for Year 8	757

(6) Balance on accumulated fund at the end of Year 8:

	£
Balance at the end of Year 7	1,674
Surplus added for Year 8	663
	2,337

Interpreting Financial
Statements: Part 1

6.1   Introduction

In the next two chapters you will be learning how to analyse and interpret a set of financial statements. You will discover what questions you should ask about the accounts, and how and where to find the answers to these questions.

In this chapter you will be focusing on the income statement and balance sheet, using them to assess the organisation's profitability, liquidity and efficiency. In Chapter 7 you will be looking at financial structure, and at how to assess a company's performance from the point of view of a shareholder or potential shareholder. In that chapter you will also be introduced to the analysis of cash flow statements.

6.2   Using ratios to analyse accounting statements

6.2.1   Why do we use ratios?

Let me tell you about my aunt Pamela. She owns a small newsagent's shop in our local town, employing one sales assistant, and seven school children who deliver morning papers. Suppose I told you that she earned £0.5 m profit from her business last year, Would you say that was a good result or a poor result?

Hopefully you would say that was a good result. It would be quite astonishing to earn an annual profit of £0.5 m from such a small, relatively low-risk enterprise!

Now consider a public limited company (plc) which owns a chain of newsagents, with an outlet in every high street and at every major railway station and airport in the UK. If I told you that this plc earned £0.5 m profit last year, would you say that was a good result or a poor result?

This time you probably said that was a poor result. With so many outlets, you would expect a return of more than £0.5 m in one year.

> *The comparison of these two organisations is reasonably valid because they are in the same line of business.*

If you agreed with my answers to these two questions, you were automatically relating the amount of profit to the size of the business earning the profit, that is you were performing a ratio analysis. A profit figure viewed in isolation is not very helpful in assessing an organisation's performance. However, if, for example, we relate the profit to the amount of money invested in the business (i.e. the size of the business) we can begin to judge whether or not the profit figure is adequate. Furthermore we can then legitimately compare the performance of two businesses.

A direct comparison of my aunt Pamela's profits with those of the large plc would obviously be unrealistic. We would expect that the plc's profits would be larger, but it would be difficult to state, in absolute terms, how much larger we expect them to be. However, if we express the profits in relation to some other figure, for example the business sales or the capital invested in the business, the resulting ratios would be comparable and would enable us to make some judgements about the businesses' performance.

6.2.2 Making comparisons

A ratio calculated in isolation is of little use unless there is some sort of yardstick or benchmark to compare it with. Suppose that the company you work for earned a return on the money invested in it (the capital employed) of 20 per cent last year, Would you say that was a good result or a poor result?

It is not possible for you to answer that question without making some sort of comparison. You probably answered 'it depends'. On what does it depend?

Exercise

Can you think of any bases that could be used to assess whether the 20 per cent return was a good result or a poor result?

Solution

You may have thought of the following bases:

◆ Compare with the same ratio for past periods. It may be possible to see whether there is a trend in the ratio over time.
◆ Compare with the budgeted or planned ratio for the period.
◆ Compare with the performance of other similar businesses.

6.2.3 The most common groups of ratios

There are dozens of ratios that could be used to analyse the performance of a business. In this book we will look at how to calculate and interpret the most common ratios.

The easiest way to approach a full ratio analysis is to group the ratios according to the particular aspect of business performance or financial position that they are attempting to monitor. We will consider five groups of ratios as follows:

◆ *Profitability*: Did the organisation make profitable use of the capital available to it? Was revenue adequate in relation to the amount of capital employed? Was the sales activity profitable?
◆ *Efficiency*: Is the business making efficient use of its resources?
◆ *Liquidity*: Can the company meet its current obligations as they fall due? How well equipped is it to pay its way in the short term?
◆ *Financial structure*: How much of the business's capital is contributed by the owners, and how much is contributed by outsiders? How easily did the business meet its commitments to pay interest on its borrowings?
◆ *Investment*: What returns are shareholders receiving on their investment? Is investor confidence in the company high or low?

The last two groups of ratios, financial structure and investment, will be reviewed in Chapter 7. In this chapter we will be discussing the assessment of profitability, efficiency and liquidity.

6.3 LMN plc's financial statements

The best way to demonstrate the interpretation of financial statements is to work through an example. Throughout this chapter and the next we will be referring to the following summarised income statements and balance sheets for LMN plc.

LMN plc: Income statements for the year ended 31 December

	Year 2 (£m)	Year 3 (£m)
Revenue	150.0	250
Cost of sales	100.0	175
Gross profit	50.0	75
Operating expenses	38.0	49
Operating profit	12.0	26
Finance costs: interest payable	–	1
	12.0	25
Taxation	5.0	11
Profit for the year	7.0	14

A reminder: Operating profit is another term used to describe 'profit before interest and tax'.

LMN plc: Balance sheet as at 31 December

	Year 2 £m	Year 2 £m	Year 3 £m	Year 3 £m
Non-current assets		52.0		85
Current assets				
Inventories	12.0		16	
Trade receivables	18.0		40	
Cash and cash equivalents	10.0		4	
	40.0		60	
Current liabilities				
Trade payables	(10.2)		(28)	
Other creditors	(9.8)		(17)	
	(20.0)		(45)	
Net current assets		20.0		15
		72.0		100
Financed by:				
Ordinary £1 shares		60.0		60
Reserves – retained profit		12.0		20
Shareholders' equity		72.0		80
Non-current liabilities:				
loan capital/borrowings		–		20
Capital employed		72.0		100

6.4 Begin with an overview

It is too easy to launch into calculating ratios without first stopping to look at the general trend in the organisation's performance and financial position: you should try to obtain a 'feel' for what has been happening. This will help you to interpret the ratios once they are calculated.

Exercise

Look at LMN plc's financial statements and write the answers to the following general questions.

- What is the movement in revenue?
- What is the movement in gross profit and in operating profit?
- Is the company investing in non-current assets?

Solution

LMN's activity has expanded dramatically. Revenue and profits have increased. The operating profit has increased proportionately more than the gross profit.

The company is investing in non-current assets. The balance sheet value of non-current assets has increased by more than 50 per cent, despite the depreciation charge for the year (you can also tell this by looking at the cash flow statement which is shown in Chapter 7).

6.4.1 Common size statements

A technique that you might find useful when you are at the early stages of analysing a company's financial statements is to prepare a common size statement. This is a statement which simply expresses each figure within the income statement or balance sheet as a percentage of a total.

For example, a common size income statement might express each figure in the statement as a percentage of the revenue. A common size balance sheet might express each figure in the balance sheet as a percentage of the total assets.

When you are looking at the results for more than one year, a common size statement can sometimes help you to identify the major changes that have occurred between the two years. It is usually possible to get a general feel for the changes by looking at the absolute figures but a common size statement can help to really focus your attention on the major changes that might be worthy of further analysis.

Example: Common size balance sheets

To begin the preparation of two common size balance sheets for LMN plc we need to know the value of the total assets at the end of each of the two years. The total asset value is the sum of the balance sheet value of the non-current assets and the current assets. Therefore the total asset value at the end of Year 2 is £92 m (52 + 40) and at the end of Year 3 is £145 m (85 + 60).

Beginning with Year 2, the non-current asset balance as a percentage of the total assets of £92m is 56.5 per cent (52/92 × 100%). Performing the same calculation for each figure on the balance sheet, that is expressing it as a percentage of £92 m, produces the following results.

LMN plc: Common size balance sheets as at 31 December

	Year 2 (%)	Year 3 (%)
Non-current assets	56.5	58.6
Current assets		
Inventories	13.0	11.0
Trade receivables	19.6	27.6
Cash and cash equivalents	10.9	2.8
Total assets	**100.0**	**100.0**
Trade payables	11.1	19.3
Other creditors	10.7	11.7
Ordinary shares	65.2	41.4
Retained profit	13.0	13.8
Loan capital	–	13.8
	100.0	**100.0**

The Year 3 figures are calculated by expressing each Year 3 balance sheet figure as a percentage of the total assets of £145 m.

Exercise

What information can we obtain from these common size statements?

Solution

The common size statements assist our initial analysis by helping us to see the significance of the major changes that have occurred between the two years.

◆ Although the absolute amount of money invested in non-current assets has increased (from £52 m to £85 m), the percentage of total assets represented by non-current assets has increased by only just over 2 per cent (from 56.5% to 58.6%).

◆ There is a significant increase in the proportion of the investment in total assets which is tied up in receivables. This has increased from 19.6 per cent to 27.6 per cent.

◆ This increase in receivables has been partly funded by a significant increase in trade payables, from 11.1 per cent to 19.3 per cent.

◆ Only 2.8 per cent of total assets is represented by cash and cash equivalents in Year 3, compared with 10.9 per cent in Year 2.

◆ 13.8 per cent of the company's assets are financed by external investors (loan capital) in Year 3. What is the potential impact of this?

In conclusion, the common size statement has signalled that we might need to pay particular attention to the company's control of its receivables, its liquidity and the impact of the new reliance on external long-term borrowing.

Common size balance sheets can also be useful when comparing the balance sheets of two different-sized companies. For example if one company's balance sheet is expressed in units of £'000 and the other company's balance sheet is expressed in £million it can be difficult to pinpoint any differences between the relative magnitude of the companies' assets and liabilities. Perhaps one company has proportionately more of its capital invested in non-current assets and a relatively high level of current liabilities compared with the other company. This can be difficult to spot using the absolute figures when comparing £'000 with £million. The preparation of a common size balance sheet for each company converts all figures to percentages which can be compared directly and are not affected by the relative size of the companies.

6.5 Assessing profitability

The following ratios may be used to evaluate the organisation's profitability:

- ◆ Return on capital employed
- ◆ Operating profit margin
- ◆ Asset turnover
- ◆ Gross profit margin

Strictly speaking, asset turnover is an efficiency ratio rather than a profitability ratio. However, it has been included here because, as you will see, it helps to explain the movement in the key profitability ratio: return on capital employed.

6.5.1 Return on capital employed

This is a fundamental ratio which is used to monitor business performance. It measures the amount of profit earned as a percentage of capital employed, that is it helps to provide the answer to the question that we were considering when evaluating the performance of my aunt Pamela's newsagent's shop: 'Is the profit sufficient considering the amount of capital invested to earn that profit?'

The return on capital employed (ROCE) is calculated as follows:

$$ROCE = \frac{\text{Profit before interest and taxation}}{\text{Share capital} + \text{reserves} + \text{long-term loans}} \times 100\%$$

The profit figure is usually taken before interest because this is the profit that has been earned to pay all the providers of finance, that is the profit on the top of the calculation 'belongs' to the providers of finance on the bottom of the calculation.

Some analysts argue that profit before interest and tax (operating profit) is the most appropriate measure of an organisation's performance because it is the profit over which operational managers can exercise day-to-day control: they have some influence over this profit measure. If we chose profit after interest, the performance would be distorted by the way in which the organisation is financed, that is by how much interest has to be paid. Operational managers have no direct influence over this. If we used the profit after taxation the performance would be distorted by the vagaries of the taxation charge, which again is outside the control of operational managers.

The ROCE for LMN for Year 2 is

$$\frac{12}{72} \times 100\% = 16.7\%$$

Exercise

Calculate LMN's ROCE for Year 3.

Solution

$$\text{ROCE for Year 3} = \frac{26}{100} \times 100\% = 26\%$$

The ROCE has improved dramatically. So now we need to start to look at why this has happened. We are going to perform a subanalysis of the ROCE, that is break it down into its constituent parts.

6.5.2   The constituent parts of ROCE

Returning for a moment to the example of a small newsagent's shop, suppose that you wanted to improve the shop's ROCE. What basic steps could you take to try to achieve an improvement?

Exercise

Name four basic steps that you could take to improve the ROCE of a newsagent's shop.

Solution

(1)   Put the prices up (assuming that this does not adversely affect sales volume)

(2)   Reduce costs

(3)   Sell more newspapers, etc.

(4)   Reduce the amount of capital employed.

Steps 1 and 2 in the above solution can effectively be combined into one simple statement: 'earn more profit from each sale that is made'. This aspect of profitability is monitored by the operating profit margin. This ratio relates the operating profit to the sales value.

$$\text{Operating profit margin} = \frac{\text{Profit before interest and taxation} \times 100\%}{\text{Revenue}}$$

Remember that we are trying to perform a subanalysis of the ROCE. Therefore we must use the same profit measure that we used in the ROCE calculation.

Steps 3 and 4 could be stated in general terms as 'generate more sales per £1 of capital invested'.

This aspect of performance is measured by the asset turnover ratio, which monitors the level of sales revenue relative to capital employed.

$$\text{Asset turnover} = \frac{\text{Revenue}}{\text{Share capital} + \text{reserves} + \text{long-term loans}}$$

Remember again that we are still performing a subanalysis of the ROCE. Therefore the figure for the capital employed (the denominator) must be the same as in the ROCE calculation.

Now we can put all this together to see the constituent parts of ROCE.

$$\text{ROCE} = \frac{\text{Profit before interest and taxation}}{\text{Captial employed}}$$
$$= \frac{\text{Profit before interest and taxation}}{\text{Revenue}} \times \frac{\text{Revenue}}{\text{Capital employed}}$$
$$\text{ROCE} = \text{operating profit margin} \times \text{asset turnover}$$

You should be able to see that when the formulae for operating profit margin and asset turnover are multiplied together, the revenue on the top and bottom of the calculation cancels out, leaving the basic formula for the ROCE.

Therefore when we want to explore the reasons for changes in the ROCE, we can break it down between the profitability of sales (the operating profit margin) and the level of sales revenue achieved from the assets (the asset turnover).

Exercise

Use the data below to calculate the following ratios for Year 4 for the two businesses:

◆ Return on capital employed
◆ Operating profit margin
◆ Asset turnover

Year 4	The Posh Food Company	The Discount Food Company
	£'000	£'000
Sales revenue	200	1,275
Operating profit	40	65
Capital employed	335	540

Solution

ROCE	$(^{40}/_{335})$ 11.9%	$(^{65}/_{540})$ 12.0%
Operating profit margin	$(^{40}/_{200})$ 20.0%	$(^{65}/_{1,275})$ 5.1%
Asset turnover	$(^{200}/_{335})$ 0.6 times	$(^{1,275}/_{540})$ 2.4 times

For each company, you could check the following:

operating profit margin × asset turnover = ROCE (approx.)

Notice that the asset turnover is usually expressed in terms of a number of times, rather than as a percentage.

It is worth looking in more detail at the results of this exercise. The ROCE is similar for both companies: about 12 per cent. Both companies are in the same business and therefore we might expect to see them earning the same sort of return for the same level of business risk.

However, you can see that each company has earned the overall ROCE in a quite different way. The Posh Food Company has earned a high margin on sales (20 per cent), possibly by charging higher prices, whereas The Discount Food Company has a comparatively low operating profit margin (5.1 per cent) – their selling prices are probably relatively low. But The Discount Food Company has generated a much higher level of sales revenue compared to capital employed (higher asset turnover) and this has compensated for the lower profit margin to produce a comparable overall ROCE.

You should now be in a position to analyse LMN's ROCE into its constituent parts.

6.5.3 Operating profit margin for LMN

Exercise

Calculate LMN's operating profit margin for Years 2 and 3.

Solution

$$\text{Operating profit margin for Year 2} = \frac{12 \times 100\%}{150} = 8.0\%$$

$$\text{Operating profit margin for Year 3} = \frac{26 \times 100\%}{250} = 10.4\%$$

The operating profit margin has improved in Year 3 compared with Year 2. This means that sales are being achieved more profitably. A smaller proportion of the sales revenue is being absorbed as costs. This has been a contributory factor in the improvement in ROCE.

6.5.4 Asset turnover for LMN

Exercise

Calculate LMN's asset turnover for Years 2 and 3.

Solution

$$\text{Asset turnover for Year 2} = \frac{150}{72} = 2.1 \text{ times}$$

$$\text{Asset turnover for Year 3} = \frac{250}{100} = 2.5 \text{ times}$$

Sales achieved during Year 2 were 2.1 times the level of capital employed. This is a measure of how efficiently the assets of the business were being used to generate sales. Generally, the higher the asset turnover, the more productively the assets were being used.

The asset turnover has improved in Year 3 compared with Year 2. This means that LMN's assets are being used more productively in Year 3. More sales are being generated per £1 of capital invested in the assets. This has also been a contributory factor in the improvement in LMN's ROCE.

6.5.5   Gross profit margin

The gross profit margin relates the gross profit to the sales revenue for the period:

$$\text{Gross profit margin} = \frac{\text{Gross profit}}{\text{Sales revenue}} \times 100\%$$

Look back to Chapter 2 if you have forgotten the difference between gross profit and operating profit.

For many retailing and manufacturing organisations, the cost of sales or the cost of the goods sold is a major part of total cost. Therefore this ratio can be of vital importance to the overall performance of this type of business.

$$\text{Gross profit margin for Year 2} = \frac{50}{150} \times 100\% = 33.3\%$$

Exercise

Calculate LMN's gross profit margin for Year 3.

Solution

$$\text{Gross profit margin for Year 3} = \frac{75}{250} \times 100\% = 30\%$$

6.5.6   LMN's profitability ratios: Summary

The ratios that we have calculated for Years 2 and 3 are as follows:

	Year 2	Year 3
Return on capital employed	16.7%	26.0%
Operating profit margin	8.0%	10.4%
Asset turnover	2.1 times	2.5 times
Gross profit margin	33.3%	30.0%

Exercise

What general conclusions can you draw about LMN's profitability during Year 3?

Solution

ROCE has improved dramatically, due to increases in both the asset turnover and the operating profit margin. Not only is more being sold in Year 3, but it is also being sold more profitably than in Year 2.

The gross profit percentage has decreased. This could be due to an increase in the cost of goods sold. However, it is perhaps more likely in this particular case that the selling price of goods has been reduced in order to stimulate the increase in sales revenue. This has reduced the gross profitability of sales, but the extra volume has helped to make sales more profitable at the operating profit level.

Later in this text you will learn that part of the reason for this increase in profitability is the spreading of fixed costs (those costs that do not increase with sales volume) over a higher level of sales.

6.5.7   Problems with the use and interpretation of ROCE

A number of problems arise with the use and interpretation of ROCE:

(a)   The main problem with ROCE is that the definition of capital employed can vary as can the profit figure used for the numerator. Different analysts will calculate the ratio in different ways, therefore care is needed when comparing two calculated ROCEs. It is essential to ensure that they both are calculated using the same method.

(b) ROCE can give a misleading guide to efficiency if a company's assets are not valued at current prices, for example if a company's land and buildings have increased in value but this increase is not reflected on the balance sheet.

(c) Linked to problem (b), capital investment often results in low returns in the early years and an annual calculation of ROCE may therefore be distorted in the short term by investment in longer term projects. The following example will help to illustrate this point.

Example

A company is about to invest in a new machine. This will cost £1,000 and will last for five years, after which time it will have no value. During its five-year life the machine will generate an annual profit of £100, after taking account of depreciation.

The return on the capital employed in this machine for each of the five years could be calculated as follows:

End of year		Net book value of machine (£)		ROCE (%)
1	(£1,000 − £200)	800	$(^{100}/_{800})$	12.5
2	(£800 − £200)	600	$(^{100}/_{600})$	16.7
3	(£600 − £200)	400	$(^{100}/_{400})$	25.0
4	(£400 − £200)	200	$(^{100}/_{200})$	50.0
5	(£200 − £200)	0	$(^{100}/_{0})$	Infinite

The annual depreciation charge is (£1,000 ÷ 5 =) £200. This is the amount by which the net book value is reduced each year.

This simple example demonstrates that the lower the net book value of the asset, the higher will be the ROCE for a given level of profit. Therefore new capital investment can depress the ROCE in the short term, and if assets are undervalued then the ROCE may be misleadingly high.

6.6 Assessing efficiency

This group of ratios assesses whether the organisation is making efficient use of its resources. We have already seen that LMN's asset utilisation, as measured by its asset turnover, improved in Year 3.

Now we will investigate separately how LMN managed each of its main groups of assets.

Ratios that may be calculated under this category include the following:

◆ Inventory turnover period
◆ Receivables collection period
◆ Payables payment period
◆ Non-current asset turnover

6.6.1   Inventory turnover period

This ratio measures the average number of days' inventory held on the balance sheet date. It can be calculated for LMN in Year 2 as follows:

$$\text{Inventory turnover period} = \frac{\text{Inventory}}{\text{Cost of sales per day}} = \frac{12}{\left(\frac{100}{365}\right)}$$
$$= 44 \text{ days}$$

This means that, based on the average cost of sales per day during Year 2, the year-end inventories represented 44 days' worth of sales.

However, it is important to bear in mind that this ratio is based on year-end balance sheet data. The inventory held on this particular date may not be representative of what has been held during the year. Another problem with the calculation is that it assumes that sales are made at an even rate throughout the year.

Therefore the result of the calculation is not particularly accurate. However, it is the best we can do with the data that is available from a published income statement and balance sheet.

Exercise

Calculate LMN's inventory turnover period for Year 3.

Solution

$$\text{Inventory turnover period for Year 3} = \frac{16}{\left(\frac{175}{365}\right)} = 33 \text{ days}$$

Generally a low inventory turnover period is preferable, that is inventory should be held for the shortest time possible. The ability to manage a business on very low inventories depends, among other things, on the quality of the management information systems and on the closeness of relationships with suppliers and their reliability.

Exercise

Can you think of reasons why inventory should be held for the shortest time possible? And can you think of when this policy might lead to problems?

Solution

Your reasons for a short inventory period may have included the following:

◆ Capital tied up in inventory could be used more effectively elsewhere.
◆ The longer inventory is held, the more likely it is to become unusable or obsolete. This is particularly important with perishable items or fashion goods.
◆ Higher inventory will generally incur higher storage costs, higher insurance costs, etc.

If inventories are too low this could lead to the following problems:

◆ Inventory may run out, leading to lost opportunities or the need to make emergency purchases at higher prices.
◆ If goods are purchased in small quantities, bulk discounts may be forgone and ordering costs may be high.

6.6.2 Receivables collection period

The receivables collection period measures how long, on average, credit customers take to settle their bill and is calculated as follows:

$$\text{Receivables collection period} = \frac{\text{Trade receivables}}{\text{Credit sales per day}}$$

> **Exercise**
>
> Assuming that all LMN's sales are made on credit, calculate the receivables collection period for Years 2 and 3.

> **Solution**
>
> $$\text{Year 2} = \frac{18}{\left(\frac{150}{365}\right)} = 44 \text{ days} \qquad \text{Year 3} = \frac{40}{\left(\frac{250}{365}\right)} = 58 \text{ days}$$

On average, it took longer to collect debts from credit customers in Year 3 than in Year 2. This can have a detrimental effect on the cash flows and liquidity of the company. Furthermore, the longer a credit customer takes to pay, the higher the risk that the customer will run into financial difficulties and be unable to pay.

Once again it is important to bear in mind the inadequacies of the balance sheet figure in calculating the number of days' debt. The resulting figure is an average which may not be representative of the year as a whole. Also it might be distorted by the existence of, say, one large customer who is exceptionally slow to pay.

6.6.3 Payables payment period

The receivables collection period could be compared with the payables payment period:

$$\text{Payables payment period} = \frac{\text{Trade payables}}{\text{Credit purchases per day}}$$

Management sometimes try to ensure that the two periods are roughly equal, or that the payables period is slightly longer, that is the organisation takes longer to pay its bills than it takes to collect money from its customers, resulting in interest-free credit for a period.

However, this policy should not be pursued to extremes. The organisation may gain a reputation for being a slow payer resulting in higher prices, or the supplier might even curtail supplies.

The data that we have for LMN does not show the purchases made each year. This is often the case with published accounts and it is commonly accepted that a reasonable approximation is to use instead the figures for cost of goods sold.

Exercise

Using cost of goods sold instead of purchases in the above formula, calculate the average payables payment period for LMN in Years 2 and 3.

Solution

$$\text{Year 2} = \frac{10.2}{\left(\frac{100}{365}\right)} = 37 \text{ days} \qquad \text{Year 3} = \frac{28}{\left(\frac{175}{365}\right)} = 58 \text{ days}$$

The average payment period for suppliers has shown a substantial increase. In Year 3 LMN took, on average, nearly two months to pay for its credit purchases.

Remember that the use of balance sheet data presents the same interpretation problems with this ratio as with the receivables collection period. For example, the calculation can be distorted by the company taking a longer period of credit from one or two larger suppliers.

6.6.4 Cash operating cycle

The cash operating cycle, also known as the working capital cycle, provides a useful measure to monitor approximately how much time passes between a payment being made by the company to purchase inventory and the cash being received from the final customer.

The cash operating cycle is usually expressed in terms of a number of days and its calculation is based on the working capital ratios that we have already calculated.

Cash operating cycle	=	inventory turnover period	+	receivables collection period	−	payables payment period

The payables payment period is deducted because the credit granted by suppliers reduces the length of time for which the company's own money is tied up in the cash operating cycle.

Exercise

Calculate LMN's cash operating cycle for Years 2 and 3.

Solution

Year 2 = inventory 44 days + receivables 44 days
  − payables 37 days
  = 51 days

Year 3 = inventory 33 days + receivables 58 days
  − payables 58 days
  = 33 days

In general the cash operating cycle should be as short as possible. A shorter cycle means that the company's money is tied up in working capital for a shorter period of time and this will reduce the amount of capital that the company requires in order to operate at a given level of activity.

6.6.5 Non-current asset turnover

This ratio monitors how effectively a company uses its non-current assets. It is calculated as follows.

$$\text{Non-current asset turnover} = \frac{\text{Sales revenue}}{\text{Non-current assets}}$$

Exercise

Calculate the non-current asset turnover for LMN in Years 2 and 3.

Solution

$$\text{Non-current asset turnover for Year 2} = \frac{150}{52} = 2.9 \text{ times}$$

$$\text{Non-current asset turnover for Year 3} = \frac{250}{85} = 2.9 \text{ times}$$

6.6.6 LMN's efficiency ratios: Summary

The ratios and performance measures that we have calculated for Years 2 and 3 are as follows:

	Year 2	Year 3
Inventory turnover period	44 days	33 days
Receivables collection period	44 days	58 days
Payables payment period	37 days	58 days
Cash operating cycle	51 days	33 days
Non-current asset turnover	2.9 times	2.9 times

Exercise

What outline conclusions can you draw about LMN's management of its working capital and non-current asset resources in Years 2 and 3?

Solution

Receivables levels appear to be increasing out of control by the end of Year 3, although this may be a deliberate and controlled increase as part of a policy to encourage increased sales revenue.

Inventory levels appear to have reduced. This indicates efficient control of working capital, although sales may be forgone if customer requirements cannot be met from inventory. The reduction in the inventory turnover period has contributed to the improvement in the company's asset turnover. It has also contributed to the reduction in the cash operating cycle.

Payables levels have been reasonably well matched with receivables. However, supplier relationships may be harmed if the credit period becomes excessive and the large increase in the period of credit taken from suppliers may have arisen simply because of LMN's inability to pay by the due date because of a shortage of cash. The increase in the period of credit taken from suppliers in Year 3 has contributed towards the improvement in the company's asset turnover and towards the reduction in the cash operating cycle.

The cash operating cycle has reduced in Year 3 which means that less money is required for the working capital to operate at a given level of activity. This is usually a good sign but a major factor causing this change is the increase in the period of credit apparently being taken from suppliers in Year 3. This does carry risks, as described earlier.

The utilisation of non-current assets continues at approximately the same level in both years. The level of investment in non-current assets has increased but the revenues have increased correspondingly and a broad conclusion can be drawn that it appears that the new assets are being used in an efficient way to generate revenue.

6.7 Assessing liquidity

The liquidity of an organisation refers to its ability to meet its current liabilities as they fall due. A bank manager might be interested in an organisation's liquidity if they have requested overdraft facilities. Or perhaps a company has been approached by a new customer who requires credit for all supplies. The supplying company may first review the customer's liquidity position before deciding to grant credit facilities.

The following ratios may be used to evaluate the organisation's liquidity:

◆ Current ratio
◆ Acid test ratio (also called the quick ratio or the liquid ratio)

6.7.1 Current ratio

This ratio relates an organisation's current assets to its current liabilities to assess its ability to meet its short-term obligations and is calculated as follows:

$$\text{Current ratio} = \frac{\text{Current assets}}{\text{Current liabilities}}$$

The current ratio for LMN for Year 2 is:

$$\frac{40}{20} = 2 \text{ times}$$

This means that the current assets cover the current liabilities twice at the end of Year 2.

Exercise

Calculate LMN's current ratio for Year 3.

Solution

$$\text{Current ratio} = \frac{60}{45} = 1.3 \text{ times}$$

The current assets covered the current liabilities 1.3 times at the end of Year 3.

6.7.2 Is there an 'ideal' size for the current ratio?

The 'ideal' size for the current ratio depends on a number of factors, including the following:

◆ *The past record for the company*: It is preferable to look at the trend in the current ratio over a number of years. Generally, the higher the current ratio, the more liquid the organisation. Since liquidity is important to the organisation's survival, it may be a cause for concern if the current ratio is reducing. If the current ratio falls too low, the organisation may be in danger of overtrading. This happens when the organisation enters into commitments which are in excess of its available short-term resources. However, if the current ratio is too high, funds may be unnecessarily tied up in inventories or receivables that could be used more efficiently elsewhere in the organisation.

◆ *The type of business and the 'norm' for the industry*: For example, a retailing company might be expected to have a lower current ratio than a manufacturing company. In fact, many retailing companies have a current ratio of less than 1.0, indicating that the current liabilities exceed the current assets, that is these companies have net current liabilities or negative working capital.

Exercise

Explain why retailing companies tend to have a lower current ratio than manufacturing companies.

Solution

The current asset balances of retailing companies tend to be relatively lower than the current asset balances of manufacturing companies for the following reasons:

◆ Retailing companies do not hold inventories of raw materials or work in progress.
◆ Retailing companies sell mostly on a cash basis and so have very few receivables on their balance sheet. Manufacturing companies may have to wait for several weeks before cash payment is received from their customers.

6.7.3 The acid test ratio

This ratio may also be called the quick ratio or the liquid ratio. It is used to give a more stringent assessment of an organisation's liquidity.

In many organisations it may take quite a long time to convert inventories into cash. For example, the manufacturing process may be such that it takes several days or even weeks to produce a finished product, and on top of this customers may expect a lengthy period of credit. Therefore it could be argued that in this type of organisation, inventories are not a liquid asset: they cannot be quickly liquidated to meet current liabilities as they become due. The 'acid test' of an organisation's liquidity is whether it can cover its current liabilities without having to sell its inventories, and so this ratio includes only the more liquid assets in the calculation:

$$\text{Acid test ratio} = \frac{\text{Current assets } \textit{excluding } \text{inventory}}{\text{Current liabilities}}$$

Exercise

Calculate LMN's acid test ratio for Years 2 and 3.

Solution

$$\text{Year 2} = \frac{28}{20} = 1.4 \text{ times} \qquad \text{Year 3} = \frac{44}{45} = 0.98 \text{ times}$$

In Year 2, LMN's liquid assets covered its current liabilities 1.4 times. However, in Year 3 the ratio has fallen below 1.0 therefore LMN would have to sell some of the inventory to meet all its current liabilities.

6.7.4   Using balance sheet information

The use of balance sheet data to assess liquidity presents the same problems as with the assessment of the efficiency of asset management. It is important to appreciate that the liquidity ratios that we have calculated in this section are based on balance sheet data. The balance sheet is like a photograph taken of the organisation's assets and liabilities at the end of the financial year.

Therefore the working capital balances may not be representative of the liquidity position during the year. There may have been exceptional events at the end of the year or the business may be seasonal, leading to higher or lower than average working capital balances at the end of the year.

6.7.5   LMN's liquidity ratios: Summary

The ratios that we have calculated for Years 2 and 3 are as follows:

	Year 2	Year 3
Current ratio	2.0 times	1.30 times
Acid test ratio	1.4 times	0.98 times

Exercise

What outline conclusions can you draw about LMN's short-term liquidity position at the end of Year 3?

Solution

We do not know what business LMN is in, therefore we cannot comment on what would be a suitable current ratio. However, the change in the two liquidity ratios may be a cause for concern. They have both deteriorated and in Year 3 it is not possible for LMN to meet its current liabilities without having to sell some inventory.

The Year 3 ratios in themselves are not necessarily too low and it is difficult to draw firm conclusions without knowing the sort of business that LMN is in. However, the change from Year 2 levels could indicate liquidity problems if it is not a controlled change. The company appears to be in danger of overtrading.

Since we have seen from earlier calculations that in Year 3 an average item is held for 33 days in inventory (the inventory turnover period) and then customers take an average of 58 days to settle their account (the receivables collection period), we might conclude that inventory is not a particularly liquid asset for LMN. They cannot rely on selling it quickly to generate cash rapidly to meet their short-term liabilities.

Therefore perhaps we should place more weight on the acid test ratio than on the current ratio when assessing this particular company's liquidity. Accordingly, we might conclude that the company could be heading for liquidity problems when attempting to meet its short-term commitments.

Notice how our interpretation of the liquidity ratios referred back to the information obtained from the efficiency ratios. Although you are calculating separate groups of ratios in order to give your analysis some structure, do not view each group of ratios in isolation. Each group can help you with the interpretation of the results of other groups of ratios.

6.8 Segment reporting

Many large companies produce a wide range of different products and services, often in a number of different countries. The problem for the user of the financial statements is that the income statement and balance sheet provide only the aggregated results of all the company's activities.

In order to get a better idea of the returns and risks of the company as a whole, the reader should be able to find information about the results of each major segment of the company.

The company's different products or services and the different geographical areas in which they operate are probably subject to differing risks and growth opportunities as well as to differing current and future levels of profitability.

This is the reason for providing supplementary information about the company's major segments. This information is provided in addition to the income statements and balance sheets that we have covered in earlier chapters.

Listed companies provide segment information about their separate business segments and about their separate geographical segments.

Exercise

Can you think of reasons why it might be important to have separate information about the geographical segments of a particular company?

Solution

You might have thought of some of the following reasons, or other reasons that are equally valid:

◆ If a significant proportion of revenue and profit is generated in a country where there are signs of political unrest this would affect the reader's assessment of the level of risk associated with the company's activities.
◆ Some geographical segments might have better growth prospects than others.
◆ Rapid inflation in one geographical segment might impact upon the group's results in future.
◆ The potential impact of currency fluctuations could be more easily assessed.

6.8.1　Example: A segment report

The following segment information is provided concerning the business segments of Vend plc, a company which manufactures food and drink products for use in vending machines. The company's two business segments are food products and drink products.

Segment information for the year to 30 June Year 6

	Food products (£m)	Drink products (£m)	Eliminations (£m)	Consolidated results (£m)
Revenue				
External revenue	224	109		
Inter-segment revenue	30	12	(42)	
Total revenue	254	121	(42)	333
Results				
Segment profit	15	17	(1)	31
Unallocated expenses				(11)
Operating profit				20
Interest expense				(3)
Taxation				(4)
Profit				13
Other information				
Segment assets	122	65		187
Unallocated assets				13
Consolidated total assets				200
Segment liabilities	45	12		57
Unallocated liabilities				22
Consolidated total liabilities				79
Expenditure on				
non-current assets	24	4		
Depreciation	28	15		

The second line in the statement refers to inter-segment revenue. These sales relate to goods or services sold by one segment of the company to the other segment. However for the company as a whole these sales or transfers between segments do not actually generate any additional revenue. Therefore these sales between the segments are eliminated in the third column in order to derive the total revenue for the group as a whole $(254 + 121 - 42 = 333)$.

Similarly, further down the statement, the profit result for the company as a whole is the combined results of the two segments less the profit earned on transfers or sales between the segments $(15 + 17 - 1 = 31)$.

You can also see that there is £11 m of unallocated expenses. These are expenses incurred by the company that it is not possible to identify specifically with either of the two business segments. Examples might include head office expenses and legal costs.

Similarly, you will see that there are unallocated assets and unallocated liabilities. These items could not be specifically identified with either of the segments, therefore they have been included in aggregate in the total figures.

Exercise

Use the segment information provided for food products and drink products to assess the relative performance of each of the business segments.

Solution

Despite generating the majority of the total company's revenue the food products earn a lower profit than the drink products (£15 m compared with £17 m).

If we calculate the capital employed by each segment we can calculate the ratios that we have used in this chapter.

Capital employed by food products = 122 assets − 45 liabilities
= £77 m

Capital employed by drink products = 65 assets − 12 liabilities
= £53 m

Return on capital employed

Food products = 15/77 × 100% = 19.5%
Drink products = 17/53 × 100% = 32.1%

Operating profit margin
> Food products = 15/254 × 100% = 5.9%
> Drink products = 17/121 × 100% = 14.0%

Asset turnover
> Food products = 254/77 = 3.3 times
> Drink products = 121/53 = 2.3 times

Drink products generate a much higher ROCE despite a lower asset turnover. This is because drink products earn a considerably higher operating profit margin than food products. Is this due to an ability to command higher sales prices or is cost control of drink products better than that of food products? The reasons for the lower margins on food products should be investigated, particularly since the majority of the company's revenue comes from this segment.

It is surprising to see that the highest expenditure on non-current assets was incurred in the food products segment, despite the lower margins that are earned in this segment. Perhaps some of this expenditure will lead to cost savings in future which will help to improve the food products margin. Otherwise it might be sensible to focus on expansion of the higher margin drink products.

The depreciation as a percentage of total assets is approximately 23 per cent for both business segments. This suggests that the segments probably employ a comparable mix of assets and use a similar depreciation policy.

For reporting periods beginning on or after 1 January 2009 the method of identifying the individual segments for which additional information must be reported focuses more on a 'managerial approach', although the information to be reported for each segment remains broadly the same. The managerial approach requires that information should be disclosed for separate products and services, geographical areas and even major customers, using the same segments that are used by the company's managers in the internal information system.

This means that the company is effectively providing additional information that is equivalent to the information that the management of the company would be using to assess and control the performance of different areas of business within the company as a whole.

6.9   Summary

(1) Ratios are widely used in the analysis of financial statements. They enable one figure to be related to another and facilitate comparison between organisations of different size.

(2) The following five groups of ratios may be used to analyse a set of financial statements:

◆ Profitability
◆ Efficiency
◆ Liquidity
◆ Financial structure
◆ Investment

(3) Before beginning on a ratio analysis it is important to look at the financial statements to obtain an overall 'feel' for what has been happening during the period covered by the statements.

(4) A common size statement can help to focus the analyst's attention on the major changes that have occurred over the period covered by the statements.

(5) Additional information is provided by a segment analysis so that the users of financial statements can see how the total figures are made up in terms of geographical segments and product or service segments.

Review questions

(1) How is the return on capital employed (ROCE) calculated? (Section 6.5.1)

(2) If there has been a change in the ROCE which is worth further investigation, which two ratios can be used to subanalyse the ROCE? (Section 6.5.2)

(3) If a company's assets are undervalued, will ROCE tend to be under- or over-stated? (Section 6.5.7)

(4) How is the inventory turnover period calculated and what is the significance of a relatively long inventory turnover period? (Section 6.6.1)

Accounting in a Nutshell

(5)   What is the difference between the two main ratios used to assess liquidity: the current ratio and the acid test ratio? (Sections 6.7.1 and 6.7.3)

(6)   What is meant by unallocated expenses in a segment report? (Section 6.8)

Self-test questions

(1)   Other things being equal, would the following events, each considered separately, cause the return on capital employed to increase or decrease?

(a)   Increase in inventory
(b)   Decrease in asset turnover
(c)   Decrease in receivables
(d)   Increase in operating profit margin
(e)   Increase in payables

(2)   Use the following information to produce two common size balance sheets for the A Company as at the end of Years 3 and 4. Comment on whether you think the A Company's balance sheet has improved or deteriorated between Years 3 and 4.

The A Company: Balance sheets as at 31 December

	Year 4		Year 3	
	£m	£m	£m	£m
Non-current assets		35.8		33.1
Current assets				
Inventory	6.8		7.0	
Receivables	5.4		5.1	
Bank	4.5		10.5	
	16.7		22.6	
Current liabilities				
Trade payables	(20.0)		16.4	
Net current assets/(liabilities)		(3.3)		6.2
		32.5		39.3
Ordinary share capital		4.0		4.0
Reserves		22.6		26.4
Shareholders' equity		26.6		30.4
Non-current liabilities: loan capital		5.9		8.9
		32.5		39.3

(3) RC Limited manufactures and sells non-perishable food products to the retail trade. A summary of the latest income statements and balance sheets is as follows:

RC Limited: Income statements for the year ended 31 March

	Year 7 £'000	Year 8 £'000
Revenue	183	170
Cost of sales	71	55
Gross profit	112	115
Operating expenses	76	78
Operating profit	36	37
Finance costs: interest payable	4	6
Profit before tax	32	31
Taxation	8	7
Profit for the period	24	24

RC Limited: Balance sheets as at 31 March

	Year 7 £'000	Year 7 £'000	Year 8 £'000	Year 8 £'000
Non-current assets		94		130
Current assets				
Inventory	8		5	
Receivables	22		15	
Bank	16		12	
	46		32	
Current liabilities				
Trade payables	(8)		(8)	
Other creditors and accruals	(26)		(19)	
	(34)		(27)	
Net current assets		12		5
		106		135
Non-current liabilities: bank loans		(25)		(40)
		81		95
Ordinary £1 shares		50		50
Reserves – retained profit		31		45
Shareholders' equity		81		95

Required

Prepare an analysis of RC Limited's profitability, efficiency of asset management and liquidity for Years 7 and 8.

(4) J Limited manufactures and sells woven carpets to the wholesale trade. J Limited is a member of a trade association and has obtained average performance ratios for carpet manufacturers for the latest year. A comparison of J Limited's results with the industry averages is as follows:

	J Limited	Industry average
Return on capital employed	16.5%	21.1%
Operating profit margin	7.2%	5.0%
Gross profit margin	41.7%	25.4%
Non-current asset turnover	5.4 times	8.2 times
Inventory turnover period	89 days	37 days
Receivables collection period	69 days	42 days
Payables payment period	48 days	37 days
Current ratio	3.9 times	2.6 times

Required

Comment on J Limited's performance in the latest year compared with the industry average, as far as the available information will allow.

Answers to self-test questions

(1)

(a) An increase in inventory would cause the return on capital employed (ROCE) to decrease, because the amount of capital employed (the denominator in the ROCE calculation) would increase.

(b) A decrease in asset turnover would tend to cause the ROCE to decrease because lower sales revenue is being achieved for a given level of capital employed.

(c) A decrease in receivables would cause the ROCE to increase, because the amount of capital employed (the denominator in the ROCE calculation) would decrease.

(d) An increase in operating profit margin would cause the ROCE to increase. The operating profit margin and the asset turnover can be multiplied together to determine the ROCE. Other things being equal, if the operating profit margin increases then so will the ROCE.

(e) An increase in payables would cause the ROCE to increase, because the amount of capital employed (the denominator in the ROCE calculation) would decrease.

(2) Total asset value for Year 4 = 35.8 + 16.7 = £52.5 m
Total asset value for Year 3 = 33.1 + 22.6 = £55.7 m

Expressing each figure in the balance sheets as a percentage of these totals produces the following results.

The A Company: Common size balance sheets as at 31 December

	Year 4 (%)	Year 3 (%)
Non-current assets	68	59
Current assets		
Inventory	13	13
Receivables	10	9
Bank	9	19
	100	100
Trade payables	38	30
Ordinary share capital	8	7
Reserves	43	47
Non-current liabilities: loan capital	11	16
	100	100

The A Company's balance sheet has deteriorated. In Year 4 the company relies more heavily on short-term funding in the form of trade payables (38 per cent compared with 30 per cent) while at the same time investing proportionately more in non-current assets (68 per cent compared with 59 per cent). This is a mismatch of funding since longer-term asset investments should preferably be funded with correspondingly longer-term sources of finance.

The proportion of assets financed by the shareholders' equity has reduced (51 per cent (8 + 43) in Year 4 compared with 54 per cent (7 + 47) in Year 3). This could represent a riskier situ-ation for the shareholders.

In the next chapter we will investigate further the risk aspect of relying more heavily on external finance rather than on shareholders' equity.

(3) The first thing to notice is that RC Limited's balance sheet is arranged slightly differently. The long-term bank loans are shown as a deduction from the 'assets side' of the balance sheet. This is a common form of presentation which highlights the shareholders' investment in the company, as we saw in Chapter 3. It does not affect the analysis, but it does mean that a little more care is needed in determining the correct figure for capital employed.

Profitability

		Year 7	Year 8
ROCE $=$	$\dfrac{\text{profit before interest and taxation}}{\text{share capital + reserves + long-term loans}} \times 100\%$	$\dfrac{36}{106} \times 100\%$ $= 34.0\%$	$\dfrac{37}{135} \times 100\%$ $= 27.4\%$
Operating profit margin $=$	$\dfrac{\text{profit before interest and taxation}}{\text{revenue}} \times 100\%$	$\dfrac{36}{183} \times 100\%$ $= 19.7\%$	$\dfrac{37}{170} \times 100\%$ $= 21.8\%$
Asset turnover $=$	$\dfrac{\text{revenue}}{\text{share capital + reserves + long-term loans}}$	$\dfrac{183}{106}$ $= 1.7$ times	$\dfrac{170}{135}$ $= 1.3$ times
Gross profit margin $=$	$\dfrac{\text{gross profit}}{\text{revenue}} \times 100\%$	$\dfrac{112}{183} \times 100\%$ $= 61.2\%$	$\dfrac{115}{170} \times 100\%$ $= 67.6\%$

RC Limited's return on capital employed deteriorated in Year 8, due to a reduction in the asset turnover. A lower level of sales was combined with an increase in the capital employed (there was a substantial increase in the level of non-current asset investment).

The profitability of sales, at the operating profit level and at the gross profit level, improved and this lessened the impact of the reduced asset turnover.

Liquidity

		Year 7	Year 8
Current ratio	$= \dfrac{\text{Current assets}}{\text{Current liabilities}}$	$\dfrac{46}{34} = 1.4$ times	$\dfrac{32}{27} = 1.2$ times
Acid test ratio	$= \dfrac{\text{Current assets} - \text{inventory}}{\text{Current liabilities}}$	$\dfrac{38}{34} = 1.1$ times	$\dfrac{27}{27} = 1.0$ times

RC Limited's liquidity has deteriorated slightly but the current assets are sufficient to cover the current liabilities in Year 8, even without the inventory.

Efficiency of asset management

		Year 7	Year 8
Inventory turnover period	$= \dfrac{\text{Inventory}}{\text{Cost of sales per day}}$	$\dfrac{8}{71/365} = 41$ days	$\dfrac{5}{55/365} = 33$ days
Receivable collection period	$= \dfrac{\text{Receivables}}{\text{Sales per day}}$	$\dfrac{22}{183/365} = 44$ days	$\dfrac{15}{170/365} = 32$ days
Payables payment period	$= \dfrac{\text{Trade payables}}{\text{Cost of sales per day}}$	$\dfrac{8}{71/365} = 41$ days	$\dfrac{8}{55/365} = 53$ days
Cash operating cycle = inventory turnover period + receivables collection period − payables payment period		$41 + 44 - 41 =$ 44 days	$33 + 32 - 53 =$ 12 days
Non-current asset turnover	$= \dfrac{\text{Sales revenue}}{\text{Non-current assets}}$	$\dfrac{183}{94} = 1.9$ times	$\dfrac{170}{130} = 1.3$ times

The average inventory period has reduced by eight days, which is an improvement as long as customer service is maintained.

The average receivables collection period has reduced by 12 days. This demonstrates improved working capital control, but could it have contributed to the reduction in sales revenue, due to customers going elsewhere to receive better credit terms?

The average payables payment period has increased by 12 days. This probably demonstrates improved working capital control, as long as it is not leading to higher purchase prices or loss of supplier goodwill.

All of the above changes in the elements of working capital have resulted in a considerable reduction in the cash operating cycle. This is a positive sign from a cash flow perspective and if the company can continue to operate effectively with this length of cycle then less capital will be required to finance its activities.

The non-current asset turnover has deteriorated. There was increased investment in non-current assets as well as a reduction in the revenue generated from the assets. This deterioration is the cause of the reduced total asset turnover in Year 8 and hence is the cause of the reduced return on capital employed.

(4) J Limited's return on capital employed is lower than average despite a higher than average operating profit margin. This indicates that the company's asset turnover must be lower than average, since ROCE = asset turnover × operating profit margin.

The company's gross profit margin is higher than the industry average but this major advantage is not maintained to the same extent at the operating margin level. This suggests that J Limited's overhead/operating expenses are much higher than the industry average.

The non-current asset turnover is lower than the industry average and indicates that J Limited could perhaps make better use of its non-current assets. However, this comparison is possibly distorted by the mix of assets compared with the industry average and by their age and the depreciation policies used. The lower non-current asset turnover contributes to the lower total asset turnover mentioned above.

J Limited's inventory turnover is very slow. This also contributed to the lower asset turnover result. The average inventory period for the industry is only just over one month whereas J Limited's holding at the year end was sufficient to last an average of nearly three months. This needs attention but perhaps J Limited buys materials in bulk in order to obtain discounts. This would help to explain the higher gross margin. On the other hand, higher storage costs might have contributed to the higher than average overhead/operating expenses.

J Limited takes much longer than the industry average to collect the amounts owing from its customers (69 days compared with 42 days). This also contributed to the lower asset turnover result. This increases the risk of bad debts and has an adverse impact on cash flow. However, the longer credit terms may be enabling J Limited to charge higher selling prices, hence the higher gross margin earned.

J Limited is slower to pay its suppliers (48 days compared with 37 days). This assists cash flow but J Limited should avoid the risk of losing supplier goodwill.

The cash operating cycle can be calculated for J Limited and for the industry average as follows.

J Limited	Industry average
$89 + 69 - 48 = 110$ days	$37 + 42 - 37 = 42$ days

Cash is tied up in J Limited's working capital cycle for more than twice as long as the industry average. This is detrimental to J Limited's cash flow and means that J Limited requires a higher investment in working capital than the industry average in order to operate at a given level of activity.

J Limited has a higher current ratio than average but this is probably an unnecessarily high cover of current liabilities with current assets. It reflects the possibly wasteful level of inventories and the higher than average receivables.

Interpreting Financial
Statements: Part 2

7.1 Introduction

In this chapter you will be learning more about how to interpret financial statements. We will be continuing our review of LMN plc, looking first at the company's financial structure and then at its performance from the point of view of shareholders and potential shareholders. We will also be interpreting the cash flow statement.

7.2 Financial structure

There are two important ratios which help in analysing a company's financial structure.

◆ The gearing ratio
◆ The interest cover ratio

7.2.1 What is financial gearing?

Gearing refers to the proportion of a company's funds that are provided by borrowings on which interest is payable regardless of how well the company performs.

If a company has a large amount of borrowings compared to shareholders' equity, it is said to be high geared.

If a company has a small amount of borrowings compared to shareholders' equity, it is said to be low geared.

Gearing has important implications for management because if the company is high geared it means that managers must react quickly if revenues start to fall. Shareholders will also be interested in the level of gearing, because any changes in revenue could have a dramatic effect on their fortunes if the company is high geared.

The following example will demonstrate why this happens.

Example: The effect of financial gearing

Two companies, High Gear Limited and Low Gear Limited, each have the same amount of capital in total, but different proportions of share capital and borrowings as follows:

	High Gear Limited £	Low Gear Limited £
Share capital: £1 shares	100,000	250,000
Borrowings	200,000	50,000
	300,000	300,000

The annual interest rate on the borrowings is 10 per cent.

Notice that two-thirds of High Gear's capital comes from borrowings, whereas only one-sixth of Low Gear's capital consists of borrowings.

Suppose that the profit for the year, before interest, amounts to £30,000 for each company. The profit per share (ignoring taxation) can be calculated as follows:

	£'000	£'000
Profit before interest	30	30
Less		
Interest (200,000 × 10%)	20	(50,000 × 10%) 5
Profit after interest	10	25
Profit per share (ignoring tax)	($^{10}/_{100}$) £0.10	($^{25}/_{250}$) £0.10

At this level of profits there is no difference in the fortunes of the shareholders. Although Low Gear Limited has earned more profit after interest, this higher profit has to be shared between a higher number of shares. Therefore the profit per share is the same for both companies.

Now let us see what happens if the profit before interest doubles to £60,000. The amount of interest payable on the loans will not alter but the fortunes of the shareholders will change considerably.

	£'000	£'000
Profit before interest	60	60
Less		
Interest (200,000 × 10%)	20	(50,000 × 10%) 5
Profit after interest	40	55
Profit per share (ignoring tax)	($^{40}/_{100}$) £0.40	($^{55}/_{250}$) £0.22

The profit per share has more than doubled for both companies, since both have some gearing. However, the change in profit is magnified dramatically for the high geared company, therefore the returns for shareholders increase considerably.

On the other hand, if profits begin to fall then the profit per share will reduce faster with the high geared company than with the lower geared one.

Exercise

In the above example of High Gear Limited and Low Gear Limited, calculate the profit per share for each company (ignoring tax) if annual profits before interest fall to £24,000.

Solution

	High Gear Limited £'000	Low Gear Limited £'000
Profit before interest	24	24
Less		
Interest (200,000 × 10%)	20	(50,000 × 10%) 5
Profit after interest	4	19
Profit per share (ignoring tax)	($^4/_{100}$) £0.04	($^{19}/_{250}$) £0.08

The fall in profits has caused a greater reduction in the profit per share for the highly geared company.

The managers of a highly geared company must therefore be careful to maintain the level of profits and sales and must react quickly if revenues or profits start to fall. However, if revenues and profits increase, the shareholders in a highly geared company will be proportionately much better off.

This volatility of returns which is caused by the existence of higher levels of gearing reflects the financial risk associated with high gearing.

> *You might also hear a company's gearing referred to as its financial leverage.*

7.2.2 Is there an ideal level of gearing?

The most appropriate level of gearing will depend on the type of business that the company is in. Different types of business bring with them different levels of business risk. Business risk is assessed by the potential variability in a company's profits from one year to the next.

Exercise

Which would you say has the higher level of business risk: a company which manufactures luxury fashion goods or a company which manufactures bread?

Solution

The fashion goods company would be exposed to greater business risk than would a company which manufactures bread, because the potential variability in profits is higher.

Demand for the fashion goods is likely to be more volatile than the demand for bread. The demand for fashion goods would depend on changes in fashion, on the activities of competitors and on the amount of money that consumers have to spend.

Demand for bread would probably be more stable, hence this company would experience smaller fluctuations in profit and therefore a lower level of business risk.

We have seen that high gearing leads to high financial risk because of the potentially exaggerated fluctuations in the returns to shareholders. The total risk of a company is made up of its financial risk and business risk. Potential investors and lenders will assess the total level of risk in a company. Generally, for a given level of desired total risk, the higher a company's business risk, the lower its financial risk should be, that is the lower its desirable level of gearing.

7.2.3 Calculating the gearing ratio

There are many different methods that might be used to calculate the gearing ratio. The most important thing is to be consistent and to ensure, if you are comparing gearing ratios, that they have been calculated using the same method.

In this text the following formula will be used:

$$\text{Gearing ratio} = \frac{\text{Borrowings} + \text{preference share capital}}{\text{Total capital employed}} \times 100\%$$

Overdrafts and short-term borrowings are usually included within the total borrowings figure.

Preference share capital is also usually included within the borrowings figure. You should recall that a preference share is a special type of share which is entitled to a fixed rate of dividend each year.

In contrast to lenders, preference shareholders cannot force the company to pay them their fixed annual dividend. Therefore it could be argued that preference shares should not be treated in our analysis in the same way that we are treating borrowings on which interest must be paid no matter how well or how badly the company performs.

However, in practical terms the company must pay the preference dividend in order to maintain investor confidence in the company. Therefore the fixed amount of preference dividend payable each year has the same gearing impact as the annual interest payments that must be met.

In our example, LMN's gearing ratio for Year 2 is zero, since it has no borrowing and no preference shares.

> *Exercise*
>
> Calculate LMN's gearing ratio for Year 3.

> *Solution*
>
> $$\text{Gearing Year 3} = \frac{20}{100} \times 100\% = 20\%$$

LMN's gearing ratio has increased due to the introduction of borrowings during Year 3. This has increased the financial risk associated with LMN.

We do not know what type of business LMN is engaged in, therefore it is difficult to comment on whether this is an acceptable level of financial risk commensurate with LMN's business risk. Certainly the increase in gearing may cause alarm to some investors. On the other hand, they may welcome the potentially higher returns that accompany the introduction of a modest level of gearing, particularly if LMN has opportunities for expansion which will lead to increased revenues and operating profits. Increases in operating profits will be magnified in the returns to shareholders as a result of the gearing effect.

7.2.4 Interest cover

This ratio monitors the amount of profit that was available to cover the interest payment for the year. The higher the cover, the more able the business was to meet its commitments to pay interest on its borrowings.

$$\text{Interest cover} = \frac{\text{Profit before interest and tax}}{\text{Interest payable}}$$

Exercise

Calculate LMN's interest cover ratio for Year 3 and comment on the result.

Solution

$$\text{Interest cover, Year 3} = \frac{26}{1} = 26 \text{ times}$$

This is a very high interest cover: it appears that LMN could have paid the interest 26 times over (but see the next paragraph!).

The result of this exercise could be misleading. It is important to bear in mind that the loan was probably not held for the whole of the year (this is the problem with placing too much weight on balance sheet figures). Therefore, the interest for a full year is likely to be more than £1 m and the interest cover is in reality lower than 26 times.

However, even if the interest rate was as high as 25 per cent, the annual interest on the loan would be only £5 m (£20 m × 25%). In that case the interest cover would be 5.2 times (£26 m/£5 m).

As with the gearing ratio, the desirable level of interest cover will depend on the company's business risk.

7.3 Investment ratios

The following ratios can be used to assess the company's performance from the point of view of a shareholder or potential shareholder:

◆ Return on shareholders' funds (also called the return on shareholders' equity)
◆ Ordinary dividend cover
◆ Dividend yield
◆ Earnings yield
◆ Earnings per share (EPS)
◆ Price–earnings (PE) ratio

7.3.1 Return on shareholders' funds (return on shareholders' equity)

This is very similar to ROCE, except that it focuses on the returns to ordinary shareholders. Remember that ordinary shares entitle the holders to the profits that remain after everybody else has received their entitlement, for example after tax, interest and preference dividend has been paid. They literally are 'at the bottom of the pile', in distribution of profits as well as in repayment of capital in a liquidation.

Ordinary shareholders tend to do well when business fortunes are good, because everybody else receives only their fixed return and all other returns belong to the ordinary shareholders (see our earlier discussion on gearing). On the other hand, they have no recourse if business is not going so well. They are really the 'risk-taking' investors in the business.

The level of risk taken by ordinary shareholders in any particular company will depend on the company's total risk, that is on the combination of its business risk and its financial risk.

The return on shareholders' funds (ROSF) is calculated as follows:

$$\text{ROSF} = \frac{\text{Profits after interest, tax and}}{\text{Ordinary share capital} + \text{reserves}} \times 100\%$$

Exercise

Calculate LMN's return on shareholders' funds for Years 2 and 3.

Solution

	Year 2	Year 3
Return on shareholders' funds		
($^{7}/_{72} \times 100\%$)	9.7%	
($^{14}/_{80} \times 100\%$)		17.5%

In our example LMN has no preference shareholders but if they did, we would need to deduct the preference dividend from the numerator in order to derive the final amount of the profit that was attributable to the ordinary shareholders.

7.3.2 Ordinary dividend cover

This is similar to the interest cover ratio. It measures how 'safe' the dividend payment was, that is how many times the current year's profit could have covered the dividend payout. If the dividend cover falls to very low levels, shareholders may not be able to rely on the current level of dividends being maintained in the future.

$$\text{Ordinary dividend cover} = \frac{\text{Profits after interest, tax and preference dividends}}{\text{Ordinary dividend for the year}}$$

LMN does not have any preference shares, therefore all of the dividend is ordinary dividend.

If the ordinary dividend cover is consistently low, it indicates that the directors have a general policy of paying out a large proportion of the year's profits as dividends. This means that they do not plough back a large proportion of the profits as a source of finance for the company.

Exercise

You are provided with the following additional note to accompany LMN's income statement and balance sheet.

Dividends paid and proposed

	Year 2	Year 3
	£m	£m
Interim dividend paid	2.0	2.0
Final dividend paid/proposed	2.8	4.0
Total dividend for the year	4.8	6.0

Calculate LMN's ordinary dividend cover in Years 2 and 3.

Solution

	Year 2	Year 3
Ordinary dividend cover		
$(^7/_{4.8})$	1.5 times	
$(^{14}/_6)$		2.3 times

Sometimes we might wish to focus more on the proportion of the year's profits that is paid out as dividends, rather than on how 'safe' the dividend payment was. In this case exactly the same information portrayed by the dividend cover ratio can be expressed as the dividend payout ratio. This is calculated as the reciprocal of the dividend cover ratio, expressed as a percentage.

$$\text{Dividend payout ratio} = \frac{\text{Ordinary dividend for the year}}{\text{Profit after interest, tax and preference dividends}} \times 100\%$$

Exercise

Calculate LMN's dividend payout ratio in Years 2 and 3.

Solution

	Year 2	Year 3
Dividend payout ratio		
$(4.8/_7) \times 100\%$	68.6%	
$(6/_{14}) \times 100\%$		42.9%

This focuses attention on the fact that a greater percentage of available profits was paid out as dividend in Year 2 than in Year 3.

7.3.3 Dividend yield

This is a market-related ratio which cannot be calculated based only on the information contained within a set of published accounts. A further piece of information is needed: the share's current market price. In the case of our LMN example, let us assume that the share price at 31 December of each year was as follows:

Year 2	Year 3
£1.44	£2.30

This is additional information which would not usually be available in published accounts.

The dividend yield assesses the cash return to shareholders compared with the amount of money they have invested to earn that cash return.

$$\text{Dividend yield} = \frac{\text{Dividend per share}}{\text{Market price of share}} \times 100\%$$

Exercise

Calculate LMN's shareholders' dividend yield for Years 2 and 3.

Solution		
	Year 2	Year 3
Dividend yield		
$[(^{4.8}/_{60}) \div 1.44] \times 100\%$	5.6%	
$[(^{6}/_{60}) \div 2.30] \times 100\%$		4.4%

However, the dividend is only a part of the return earned for the ordinary shareholders. The part of the profits that was taken to reserves has also been earned for them, even if they have not received it from the company in the form of a cash return. It has been invested in the company on their behalf in order to earn them a capital gain.

Therefore to gain a full assessment of the returns earned for the ordinary shareholders, the *earnings* must be taken into account.

'Earnings' is a term used to describe the profits earned for the ordinary shareholders during the year. It is the profit after deduction of interest, tax and preference dividend, that is after all other interested parties have been allocated their share of the profits. Notice that we have already been using this figure as the numerator in most of the calculations of investment ratios in this section of the chapter.

7.3.4 Earnings yield

This ratio assesses the total percentage return that shareholders have received on their investment, regardless of whether it was actually paid to shareholders as a dividend. Part of the earnings may have been paid out as dividend, the remainder has been kept in the business for reinvestment.

$$\text{Earnings yield} = \frac{\text{Current year profit attributable to each ordinary share}}{\text{Market price of share}} \times 100\%$$

'Current year profit attributable to ordinary shareholders' is the same as 'profit after deduction of interest, tax and preference dividend', which is the same as 'earnings'. Remember that we are simply describing the ordinary shareholders' return after everybody else has received their allocation. Unfortunately, in practice you will come across all these different descriptions of the same item.

Earnings yield is another ratio that cannot be calculated based on published accounts. The market price of the share is needed.

<table>
<tr><td colspan="3">Exercise

Calculate LMN's earnings yield for Years 2 and 3.</td></tr>
</table>

Solution	Year 2	Year 3
Earnings yield		
$[(^7/_{60}) \div 1.44] \times 100\%$	8.1%	
$[(^{14}/_{60}) \div 2.30] \times 100\%$		10.1%

7.3.5 Earnings per share (EPS)

This ratio relates the earnings for the year to the number of shares in issue. Many analysts regard this as a fundamental measure of a company's performance, and the trend of the EPS over time can be particularly important.

$$EPS = \frac{\text{Current year profit attributable to ordinary shareholders}}{\text{Number of ordinary shares}}$$

In practice the denominator for the EPS should be the *weighted average* number of ordinary shares in issue during the period. In the case of LMN this is the same thing, since there has been no change in the number of shares issued during the year. A company will calculate the weighted average number of shares in issue during the year and state this figure, together with the EPS calculated on this basis, in its annual report.

<table>
<tr><td colspan="3">Exercise

Calculate LMN's EPS for Years 2 and 3.</td></tr>
</table>

Solution	Year 2	Year 3
Earnings per share		
$(^7/_{60})$	11.7 pence	
$(^{14}/_{60})$		23.3 pence

Remember that if LMN had any preference shares in issue we would need to deduct the preference dividend to derive the correct earnings figure for the numerator.

Another term that you might come across in this context is the diluted earnings per share. At the end of the year, a company might have in issue certain securities that could result in more ordinary shares being issued in the future. For example, there may be share options that could be exercised in the future or a special sort of loan that is convertible into ordinary shares at some date in the future, at the option of the lender.

Although these securities are not at present entitled to a share of the company's earnings they might be entitled to a share at some point in the future. The fully diluted earnings per share is the figure that would result if the current year's earnings had to be shared between all these potential new shares as well as the existing shares.

The fully diluted earnings per share helps investors to assess the effect of a potential future dilution or 'watering down' of their returns.

7.3.6   Price–earnings (PE) ratio

This ratio relates the market price of a share to its annual earnings. It represents the number of times the annual earnings for each share that investors are willing to pay to acquire a share.

$$\text{Price–earnings ratio} = \frac{\text{Market price of share}}{\text{Earnings per share}}$$

Exercise
Calculate LMN's PE ratio based on the earnings for Years 2 and 3.

Solution		
	Year 2	Year 3
Price–earnings ratio		
$(^{1.44}/_{0.117})$	12.3 times	
$(^{2.30}/_{0.233})$		9.9 times

A high PE ratio indicates that investors have high confidence in the future prospects for a company. However, it is important to compare companies which are in the same type of business, as average PE ratios will vary from industry to industry.

In our demonstration, using LMN as an example we have based the PE ratio on the share price at the end of the year. In reality the PE ratio will change every day because the numerator is the current market price, not the year-end share price. Since the share price changes every day, so will the company's reported PE ratio.

A further complication is that the denominator or earnings per share figure used in the calculation does not stay constant all year. The earnings per share figure is updated when the company publishes its interim results part way through the year. It is updated again when the company publishes its preliminary results for the year and then again when the final annual results are available. You might also see a PE ratio based on a company's projected earnings for the year.

Therefore the PE ratio fluctuates on a daily basis to reflect the company's recent performance and investors' view of the future prospects of the company.

7.3.7 LMN's investment ratios: Summary

	Year 2	Year 3
Return on shareholders' funds	9.7%	17.5%
Ordinary dividend cover	1.5 times	2.3 times
Dividend yield	5.6%	4.4%
Earnings yield	8.1%	10.1%
Earnings per share	11.7 pence	23.3 pence
Price–earnings ratio	12.3 times	9.9 times

Exercise

Comment on LMN's performance from the point of view of a shareholder or potential shareholder.

Solution

The return on shareholders' funds has improved during Year 3, in line with the overall improvement in LMN's fortunes.

The adequacy of this return will depend on the shareholders' attitude to risk (the financial risk has increased with the level of gearing) and on the other opportunities that shareholders have for the investment of their funds.

The level of dividend cover has improved, but this also indicates that directors are retaining proportionately more of the annual earnings for reinvestment (lower dividend payout ratio in Year 3). The importance of this will depend on shareholders' need for cash returns versus capital gains.

Dividend yield has deteriorated because although the absolute amount of dividend has increased, the dividend per share has not increased at the same rate as the share's market price.

The earnings yield and the earnings per share have increased. Shareholders are achieving a higher return on their investment in LMN's shares. As above, the adequacy of these ratios will depend on the shareholders' attitude to risk and on the other investment opportunities available.

The PE ratio has deteriorated. Despite the increased earnings, the share price has not increased proportionately. This indicates a reduction in investors' assessment of the future prospects for this company. Perhaps they are not happy about the increase in gearing, or they may be disturbed by the deterioration in LMN's liquidity position.

7.4   Limitations of ratio analysis

Throughout this chapter and Chapter 6, you have seen warnings about the difficulties of making inter-company comparisons and drawing firm conclusions from an analysis based on published accounts. It will be useful to summarise in this section the main limitations of ratio analysis.

(a) Ratios are constructed from accounting data and they therefore inherit the subjective aspects of this data, for example differing depreciation policies may make it difficult to compare ratios from one company to another.

(b) If the accounts are made up to different dates, then different external factors may have influenced the figures, for example different trading conditions, which again makes comparison difficult.

(c) The results of ratios may be interpreted in different ways, for example a low inventory turnover period may indicate efficient inventory control or it may result from serious inventory shortages.

(d) If only one or two years' figures are available then there is no reference to trends over recent years.

(e) There is no reference to future prospects or plans (although the PE ratio may take account of shareholders' view of the company's future prospects).

(f) The focus tends to be on relative rather than absolute values, for example some profitability ratios can look good if the assets are undervalued (this can result in a smaller denominator).

(g) The ratios are based on balance sheet data, which may not be representative of the year as a whole.

(h) Ratios from different sources may be calculated in different ways. For example, care is needed when using an industry average ratio for comparison purposes or when interpreting ratios calculated by a company and printed in its own annual report. It is important to establish and understand the method of calculation before attempting to draw any conclusions.

(i) Ratios can indicate where changes have occurred but they do not provide the analyst with the reasons for the changes. For example a number of different factors could lead to a reduced gross profit margin, including the following.

◆ Reduced selling prices
◆ Increased costs per unit of the product or service sold
◆ A change in the mix of products or services sold, to include proportionately more of the less profitable items.

7.5 Interpreting cash flow statements

To complete our analysis of LMN's performance and financial position we will now look at the following cash flow statements for Years 2 and 3.

LMN plc: Cash flow statement for the year ended 31 December

	Year 2		Year 3	
	£m	£m	£m	£m
Cash flow from operating activities				
Operating profit for the year		12.0		26.0
Add back: Depreciation		2.7		3.8
		14.7		29.8
Decrease/(increase) in inventories	1.2		(4.0)	
Decrease/(increase) in receivables	(3.4)		(22.0)	
Increase/(decrease) in trade payables	4.1		17.8	
		1.9		(8.2)
Cash generated from operations		16.6		21.6
Interest paid		–		(0.7)
Taxation paid		(3.9)		(4.1)
Net cash from operating activities		12.7		16.8
Cash flows from investing activities				
Purchase of non-current assets		(6.2)		(36.8)
Cash flows from financing activities				
Payment of dividends	(4.8)		(6.0)	
Proceeds from long-term borrowings	–		20.0	
Net cash flow from financing activities		(4.8)		14.0
Net increase/(decrease) in cash and cash equivalents		1.7		(6.0)
Cash and cash equivalents at beginning of period		8.3		10.0
Cash and cash equivalents at end of period		10.0		4.0

The interpretation of cash flows is fraught with difficulties because cash flows are so volatile. For this reason it is important not to read too much into a single year's cash flows. However we can see the following from LMN's cash flow statements.

◆ The cash generated from operations is a positive figure for both years, despite a large cash outflow caused by the increase in receivables during Year 3.
◆ In both years the net cash from operating activities was a positive figure. This meant that the cash generated from operations was sufficient to cover the payments for interest and tax, and to contribute towards the purchase of non-current assets.
◆ In Year 3, the net cash inflow from operating activities amounted to £16.8m but this did not cover the full amount

of the investment in non-current assets. However, the net cash inflow from operating activities was probably adequate, since the investment in non-current assets during Year 3 was relatively large.

♦ After taking account of the cash flows from investing activities LMN had a net cash outflow in Year 3 of £20m (£16.8m less £36.8m). This has been financed by £20m of long-term borrowings. Given LMN's previous zero level of gearing this may not be a problem. However, the payment of dividends has effectively been financed by a decrease in cash. This may cause problems because more cash is usually needed to support increased activity.

However, remember the earlier comment that it is important not to read too much into one year's cash flows because they are so volatile.

♦ If the net cash flow from operating activities is consistently failing to contribute towards capital expenditure, or if borrowings are steadily increasing (or if cash is steadily decreasing), we would usually expect to see the company reducing its outflow on capital expenditure. With only two years' figures available for LMN, it is not possible to comment on this aspect of their cash management.

7.5.1 Free cash flow

The concept of free cash flow (FCF) can be useful in the interpretation of cash flow statements. Definitions of FCF vary and some companies will use their own formula to calculate what they believe to be the correct FCF and will include the result in their annual report.

A common calculation used to derive the FCF is as follows.

FCF = net cash from operating activities − capital expenditure

One way of understanding FCF is to view it as the cash that the company has generated during the period that its directors are free to spend, after paying for all the obligatory costs that they must meet in order to continue operating such as operating expenses, interest, taxation and capital expenditure.

A positive FCF gives directors the cash they need to pursue any profit-generating opportunities that are available to the company.

With no FCF the directors are not generating the cash required to develop new products or services or perhaps to pay back any borrowings.

However a negative FCF is not necessarily a bad thing, particularly in a new company. If a company is investing heavily in capital expenditure to bring about profit-generating opportunities in the future then this might result in a negative FCF in the short term. But it is important that the cash is invested to earn a good return on the investment and the cash outflow must be financed appropriately.

Exercise

Using the definition given above, calculate the free cash flow for LMN plc for Years 2 and 3.

Solution

Free cash flow Year 2 $= 12.7 - 6.2 = £6.5\,m$

Free cash flow Year 3 $= 16.8 - 36.8 = £20.0\,m$ negative

Notice that the definition of FCF we have discussed assumes that capital expenditure must be met before the directors are free to spend the remaining cash on other more discretionary items. Some companies and analysts use a more sophisticated definition of FCF which takes one step further the idea of the cash that the directors are free to spend after all obligatory payments. This more sophisticated version distinguishes between 'replacement' capital expenditure and 'expansion' capital expenditure.

In this context replacement capital expenditure (sometimes called maintenance capital expenditure) is necessary to replace non-current assets in order to maintain the company's existing operating capability, as non-current assets already in use reach the end of their useful lives. Expansion capital expenditure (sometimes called enhancement capital expenditure) is incurred in increasing the company's operating capability.

Free cash flow would then be calculated as follows.

$$FCF = \text{net cash from operating activities}$$
$$- \text{'replacement' capital expenditure}$$

This definition of FCF views the outlay of cash for expansion capital expenditure as a discretionary cash flow that the directors are free to incur if they wish. The replacement capital expenditure is viewed as an obligatory cash outlay in the context of calculating the FCF.

Whatever definition of FCF is used, it can be seen as a measure of the ability of a company to be self-financing. However you should remember that cash flows are volatile and it is important not to place too much weight on the interpretation of a single year's cash flow figures.

7.6   EBITDA

Before we complete this chapter on interpreting financial statements it will be useful to look at a term which has become increasingly popular as a performance measure in companies' financial statements: EBITDA.

EBITDA stands for 'earnings before interest, taxation, depreciation and amortisation'. It is calculated by taking the profit for the period and adding back the charges for interest, taxation, depreciation and amortisation.

Supporters of EBITDA as a performance measure argue that it enables a more valid comparison of performance between companies. This is because it is not affected by the way that the company is financed or by subjective accounting charges for depreciation and amortisation. They also argue that EBITDA is a good approximation for operating cash flow because it adds back depreciation and amortisation, which are often major non-cash items.

However, while EBITDA might in some circumstances be a useful measure of comparative profitability it is misleading to suggest that it is an approximation for operating cash flows. This is because it ignores the changes in working capital which can create a significant cash drain, particularly for growing companies.

EBITDA is often quoted by companies as a performance measure in their annual report. However, it should never be used as a substitute for other profit measures or as a proxy for monitoring operating cash flows. Instead it should be considered as another potentially useful performance measure among the range of measures available to the analyst.

7.7 Summary

(1) Gearing refers to the proportion of a company's funds that is provided by finance sources on which interest or a fixed amount of dividend is payable. High gearing can result in wide fluctuations in shareholders' earnings.

(2) The PE ratio is calculated by dividing the market price of a share by the earnings per share. The PE ratio fluctuates on a daily basis as the current share price changes.

(3) There are many limitations in the use of ratio analysis. Therefore the analysis should be applied thoughtfully and not mechanically.

(4) Cash flows are volatile. Therefore it is important to look at cash flow trends, and not to read too much into one or two years' cash flow figures.

(5) Free cash flow can be calculated in a number of different ways. It is a measure used to assess the amount of cash that the company has generated during the period that its directors are free to spend, after paying for all the obligatory costs that they must meet in order to continue operating.

(6) EBITDA stands for 'earnings before interest, taxation, depreciation and amortisation'.

Review questions

(1) What is financial gearing, and what are the implications of a relatively high gearing ratio? (Section 7.2.1)

(2) Name another term that might be used instead of financial gearing. (Section 7.2.1)

(3) What is another term used to describe the return on shareholders' funds? (Section 7.3.1)

(4) What is the difference between the return on shareholders' funds and ROCE? (Section 7.3.1)

(5) What is meant by 'earnings'? (Section 7.3.3)

(6) What is meant by the term 'diluted earnings per share'? (Section 7.3.5)

(7) What is the significance of a relatively high PE ratio? (Section 7.3.6)

(8) State three limitations of ratio analysis based on published financial statements. (Section 7.4)

(9) Describe one method that may be used to calculate the free cash flow for a period. (Section 7.5.1)

(10) What does the acronym EBITDA stand for? (Section 7.6)

(11) Why is it not correct to say that EBITDA provides a good approximation for a company's operating cash flow? (Section 7.6)

Self-test questions

(1) Refer to Question 3 at the end of the previous chapter (RC Ltd).

Required

(a) Use the income statements and balance sheets to calculate the following for Year 7 and Year 8 for RC Limited.
   (i) Gearing ratio
   (ii) Interest cover
   (iii) Return on shareholders' equity
   (iv) Ordinary dividend cover (see information below)
   (v) Earnings per share

The following additional information is provided concerning dividends paid and proposed.

	Year 7 £'000	Year 8 £'000
Interim dividend paid	6.0	5.0
Final dividend paid/proposed	9.0	5.0
Total dividend for year	15.0	10.0

(b) Comment on the results of your calculations.

(2) The PE ratios for two companies in the same industry are as follows:

	31 March Year 2	31 March Year 3
Company A	9.5	14.6
Company B	10.8	12.9

What broad conclusions can be drawn from this information?

(3) The following extracts are taken from the latest results of F plc.

Income statement (extract) for latest year

	£'000
Operating profit	37.5
Interest payable	(6.4)
	31.1
Taxation	(8.3)
Profit for the period	22.8

Balance sheet (extract) as at end of latest year

	£'000
Ordinary 50p shares	43
Reserves	24
Ordinary shareholders' equity	67
8% £1 preference shares	15
	82
Non-current liabilities: borrowings	12
	94

The company has no other borrowings in addition to those shown on the balance sheet extract.

The preference dividend was paid in the latest year.

There was no change in the number of shares in issue and an ordinary dividend of £6,700 was paid.

Required

Use the extracts and additional information above to calculate the following for the latest year.

(a) Gearing ratio
(b) Interest cover
(c) Return on ordinary shareholders' funds (ROSF)
(d) Ordinary dividend cover
(e) Earnings per share

(4) The directors of G Limited are concerned that the company's cash balance has reduced during the latest year despite the achievement of a healthy profit result and the addition of a new long-term loan to the company's financing structure.

From the following cash flow statement for the year identify four major factors which have contributed to the reduction in the company's cash balance.

G Limited: Cash flow statement for the year ended 31 December Year 7

	£m	£m
Cash flow from operating activities		
Operating profit for the year		291
Add back: Depreciation		46
		337
Decrease/(increase) in inventories	(92)	
Decrease/(increase) in receivables	19	
Increase/(decrease) in trade payables	(76)	
		(149)
Cash generated from operations		188
Interest paid		(18)
Taxation paid		(58)
Net cash from operating activities		112
Cash flows from investing activities		
Purchase of non-current assets	(87)	
Proceeds from sale of equipment	11	
Net cash outflow from investing activities		(76)
Cash flows from financing activities		
Payment of dividends	(99)	
Proceeds from long-term borrowings	40	
Net cash outflow from financing activities		(59)
Net decrease in cash and cash equivalents		(23)
Cash and cash equivalents at beginning of period		25
Cash and cash equivalents at end of period		2

Answers to self-test questions

(1) (a)

	Year 7	Year 8
Gearing ratio		
$= \dfrac{\text{Borrowings} + \text{Preference share capital}}{\text{Total capital employed}} \times 100\%$	$\dfrac{25}{106} \times 100\% = 24\%$	$\dfrac{40}{135} \times 100\% = 30\%$
Interest cover		
$= \dfrac{\text{Profit before interest and tax}}{\text{Interest payable}}$	$\dfrac{36}{4} = 9$ times	$\dfrac{37}{6} = 6$ times
Return on equity		
$= \dfrac{\text{Profit after interest, tax and preference dividend}}{\text{Ordinary share capital} + \text{reserves}} \times 100\%$	$\dfrac{24}{81} \times 100\% = 30\%$	$\dfrac{24}{95} \times 100\% = 25\%$
Ordinary dividend cover		
$= \dfrac{\text{Profit after interest, tax and preference dividend}}{\text{Ordinary dividend for the year}}$	$\dfrac{24}{15} = 1.6$ times	$\dfrac{24}{10} = 2.4$ times
Earnings per share		
$= \dfrac{\text{Profit after interest, tax and preference dividend}}{\text{Number of ordinary shares}}$	$\dfrac{24}{50} = 48$ pence	$\dfrac{24}{50} = 48$ pence

(b) (i) The gearing ratio has increased due to the introduction of more borrowings. This will increase the financial risk associated with the company, and the commitment to pay interest may cause problems if revenues continue to fall.

(ii) The interest cover has reduced because the interest cost increased by more than the operating profit.

(iii) The return on shareholders' equity reduced because the same earnings were achieved but the value of shareholders' equity increased, due to the retention of Year 7 profits.

(iv) The increase in dividend cover is a direct reflection of the reduction in dividend payments for Year 8.

(v) There was no change in the earnings per share. The wealth created for each share was the same in both years.

(2) The PE ratios for both companies increased in Year 3. This indicates a greater confidence generally in the future earning power of companies in this industry. Confidence in the future prospects of company B was higher in Year 2, but during Year 3 the confidence in company A's prospects grew. By 31 March, Year 3 company A's future prospects were viewed more favourably than those of company B.

(3)

(a) Gearing ratio

$$= \frac{\text{Borrowings} + \text{preference share capital}}{\text{Total capital employed}} \times 100\%$$

$$= \frac{(12 + 15)}{94} \times 100\%$$

$$= 28.7\%$$

(b)

$$\text{Interest cover} = \frac{\text{Profit before interest and tax}}{\text{Interest payable}}$$

$$= \frac{37.5}{6.4}$$

$$= 5.9 \text{ times}$$

(c) Return on ordinary shareholders' funds

$$= \frac{\text{Profits after interest, tax and}}{\text{preference dividend}} \times 100\%$$

Preference dividend = £15,000 × 8% = £1,200

$$\text{ROSF} = \frac{22.8 - 1.2 \text{ preference dividend}}{67} \times 100\%$$

$$= 32.2\%$$

(d) Ordinary dividend cover

$$= \frac{\text{Profits after interest, tax and preference dividend}}{\text{Ordinary dividend for the year}}$$

$$= \frac{22.8 - 1.2}{6.7}$$

$$= \frac{21.6}{6.7}$$

$$= 3.2 \text{ times}$$

(e)

$$\text{Earnings per share} = \frac{\text{Profits after interest, tax and preference dividend}}{\text{Number of ordinary shares}}$$

$$= \frac{22.8 - 1.2}{86^*}$$

$$= 25.1 \text{ pence}$$

(4) Major factors which have contributed to the reduction in the company's cash balance are as follows:

◆ Inventories have increased by £92 m. Increasing the inventory balance ties up additional cash.

◆ Trade payables have decreased by £76 m. Additional cash has been used to pay suppliers and reduce the balance owed to them.

◆ A generous dividend of £99 m has been paid. This appears to represent approximately half of the profit for the year after interest and taxation.

◆ £87 m of cash has been paid to purchase non-current assets. This has an immediate impact on the cash balance but only a proportion of the cost will have been charged as a depreciation expense in the income statement.

---

* The total nominal or par value of the 50 pence shares shown on the balance sheet is £43,000. The number of shares must therefore be 43,000 × 2 = 86,000.

Part 3

Using Financial Information to Manage a Business

Management Accounting as an Aid to Management

8.1   Introduction

In the remainder of this book we will be looking at the financial information which is necessary to help managers to run the business; that is, we will be discussing the internal management accounts which are not usually made available to the public. In this chapter we will be reviewing the need for management accounting information and discussing the differences between financial accounting and management accounting.

8.2   The need for detailed management accounting information

The financial information that you have learned about so far in this book has been in aggregate form. However, aggregate income statements and balance sheets prepared on an historical cost basis do not provide the answers to questions such as the following:

◆ What did it cost to operate Department A last period?
◆ What will it cost to operate Department B next period?
◆ If we decide to close Department C and instead outsource the work undertaken in that department, what will be the effect on the organisation's total cost?
◆ Should we accept this order for a batch of Product X?
◆ What price should we charge for a delivery from London to Edinburgh?
◆ Will the proposed investment in new computer equipment be worthwhile?

The financial accounting information that we have reviewed so far will not help managers to answer these questions. More detailed and forward-looking information is needed, and this need is met by an organisation's management accounting system. The management accounting department provides an internal information service to managers to help them to manage.

8.3 The core activities of management accounting

The main activities of the management accounting function could be described as follows:

◆ *Participation in the planning process at both strategic and operational levels.* In Chapter 11 we will be reviewing the role of financial budgets in the planning process.

◆ *The initiation of and the provision of guidance for management decisions.* Chapters 9 and 10 will demonstrate how cost information can be analysed to assist managers in their decision-making role. In Chapter 12 we will review the main investment appraisal techniques that are used as a basis for making capital investment decisions.

◆ *Contributing to the monitoring and control of performance through the provision of reports on organisational (and organisational segment) performance.* Chapter 11 will discuss the use of budgetary control reports to monitor and control the organisation's performance.

8.4 Management accounting compared with financial accounting

Before beginning our discussion of the provision of cost information as a basis for management decisions, it will be useful to review the differences between the financial accounting information that we have covered so far in this book and the management accounting information which we will be considering in the remaining chapters.

The differences between management accounting and financial accounting stem from the different information needs of the people who are using the two types of information.

> *If you have forgotten who might be included in the wide range of users of accounts, refer to Chapter 1 of this book to refresh your memory.*

The main differences could be summarised as follows:

◆ *Management accounting reports are for internal use only.* Financial accounts are prepared to satisfy the information needs of a variety of users both internal and external to the business.

♦ *Management accounting reports are usually very detailed.* If they are to be effective in supporting managers in the decision-making process, many management accounting reports need to be provided in considerable detail. Financial accounting statements provide an aggregated overview of an organisation's performance.

♦ *Management accounting reports often provide forecast information as well as historical information.* Management accounting tends to be more forward-looking whereas financial accounting statements are largely historical, providing information about past performance. However, certain types of financial accounting reports may contain projected information. For example, a company might issue forecasts to external users when it is attempting to raise more capital.

♦ *Management accounting reports are not regulated by external bodies.* Because they are prepared for internal use only, management accounting reports may contain any information that is useful for the managers who are to use it. This information may be presented in any way that suits the needs of the organisation, and there are no external regulations to restrict this freedom. In contrast, the content and presentation of published financial accounting statements are regulated by a series of accounting standards, partly by company law and, for listed companies, by additional stock exchange requirements. These regulations are designed to protect the external users of financial accounts, so that they can be sure that all organisations' accounts are prepared on a standardised basis.

> *In most companies, the production of management accounts (and many other aspects of the business) is regulated by internal audit departments – which can be more rigorous in their investigations than many external bodies.*

♦ *Many management accounting reports are prepared for a specific, one-off purpose.* For example, a management accounting report may be prepared to help with a particular decision, or a report might be addressed to and designed for a particular manager within the organisation. Financial accounting reports tend to be more general purpose. Most are prepared on a regular, routine basis and they are designed to be useful to a wide range of potential users.

◆ *Management accounting reports tend to be produced more frequently than financial accounting reports.* Most organisations publish their financial accounts once a year in their annual report. Many also publish abbreviated interim reports on a half-yearly or quarterly basis. In contrast, management accounting reports can be prepared monthly, weekly or even daily to allow managers to monitor current results on a regular basis.

8.5 Summary

(1) Management accounting provides the detailed, forward-looking information that managers need to help them to manage the business.

(2) Management accounting contains three core activities: participation in the planning process, the initiation of and the provision of guidance for management decisions, and contributing to the monitoring and control of performance.

(3) A number of differences can be identified between management accounting and financial accounting. These differences stem from the different information needs of the people who are using the two types of information.

The Analysis of Cost

9.1 Introduction

This chapter will explore a fundamental issue in management accounting: what is meant by cost? We will be looking at the different measures of cost and at what makes up the total cost of a product or service. You will also be learning about overhead absorption, which is the process of determining the overhead cost of a product or service.

9.2 The elements of cost

9.2.1 What makes up total cost?

Imagine that you work as a salesperson for a company that manufactures and sells wall-mounted hairdryers: the type that is fixed to the wall for customers' use in hotel bedrooms. You have been negotiating with the procurement manager of a chain of hotels in an attempt to secure a contract to supply a batch of hairdryers.

It is very important that you should win this contract, because it is likely that, once this first order has been fulfilled successfully, the hotel chain will place future orders for hairdryers and for your company's other products, when refurbishing its other hotels. Furthermore, other hotel chains may become interested in your company's products once they discover that this major chain is one of your customers.

Unfortunately the hotel's procurement manager is working within the constraints of a very strict budget and has made it clear that the highest price that the hotel is prepared to pay is £10 per hairdryer. Your company's normal selling price is considerably higher than this.

Undaunted, you go to see your company's management accountant who informs you that this is not an attractive proposition because the company's cost per hairdryer is £12. This seems to be the end of the matter. The company cannot afford to sell its hairdryers for £10 each if they cost £12 to produce.

Or can it? If we can find out what makes up this cost of £12 per hairdryer we will be in a better position to make a management decision about this potential order.

The elements of cost are as follows:

Direct material
+Direct labour
+Direct expense
=Total direct cost or prime cost
+Production overhead (share of)
- ◆ indirect production materials
- ◆ indirect production labour
- ◆ indirect production expenses

=Total production cost
+Other overhead (share of)
- ◆ selling and distribution overhead
- ◆ administration overhead

=Total cost

Now let us look at the sort of costs that might be incurred in manufacturing and selling a hairdryer, and how each cost would be classified in terms of the above analysis of the elements of cost.

◆ *Direct materials.* This is the material that actually becomes part of the finished hairdryer. It would include the plastic for the case and the packaging materials. If we make another batch of hairdryers then we will need to purchase another batch of these and other direct materials.

◆ *Direct labour.* This is the labour cost incurred directly as a result of making one hairdryer. Direct labour cost is not so common nowadays because many employees are paid a guaranteed wage regardless of their level of output. This guaranteed wage would not be classified as a direct labour cost in this case because it is not directly caused by the manufacture of any individual hairdryer or batch of hairdryers. However, our manufacturing staff may be paid a bonus of, say, £1 per hairdryer produced, in addition to their guaranteed wage. This bonus would be a direct labour cost because one more batch of hairdryers would lead to the payment of more £1 bonuses.

◆ *Direct expenses.* These are expenses caused directly as a result of making one more batch of hairdryers. For example, it might include the cost of the power to run the machinery to produce the batch for the hotel chain.

The three direct costs are totalled to derive the prime cost or total direct cost of a hairdryer. This is one measure of cost but there are still other costs to be added: production overheads and other overheads.

Production overheads are basically the same three costs as for direct cost, but they are identified as *indirect* costs because they cannot be specifically identified with any particular hairdryer or batch of hairdryers. Indirect costs must be shared out over all the production using a fair and equitable basis.

> *Later in this chapter you will see how indirect costs can be shared over all the production for the period.*

Indirect materials are those production materials that do not actually become part of the finished product. This might include the cleaning materials and lubricating oils for the machinery. The machines must be clean and lubricated in order to carry out production, but it will probably not be necessary to spend more on these materials in order to manufacture a further batch. This cost is therefore only indirectly related to the production of this batch.

Indirect labour is the production labour cost which cannot be directly associated with the production of any particular batch. It would include the guaranteed wage that was mentioned earlier, and the salaries of supervisors who are overseeing the production of hairdryers as well as all the other products manufactured in the factory.

Indirect expenses are all the other production overheads associated with running the factory, including factory rent and rates, heating and lighting, etc. These indirect costs must be shared out over all of the output in a period. The share of indirect production costs is added to the prime cost to derive the total production cost of a hairdryer. This is another measure of cost but there are still more costs to be added: a share of the other overheads.

Selling and distribution overhead includes the sales force salaries and commission, the cost of operating delivery vehicles and renting a storage warehouse, etc. Most of this cost must be shared over all of the products sold in a period.

Administration overhead includes the rent on the administrative office building, the depreciation of office equipment, postage and stationery costs, etc. This cost must again be shared over all the products produced and sold.

Now that you understand the nature of each of the cost elements which make up total cost we can return to our management accountant and ask for a detailed breakdown of the total cost of £12.

Total cost of a hairdryer

	£
Direct material	4
+Direct labour	2
+Direct expense	1
=Total direct cost or prime cost	7
+Production overhead (share of)	2
=Total production cost	9
+Other overhead (share of)	3
=Total cost	12

Now we are in a better position to judge the potential effect of accepting an order at a selling price of £10 per hairdryer.

Exercise

Which of the above costs would be incurred as a result of making a further batch of hairdryers?

Solution

The direct cost of £7 would definitely be incurred if another batch was produced. This is the extra material that would have to be bought, the extra labour bonuses that would have to be paid and the extra expenses for power, etc. that would be incurred.

The £2 production overhead cost would not be incurred if another batch was produced. This is the share of costs that would be incurred anyway, such as the cleaning materials, the factory rent and the supervisors' salaries.

The £3 share of 'other' overhead would probably not be incurred if another batch was produced. This includes the office costs, the depreciation on the delivery vehicles and the rent of warehousing facilities. This sort of cost would not increase as a result of producing another batch. However, there may be some incremental or extra selling and distribution costs, for example we would probably be entitled to a sales commission for all our hard work in winning the sale, and there would be some costs involved in delivering the batch to the hotel chain. For the sake of our analysis let us suppose that this incremental cost amounts to £1 per hairdryer, rather than the full amount of £3 shown in the cost breakdown.

You can see from the discussion in this exercise that in fact the only extra cost to be incurred in producing and selling a further batch of hairdryers is £8 per hairdryer (£7 direct cost + assumed £1 extra selling and distribution costs). Therefore it may be possible to sell to the hotel chain for £10 per hairdryer, and still be better off than if the sale was not made at all! At least the extra £2 per hairdryer (£10 − £8 extra cost) would contribute towards the costs which are being incurred anyway − the production overheads, administration overheads, etc.

In the next chapter you will see that the costs which would be incurred anyway and which would not be affected by the manufacture of a further batch are called the fixed costs. The costs which would increase in line with the number of batches produced are called the variable costs.

9.2.2 The need for subjective judgement

This exercise has demonstrated how more detailed cost information can help managers to make better-informed decisions. You should also appreciate that, although more information improves the ability to make the decision, it still cannot replace the need for management to exercise judgement.

Exercise

It seems that for commercial reasons it may be worthwhile selling a batch of hairdryers to the hotel chain for less than the normal selling price. But what other factors do you think managers should consider before agreeing to the sale?

Solution

You may have thought of the following factors, as well as others which would be equally worth consideration

◆ Can the batch be produced without affecting the remainder of our production, that is can it be fitted onto our existing facilities? If full-price business had to be displaced, or if overtime payments were incurred, this would increase the incremental cost of producing the batch.

◆ Will we be committing ourselves to charging this price on all business with the hotel, or is it a 'low introductory price'? Otherwise we could find that, as our level of business with the hotel grows, more and more of our sales are being priced at this low level and we will not be earning enough contribution towards the indirect, shared costs.

◆ Will our existing 'full-price' customers find out that we are selling to the hotel at a lower price, and begin to demand a discount as well?

9.2.3   A second example

Before we leave the subject of direct versus indirect cost, it will be worthwhile working through another exercise. This will ensure that you are completely clear about what constitutes a direct cost and what is an indirect cost. This time we will look at a service organisation.

Exercise

Spotless Limited is an office cleaning business, which employs a team of part-time cleaners who are paid an hourly wage. The business provides cleaning services for a number of clients, from small offices attached to high street shops to large open-plan offices in high-rise buildings.

In determining the cost of providing a cleaning service to a particular client, which of the following costs would be a direct cost of cleaning that client's office and which would be an indirect cost?

(a) The wages paid to the cleaner who is sent to the client's premises
(b) The cost of carpet shampoo used by the cleaner
(c) The salaries of Spotless Limited's accounts clerks
(d) Rent of the premises where Spotless Limited stores its cleaning materials and equipment
(e) Travelling expenses paid to the cleaner to reach the client's premises
(f) Advertising expenses incurred in attracting more clients to Spotless Limited's business.

Solution

The direct costs are (a), (b) and (e) because they can be directly identified with this particular client. The other costs are indirect because they would have to be shared among all of the clients serviced by Spotless Limited.

9.3 Overhead absorption

The process of sharing out the indirect costs over a number of products or services is called overhead absorption or overhead recovery. You will appreciate that this can be a very arbitrary task. For example in the previous exercise, who can say how much of the accounts clerks' salaries should be allocated to each client?

It may be easiest to simply divide the total salary cost by the number of clients to derive a cost per client. However, this may not reflect the true cost of servicing each client, and later in this chapter, we will see how the absorption of overheads can be more sophisticated than this simple division.

9.3.1 Why do we absorb overheads?

We have seen that the absorption or sharing out of overheads can at times be rather arbitrary. We have also seen that in certain management decisions; these absorbed costs are not relevant, and that management will often focus on the direct costs and not place so much importance on the indirect costs.

So why do we bother to undertake the task of absorption at all? Why not simply concentrate on the direct costs which can be allocated to products and services reasonably accurately?

There are two main reasons why we might need to calculate the fully absorbed cost of a product or service:

◆ *To have an understanding of the long-run average cost of our products and services.* This can be useful in many decisions, including pricing. Some organisations will take the total cost and add a percentage to this to determine their selling price. This is known as 'cost-plus' pricing but it can be a difficult practice to follow in a competitive market. In this type of market a supplier may have to set prices according to what customers are prepared to pay, rather than according to what the supplier would like to charge!

In our example of the hairdryer manufacturer in this chapter, a cost-plus price would have been determined by adding a percentage profit mark-up to the total cost of £12. However, this was not possible in the case of the potential order from the hotel chain – the market was attempting to dictate the price here.

◆ *To match cost against revenue when calculating profit.* In your studies of financial accounting in the earlier chapters of this book, you saw how the correct costs should be matched against each item of revenue to determine the profit for the period. Therefore if any inventory is carried forward at the end of a period the full cost of this inventory must be determined, including a fair share of overhead, so that the correct total cost can be matched against the sales revenue when the inventory items are sold in a later period.

This matching of costs also occurs in service industries. For example, a systems analyst may be designing a computer system for an organisation, and the system might not be completed at the end of the period, therefore no revenue will yet have been earned. It would not be fair to charge the development and overhead costs incurred to date in this year's income statement. Instead the full cost of the work done to date may be carried over and charged against the revenue which is earned in a later period when the system is completed. It is the management accountant's task to determine this full cost so that profit measurement is not distorted.

This is an example of work in progress – you learned about it in Chapter 3. The value of the work in progress would be shown as a current asset in the balance sheet at the end of the period.

9.3.2 Absorbing overheads: Traditional basis

We will now move on to look at how production overheads might be absorbed, that is shared out between products and services, in practice. We will begin by looking at the more traditional methods which are used to absorb overheads. Then we will go on to consider the criticisms of these methods in the modern operating environment, before reviewing more modern approaches to absorption costing.

Thinking back to our example of the hairdryer manufacturer, the types of indirect production cost that we described there were as follows:

◆ *Indirect materials*: cleaning materials and lubricating oils
◆ *Indirect labour*: basic wage of production employees, supervisors' salaries
◆ *Indirect expenses*: factory rent and rates, factory heating and lighting.

A simple way of sharing out these overheads would be as follows:

$$\frac{\text{Overhead charge}}{\text{per hairdryer}} = \frac{\text{Total production overheads in period}}{\text{Number of hairdryers produced in period}}$$

This method would work perfectly well if the company simply produced identical hairdryers all the time, and nothing else. However, this is not the case in this example and it is rarely the case in practice. It is unusual to find an organisation that produces homogeneous products that are similar in size and complexity. It is more likely that a range of products is produced, each of which places a different burden on the production facilities and which should each therefore carry a different amount of production overhead.

Looking at all the indirect costs described it could be argued that each of them tends to increase with time. The longer a machine is operated, the more lubricating oils and cleaning materials will be consumed. The longer a factory operates, the higher will be the salary and heating costs, etc.

The traditional methods of overhead absorption are based on the assumption that most overheads accrue with the passage of time. Therefore it makes sense that the longer an item takes to produce, the more overheads it should be charged, because it will have placed a greater burden on the factory facilities.

One measure of time taken is direct labour hours. Using this basis, an overhead absorption rate can be calculated as follows:

$$\text{Overhead absorption rate per direct labour hour} = \frac{\text{Total production overheads in period}}{\text{Total direct labour hours in period}}$$

9.3.3 Using a direct labour hour rate to absorb overheads: Example

The best way to see how to apply this absorption method is to work through an example.

Tronics Limited repairs and services specialist sports cars. Overheads incurred are £27,000 per period. Tronics absorbs overheads using a direct labour hour rate. During each period the total number of direct labour hours worked on servicing and repairs is 6,000. The following data relates to the repair job number 376.

Parts and spares used	£287
Direct labour charged to job (5 hours)	£60

Use this data to calculate the total cost of job number 376.

The first thing we will need to do is to calculate the overhead absorption rate:

$$\text{Overhead absorption rate per direct labour hour} = \frac{£27,000}{6,000} = £4.50 \text{ per labour hour}$$

This means that every time a labour hour is worked on a job, £4.50 will be charged to the job as its share of the overheads for the period. Over the whole period a total of 6,000 hours will be charged to jobs at an overhead rate of £4.50 per hour, so the total charges made for overhead will amount to 6,000 × £4.50 = £27,000.

The overhead will have been charged to the jobs as fairly as possible, using a time-based method. Jobs that have a lot of labour hours charged to them will be charged a higher share of the overhead than jobs that incur fewer labour hours.

We can now determine the total cost of repair job number 376:

	£
Parts and spares used	287.00
Direct labour charged to job (5 hours)	60.00
Prime cost	347.00
Overhead (5 labour hours × £4.50 per hour)	22.50
Total cost	369.50

Note that the prime cost for the job would remain unaltered whichever method was chosen to absorb overheads.

Exercise

Fine Furniture Limited manufactures pine bedroom furniture. The expected costs to be incurred on all orders next period are as follows:

	£
Direct materials – wood	3,800
screws, glue, etc.	250
Indirect materials	300
Direct labour	8,000
Supervisor's salary	2,300
Depreciation of machinery	200
Rent and rates	1,200
Electricity and gas	400
Telephone	150
Other overheads	250

Overheads are to be absorbed using a direct labour hour rate. A total of 800 labour hours will be worked during the next period.

A customer has requested a quotation for a king-size pine bed. The wood for the bed will cost £180 and other direct material cost will be £10. Direct labour hours will amount to 12 hours at a labour cost of £120. What will be the total cost of this order?

Solution

Total overhead = indirect materials £300 + supervisor's salary £2,300 + depreciation £200 + rent and rates £1,200 + electricity and gas £400 + telephone £150 + other £250 = £4,800

$$\text{Direct labour hour rate for overhead absorption} = \frac{£4,800}{800 \text{ hours}} = £6 \text{ per labour hour}$$

Cost of king-size bed	£
Direct materials	190
Direct labour	120
Prime cost	310
Overheads (12 hours × £6)	72
Total cost	382

9.3.4 Absorbing overheads based on machine hours

Another time-based absorption rate that is widely used is a machine hour rate. This works in exactly the same way as a direct labour hour rate, except that the absorption is based on the number of machine hours taken to produce each item. The machine hour rate would be calculated as follows:

$$\text{Overhead absorption rate per machine hour} = \frac{\text{Total production overheads in period}}{\text{Total machine hours in period}}$$

The machine time would be recorded for each item produced. The number of machine hours would be multiplied by the machine hour rate of overhead absorption, as calculated using the above formula, to derive the overhead cost for the item.

This method is obviously most suitable when production is more mechanised. In a mechanised environment, many overheads will be related to the number of machine hours used.

Exercise

Can you think of types of overhead cost that would tend to be higher when production is highly mechanised?

Solution

You may have thought of the following costs:

◆ Depreciation of machinery
◆ Power costs
◆ Indirect materials: lubricating oils, etc.
◆ Insurance of machinery
◆ Machinery maintenance costs

9.3.5 Departmental overhead absorption rates

The examples we have seen so far calculated a single rate of overhead absorption to be applied to all production. However, in practice an organisation might be divided into many different departments which undertake various activities to produce the final output.

For example, for Fine Furniture Limited a king-size bed might pass through the following departments during the production process:

Cutting department – the wood is cut to size

↓

Joining department – the wood is joined by skilled carpenters

↓

Finishing department – the bed is finished, the edges are smoothed, etc.

↓

Packing department – the bed is packed in cardboard ready for despatch to the customer.

The rate of incidence of overhead in each department is likely to be different. Some departments would incur a higher level of overhead cost and others would have a lower level. Furthermore, it is possible that, over the range of products manufactured by Fine Furniture Limited, certain products would spend longer in some departments than in others. Therefore the overhead charge would represent a more accurate reflection of the burden placed on the facilities if a separate charge was made for each department.

To further complicate matters, perhaps the cutting department is machine intensive whereas the other three departments might be more labour intensive. Therefore a machine hour rate would be most appropriate in the cutting department, with a labour hour rate being used in the other three departments.

In a system which uses departmental absorption rates, the overhead would be recorded separately for each department, as would the hours worked on production, that is machine hours in the cutting department and labour hours in the other three departments. A separate hourly rate would be calculated for each department with the result that a product which passes through all four departments would be charged with four separate amounts of overhead, that is one for each department, based on the time taken in each department.

Exercise

Separate departmental hourly rates of overhead absorption have now been determined for the forthcoming period for Fine Furniture Limited:

Cutting department	£7 per machine hour
Joining department	£5 per direct labour hour
Finishing department	£6 per direct labour hour
Packing department	£4 per direct labour hour

The proposed order for the king-size pine bed will require the following hours in each department:

Cutting department	3 machine hours
Joining department	6 direct labour hours
Finishing department	2 direct labour hours
Packing department	1 direct labour hour

The estimated prime cost for the order will remain as before, that is £310. What is the revised total cost of the king-size bed?

Solution

Cost of king-size bed	£	£
Direct materials		190
Direct labour		120
Prime cost		310
Overhead cost		
cutting dept (3 hours × £7)	21	
joining dept (6 hours × £5)	30	
finishing dept (2 hours × £6)	12	
packing dept (1 hours × £4)	4	67
Total cost		377

The use of separate departmental overhead absorption rates has led to a lower overhead charge for this particular order. However, it is important to realise that the same total overhead for Fine Furniture Limited is to be shared over all the products manufactured in the period. Therefore if this particular bed is to absorb a smaller amount of overhead, other products manufactured in the period will absorb a higher amount of overhead than they would have done using the single absorption rate. The overall result will be the same. The total overhead for the period will be absorbed by all the output or production.

9.3.6 Using predetermined overhead absorption rates

You may have noticed that in all the exercises and examples we have been calculating the overhead absorption rates for the forthcoming period, that is we have been using predetermined absorption rates. Predetermined rates are used for the following reasons:

◆ Managers need to have an overhead rate readily available throughout the period for quotations, cost estimates, etc. It would be very time-consuming to have to calculate a new rate several times during the period and managers would not be able to wait until the end of the period to see what the overhead rate should be. Therefore the rate is estimated in advance for the forthcoming period.

◆ Overhead costs tend to be incurred at uneven time intervals. For example, gas and telephone bills are paid quarterly whereas rent and salary bills may be paid monthly. The result would be very high overhead rates in some weeks and very low overhead rates in others. Calculating an overall rate for a longer period smooths out these fluctuations in timing.

Clearly, the actual overhead rate will often turn out to be different from the predetermined rate that has been applied throughout the period. Therefore the overheads that have been absorbed into production will be higher or lower than the actual overheads incurred. The difference between the two amounts is called the over- or under-absorbed overhead.

This might happen if the actual overhead expenditure is different from forecast, and/or if the actual hours are different from forcast. If more overhead is absorbed than was incurred, this is called an over-absorption. The opposite situation is called an under-absorption.

An adjustment for this under- or over-absorption can be made in the accounts at the end of the period. However, it is obviously undesirable for the over- or under-absorption to be very high; other-wise, managers have been using very inaccurate cost rates as a basis for pricing and other decisions during the period. This situation can be avoided by regular reviews of the absorption rates throughout the period to check that they are as accurate as possible at all times.

9.4 Recent developments in absorption costing methods

9.4.1 The criticisms of the traditional approach

Historically, the most common methods of absorbing production overhead have been based on an hourly rate: either labour hours or machine hours, for reasons discussed earlier in this chapter. However, the nature of the competitive environment is changing for many companies. The result is that customer needs are changing more rapidly and their requirements are becoming more complex.

For example, Fine Furniture Limited may previously have found that, apart from small changes required in the size of their pine beds, their output was fairly standard and that operations were reasonably standardised. However, more recently they may have been receiving requests for different-shaped headboards on the beds, perhaps with personalised carvings. Responding to these more complex and individual requirements results in a much more complex operation. Not only is it more difficult to produce the bed, but the liaison with the customer becomes more involved and the quality control activity needs to be redesigned.

The end result is that overheads are not necessarily incurred in relation to the actual time taken to produce the bed. Instead overheads are incurred in relation to the relative complexity of the activities that have to be undertaken during all the dealings with the customer, right from the first receipt of the request for a quotation to the receipt of payment from the customer.

Exercise

Can you think of, say, three additional activities that would have to be undertaken within Fine Furniture Limited as the result of a customer's order for a bed with a personalised carved headboard?

Solution

You may have thought of activities such as the following:

◆ Initial liaison with the customer to ascertain the exact design required.
◆ Consultation with a specialist carver to determine the cost of personalisation.
◆ Quality control checking to ensure that the product meets the specific customer requirements.
◆ Separate inventory control procedures for non-standard items.
◆ Invoice checking to ensure that the customer is charged for the specialist services received.

The traditional overhead absorption methods based on time taken are not sufficiently flexible to deal with such complexity in the modern operating environment. One method that has been developed to attempt to cope with this complexity is activity-based costing (ABC).

9.4.2 Activity-based costing

Activity-based costing analyses all the activities undertaken by an organisation to identify what drives the costs incurred, that is what causes the costs to increase. These cost drivers may be labour hours or machine hours but they could also be a variety of other factors.

For example, an analysis of quality control activity might identify that quality control costs are driven by the number of special customer requests. The higher the number of special requests, the higher are the quality control costs. Therefore a relatively standard product would not be associated with a high incidence of the cost driver 'specific requests' and so would receive a relatively low charge for quality control overhead. A product which involved a high number of 'specific requests' would be charged a relatively high amount of the quality control cost.

The strength of an ABC system is that it can be applied to all overhead costs incurred, and not just to the production overheads which are traditionally absorbed using a time-based method. Look back to the question that was posed at the beginning of Section 9.3. 'Who can say how much of the accounts clerks' salaries should be allocated to each client?'

Using an activity-based analysis, it might be possible to identify what *drives* the cost of employing accounts clerks in an office cleaning business. For example, we might ask the simple question 'what causes an accounts clerk to become more busy and in what circumstances would it be necessary to employ more accounts clerks?' By asking these questions we are attempting to determine the *cost drivers* for the activities undertaken by the accounts clerks.

We might be surprised to learn that perhaps it is not the number of clients which drives costs, but some other factor. For example, our accounts clerks might tell us that they are made more busy when the company takes on larger clients. Larger clients might mean that they need to process and account for more requisitions for materials, they have to account for the hiring of more heavy-duty cleaning equipment, and perhaps larger clients require more attention in terms of credit control!

An easily measured cost driver for the accounts clerks' salaries might therefore be 'square metres of floor space to be cleaned' rather than 'number of clients'. Larger clients would then be charged with more of the accounts clerks' salaries and smaller clients would be charged less. This would lead to a better analysis of cost and therefore better information for managers to use in their day-to-day planning and control of the business.

9.4.3 Establishing cost pools

We saw in the example of Fine Furniture Limited that the traditional overhead absorption method involved gathering together the overhead cost of each department (the cutting department, the joining department, etc.) and calculating a single rate of overhead absorption for each department.

In an ABC system a cost pool is established for each activity rather than for each department. Examples of cost pools related to particular activities are as follows:

◆ Materials handling
◆ Order processing
◆ Quality control
◆ Machine set-up

A separate cost driver would then be identified for each activity. Examples of cost drivers for the activities identified above might be as follows:

Activity cost pool	Cost driver identified
Materials handling	Number of materials deliveries received
Order processing	Number of customer orders
Quality control	Number of quality control inspections
Machine set-up	Number of machine set-ups

The costs associated with each activity would be allocated to the relevant cost pool. The total of each activity cost might consist of costs incurred in several different individual departments.

The total activity cost would then be divided by the number of cost drivers to determine an overhead rate per cost driver. Activity costs would be absorbed into individual product and service costs according to the number of cost drivers generated by each product or service.

The best way to see the difference between an ABC system and a traditional overhead costing system is to look at a simple example.

9.4.4 Activity-based costing: A simple example

A company manufactures two products in one production department.

Forecast data concerning the products for the next period include the following.

	Product A	Product B
Forecast output (units)	10,800	21,400
Machine hours per unit	6	2
Number of customer orders during period	12	36
Number of quality control inspections during period	25	75

Cost pools and related cost drivers

Cost pool	£	Cost driver
Machine operating	102,220	Machine hours
Order processing	20,160	Number of customer orders
Quality control	22,880	Number of quality control inspections
Total overhead costs	145,260	

Required

Calculate the overhead cost to be absorbed by each of the products using the following absorption costing methods.

(a) A traditional absorption method based on a machine hour rate.
(b) An activity-based method, using the relevant cost drivers to trace overhead costs to the individual products.

Solution

(a) Using a traditional absorption method

Forecast total number of machine hours
= A $(10, 800 \times 6)$ + B $(21, 400 \times 2)$ = $107, 600$
Overhead absorption rate = £145, 260/107, 600
= £1.35 per machine hour

Now the overhead absorption rate can be used to absorb the total overhead cost into the individual product costs.

Product A = 6 hours × £1.35 = £8.10 per unit
Product B = 2 hours × £1.35 = £2.70 per unit

(b) Using an activity-based method

Machine operating costs	£102,220/107,600 hours	£0.95 per machine hour
Order processing costs	£20,160/(12 + 36) orders	£420 per customer order
Quality control costs	£22,880/(25 + 75) inspections	£228.80 per inspection

Now the cost driver rates can be used to trace the activity costs into the individual product costs.

		Product A £		Product B £
Machine operating costs @ £0.95 per machine hour	(×10,800 × 6)	61,560	(×21,400 × 2)	40,660
Order processing costs @ £420 per customer order	(×12)	5,040	(×36)	15,120
Quality control costs @ £228.80 per inspection	(×25)	5,720	(×75)	17,160
		72,320		72,940
Output units		10,800		21,400
Overhead cost per unit		£6.70		£3.41

Let us summarise the results of the analysis to see the effect of changing the overhead absorption method.

	Product A overhead cost £ per unit	Product B overhead cost £ per unit
Traditional absorption method based on machine hour rate	8.10	2.70
Activity-based costing method	6.70	3.41

> *Remember: The total overhead cost has not changed, merely the way in which the total cost is allocated between the two products.*

The more detailed calculations using an activity-based analysis reveal that Product A absorbs too much overhead using a traditional method whereas Product B absorbs too little. This has implications for product pricing as well as for managers' understanding of what drives costs.

> *In the next chapter we will see how important it is for managers to have a thorough understanding of the way in which costs change in relation to the level of activity.*

The reason for the change in the overhead cost absorbed by each product can be seen by reviewing the original data. Product A generates more machine hours than Product B and will therefore absorb more overheads when machine hours are used as the overhead absorption base.

However, Product A generates proportionately fewer customer orders and quality control inspections. When these costs are traced separately using ABC the different usage of the resources is reflected more accurately in the product costs.

9.4.5 Criticisms of activity-based costing

While it is accepted that ABC results generally in more accurate product and service costs than an absorption costing system based on simple hourly rates, ABC should not be viewed as a panacea for all product and service costing problems. Activity-based costing does have its critics.

◆ Many critics of ABC argue that the determination of cost pools and their associated cost drivers is too complicated and time-consuming and that the cost involved outweighs any benefits that might be derived from the improved cost allocation.

◆ Some arbitrary cost apportionment is still involved at the initial stages when determining the total cost associated with each cost pool. For example, it might be difficult to apportion the factory rent accurately between the various cost pools.

◆ It is likely that more than one cost driver can be identified for a particular cost pool. Conversely it is unlikely that all of the costs allocated to each cost pool are driven by a single cost driver.

9.5 Summary

(1) The total cost of a product or service is made up of its direct cost plus a share of indirect costs or overheads.

(2) The process of assigning overhead costs to products or services is known as overhead absorption.

(3) Overhead absorption has traditionally used direct labour hours or machine hours as an absorption basis.

(4) More recent developments in overhead absorption techniques attempt to identify what drives overhead costs in order to determine more appropriate bases for the attribution of overhead costs to individual products and services.

Review questions

(1) What are the elements of cost? (Section 9.2.1)

(2) Why is overhead absorption necessary? (Section 9.3.1)

(3) Why has overhead absorption traditionally been based on time? (Section 9.3.2)

(4) Explain how a direct labour hour rate is used to absorb overheads. (Section 9.3.3)

(5) Why are overhead absorption rates determined in advance of each period? (Section 9.3.6)

(6) What is a cost driver? (Section 9.4.2)

(7) What is a cost pool? (Section 9.4.3)

Self-test questions

(1) CT Limited manufactures traditional teddy bears for the retail trade and for the collectors' market. Place each of the costs listed below into one of the following cost classifications:

◆ direct material
◆ direct labour
◆ direct expense
◆ production overhead
◆ other overhead

    (a) Rental of the vending machine located in the office
    (b) Depreciation of a sewing machine
    (c) Productivity bonus paid to production workers for each large brown bear produced
    (d) Fur fabric purchased
    (e) Salary of the production supervisor
    (f) Royalty paid to the designer of a small rainbow-coloured teddy
    (g) Cost of advertisement placed in 'Teddy Collectors' a weekly magazine

(2) S Limited manufactures self-assembly garden sheds and log cabins to customers' individual requirements. Forecast production overhead costs for the forthcoming period are

	£
Indirect labour	20,000
Rent and rates	12,000
Electricity and gas	4,500
Indirect material	2,200
Machine running costs (7,000 hours)	8,800
Other indirect production costs	1,500

S Limited adds 10 per cent to the total production cost of each job in order to absorb non-production overheads.

A customer has ordered a log cabin, job number 771, which will incur the following costs.

Direct material	£400
Direct labour	£180
Machine running time	8 hours

What is the total cost of job number 771?

Answer to self-test questions

(1)

    (a) The rental of the vending machine in an office is an administration overhead that would be classified as *other overhead*.

    (b) Depreciation of a sewing machine is a production cost that cannot be identified with any specific product unit. Therefore it is classified as an indirect production expense or a *production overhead cost*.

    (c) The productivity bonus can be identified with specific product units therefore it is a *direct labour cost*.

    (d) The fur fabric purchased is a *direct material cost*.

    (e) The salary of the production supervisor is a production cost that cannot be identified with any specific cost unit. Therefore it is classified as an indirect labour cost or a *production overhead cost*.

    (f) The royalty can be identified with specific product units therefore it is a *direct expense*.

    (g) The cost of the advertisement is a marketing overhead cost that would be classified as *other overhead*.

(2)   Total production overhead cost for forthcoming period   = £49,000

       Production overhead cost per machine running hour   = £49,000/7,000

                               = £7 per machine hour

Total cost of job 771	£
Direct material	400.00
Direct labour	180.00
Total direct cost	580.00
Production overheads (8 hours × £7)	56.00
Total production cost	636.00
Non-production overheads 10%	63.60
Total cost	699.60

Using Costs for Decision-making

10.1 Introduction

In this chapter you will find out more about how costs can be used to assist managers in their decision-making activities. You will learn about cost behaviour patterns and different classifications of cost for decision-making, including relevant costs and opportunity costs.

10.2 Cost behaviour patterns

The term 'cost behaviour patterns' is used to describe the way in which costs behave in relation to the level of activity. For example, the question 'does this cost increase in line with activity or does it remain constant?' is the same as asking 'what is the cost behaviour pattern for this cost?'

A variety of different factors can cause costs to increase or change, for example inflation or a scarcity in supply. However, in management accounting, when we talk about cost behaviour patterns we mean the way that they behave in relation to the level of activity. Activity can be measured in a variety of ways depending on the organisation, the type of cost being analysed and the reason for analysing the cost. Common measures of activity include the level of sales, the level of production, number of customers, number of employees, etc.

10.2.1 Fixed costs

A fixed cost is one which tends to be unaffected by fluctuations in the level of activity. Figure 10.1 shows a fixed cost of £10,000.

Notice that the total cost incurred in the period is £10,000 for all activity levels, even at zero activity. Therefore in the short term, an organisation will have to pay all its fixed bills, even if activity drops to zero.

Another term which is sometimes used to describe a fixed cost is 'period cost'. This highlights the fact that a fixed cost is incurred according to the time elapsed, rather than according to the level of activity.

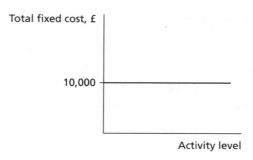

Figure 10.1 Fixed cost

Exercise

Can you name two costs that are likely to be fixed costs for a small restaurant business?

Solution

You may have thought of costs such as the following:

◆ Rent and rates
◆ Salaries of kitchen staff
◆ Insurance
◆ Depreciation of equipment.

Looking at the costs listed in this solution, they will all tend to be unaffected by the number of customers served in a period. However, you have probably realised that there may come a point when the business has expanded so much that more kitchen staff are needed to cope with the demand, or perhaps bigger premises will be necessary. There will then be corresponding increases in the costs of salaries, rent and rates, etc. So how can we describe these as fixed costs?

A fixed cost will be unaffected by activity changes *within a relevant range of activity*. If activity extends beyond this range then the identified fixed cost behaviour pattern may not be applicable. Figure 10.2 demonstrates this.

This could be depicting the cost of kitchen staff's salaries. The cost remains fixed for a certain range of activity. Within this range it is possible to serve more customers without needing extra kitchen

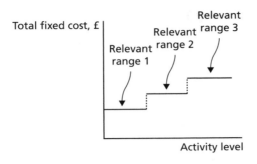

Figure 10.2 Stepped fixed cost

staff and therefore the salary cost remains constant. However, if activity is expanded to the critical point where another staff member is needed then the salary cost increases to a new, higher level. The cost then remains constant for a further range of increases in activity until another staff member is needed and another step occurs, etc.

The possibility of changes occurring in cost behaviour patterns means that it is unreliable to attempt to predict costs for activity levels which are outside the relevant range. For example, our records might show the staff levels needed at various activity levels between, say, 150 and 250 customers. We should therefore try to avoid using this information as the basis for forecasting the level of cost which would be incurred at an activity of, say, 350 customers, which is outside the relevant range.

This warning does not apply only to fixed costs. It is never wise to attempt to predict costs for activity levels outside the range for which cost behaviour patterns have been established.

10.2.2 Variable costs

A variable cost is one which varies in line with the level of activity. The higher the level of activity, the higher will be the cost incurred. Figure 10.3 depicts a linear variable cost.

The graph is a straight line through the origin which means that the cost is nil at zero activity level. When activity increases the total variable cost increases in direct proportion, that is if activity goes up by 10 per cent, then the total variable cost also increases by 10 per cent, as long as the activity level is still within the relevant range.

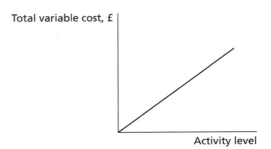

Total variable cost, £

Activity level

Figure 10.3 Linear variable cost

Accounting in a Nutshell

Exercise

Can you name two costs that are likely to be variable costs for the restaurant business?

Solution

You may have thought of costs such as the following:

◆ Food
◆ Laundry costs for napkins and tablecloths.

These costs will both tend to increase as the level of activity increases.

In many planning and decision-making situations, variable costs are assumed to be linear. Although many variable costs do approximate to a linear pattern this assumption may not always be realistic.

> *The important point is that managers should be aware of any assumptions that have been made in estimating cost behaviour patterns. They can then use the information which is based on these assumptions with a full awareness of its possible limitations.*

A variable cost may be non-linear as depicted in either of the diagrams in Figure 10.4.

> *These costs are sometimes called curvilinear variable costs.*

The graph of cost A becomes steeper as the activity level rises. This indicates that each successive unit of activity is adding more to the total variable cost than the previous unit. An example of a

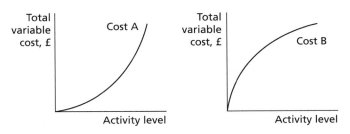

Figure 10.4 Non-linear variable cost

variable cost which follows this pattern could be where specialist food ingredients are in short supply and it is necessary to pay higher prices to acquire the larger quantities needed when more customers are served.

The graph of cost B becomes less steep as the activity level increases. Each successive unit of activity adds less to total variable cost than the previous unit. An example of a variable cost which follows this pattern could be the cost of readily obtained food ingredients where quantity discounts are available.

Exercise

The costs depicted in the figures so far in this chapter have all been total costs over a range of activity. Can you sketch graphs for the following costs over a range of activity?

◆ Fixed cost per unit
◆ Variable cost per unit.

Solution

Fixed cost per unit:

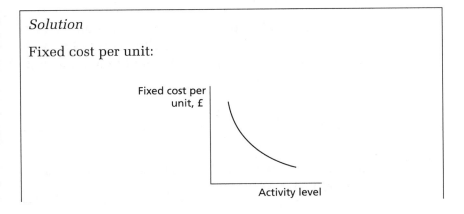

Variable cost per unit:

Variable cost
per unit, £

Activity level

The fixed cost per unit reduces as the activity level is increased. This is because the same amount of fixed cost is being spread over an increasing number of units. For the variable cost per unit, the straight line parallel to the horizontal axis depicts a constant variable cost per unit, within the relevant range.

The similarity between these graphs and those depicted earlier in the chapter should demonstrate to you the importance of reading the labels on the axes before attempting to interpret a graph of a cost behaviour pattern.

10.2.3 Semi-variable costs

A semi-variable cost is also referred to as a semi-fixed or mixed cost. It is a cost which contains both fixed and variable components and which is therefore partly affected by fluctuations in the level of activity. A graph of a semi-variable cost might appear as shown in Figure 10.5.

This particular semi-variable cost has a basic fixed component of £60,000, which is incurred even at zero activity. As activity levels increase, a variable component is incurred in addition to the basic fixed cost.

Exercise

Can you name two costs that are likely to be semi-variable costs for the restaurant business?

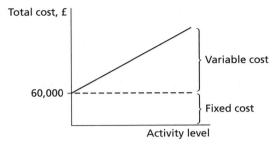

Figure 10.5 Semi-variable cost

Solution

You may have thought of costs such as the following.

◆ Telephone
◆ Gas
◆ Electricity

All these costs have a basic fixed component, which must be paid irrespective of usage. As activity increases, so does the total cost incurred but the basic fixed element remains the same.

Now that you have learned about the main cost behaviour patterns that are found in business we can look at cost-volume-profit analysis, which depends on an understanding of cost behaviour.

10.3 Cost-volume-profit analysis

Cost-volume-profit (CVP) analysis is:

> The study of the effects on future profit of changes in fixed cost, variable cost, sales price, quantity and mix.
>
> CIMA *Official Terminology*

Suppose that you are considering opening your own small restaurant. Before commencing on your new venture you will need to consider many factors, both financial and non-financial. One key decision factor will probably be: 'How many customers do I need to attract in order to break even each month?'

With a basic understanding of your likely prices, as well as your costs and their behaviour patterns, you should be able to estimate your breakeven point.

10.3.1 Calculating the breakeven point: Example

Suppose that you have produced the following estimates of your monthly costs.

Fixed costs	£ per month
Rent and rates	800
Salaries	4,000
Insurance	115
Other	100
	5,015

Variable costs	£ per customer (average)
Food and beverages	5
Laundry	2
Other	1
	8

Notice that the fixed costs are expressed in terms of the amount for a time period, whereas variable costs are expressed in relation to a unit of activity, that is a customer.

You have also estimated that the average income from each customer will be £25.

We can now calculate the breakeven point. The first step is to calculate the contribution from each customer.

Every time we serve a customer we receive £25 and we have to pay out £8 for food, etc. The management accounting term for this difference of £17 is the 'contribution'. Therefore we earn a contribution of £17 per customer:

$$\text{Contribution} = \text{Sales income} - \text{Variable costs}$$
$$= £25 - £8$$
$$= £17$$

This amount is called the contribution, because it literally does contribute towards the fixed costs, which we incur no matter how many customers we serve. Therefore if we have one customer, we have £17 contribution towards the fixed costs of £5,015. If we have two customers, we have £34 contribution towards the fixed costs, etc.

To break even we need just sufficient contribution to pay all the fixed costs. Then we will have nothing left: no profit and no loss. We will have reached the breakeven point.

$$\text{Breakeven point} = \frac{\text{Fixed costs}}{\text{Contribution per customer}}$$
$$= \frac{£5,015}{£17}$$
$$= 295 \text{ customers per month}$$

10.3.2 Margin of safety

Now that we have an estimate of the breakeven point for our proposed business, we can start to think about whether it seems to be a sound proposition. Based on our knowledge of the potential customer demand for our restaurant, we can calculate the margin of safety.

The margin of safety is the difference between what we need to achieve to break even and what we believe we can achieve. The larger the margin of safety, the more likely we are to be able to earn some sort of profit. Suppose that we predict that we will be able to attract, on average, 400 customers each month.

$$\text{Margin of safety} = \text{Forecast level of demand} - \text{Breakeven level of demand}$$
$$= 400 - 295$$
$$= 105 \text{ customers}$$

This means that we can afford to attract 105 fewer customers than we are estimating, before we begin to make losses in any one month. Our margin of safety is approximately 26 per cent of our forecast demand.

$$\text{Percentage margin of safety} = \frac{105}{400} \times 100\% = 26\%$$

> *Exercise*
>
> What factors do you think would affect your assessment of whether this was an adequate safety margin for your forecast demand?

Solution

◆ What is your attitude to risk?
◆ How accurate is the demand forecast likely to be? Is your knowledge of the market so poor that you could well have overestimated demand by 26 per cent?
◆ How accurate are your estimates of cost and revenue?

The margin of safety also helps us to calculate the likely monthly profit for our restaurant business. Once the breakeven point has been reached, each customer's contribution will go towards profit, because there are no more fixed bills to pay.

Therefore the monthly profit from 400 customers per month can be forecast as follows:

105 customers above breakeven × £17 contribution per customer
= £1,785 profit per month

Your assessment of the adequacy of this profit will depend on a number of factors including any other opportunities that are available to you, the level of risk that you are taking, etc.

This exercise demonstrates that breakeven analysis can help you to make better-informed business decisions, but the analysis itself will not produce a definitive answer as to whether this is a worthwhile proposition. Your own management judgement is still required.

10.3.3 Graphical breakeven analysis

The example that we have just worked through can be depicted graphically in a breakeven chart as shown in Figure 10.6.

◆ The fixed cost line is drawn as £5,015 per month.
◆ The total cost line is then superimposed on this. It joins the total cost at zero activity (i.e. the fixed cost of £5,015) to the total cost of £8,215 at the forecast activity of 400 customers per month.

Variable cost (400 × £8)	£3,200
Fixed cost	£5,015
Total cost	£8,215

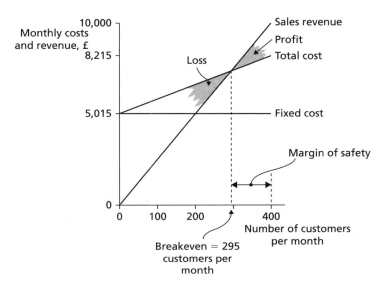

Figure 10.6 Breakeven chart for restaurant business

267

◆ The sales line joins the origin (zero customers = zero revenue) to the total sales revenue at the forecast activity of 400 customers, that is 400 × £25 = £10,000 per month.

The point where the sales revenue line cuts the total cost line is the breakeven point that is 295 customers per month, as we have already calculated. The areas of profit and loss can also be identified, and the margin of safety can be read off as the difference between the forecast number of customers and the breakeven point.

A breakeven chart like this one can often be helpful in assisting less numerate managers to appreciate the significance of the cost behaviour patterns, the size of the margin of safety, etc.

10.3.4 Breakeven analysis: Another example

LearnFast is a driving school, which employs a number of part-time driving instructors and leases a fleet of vehicles. The driving instructors are paid an hourly rate and they work flexible hours, which depend on the demand for their services. At present the school's pupils pay £20 per one-hour lesson and LearnFast's cost structure is as follows:

	£
Variable cost per lesson	15
Fixed cost per month	20,000

Current sales are 12,000 lessons per month.

Exercise

What costs might be variable for this driving school, and what costs might be fixed?

Solution

For variable costs you might have thought of fuel and instructors' wages. This sort of cost would increase with the number of lessons sold and in this example they amount to £15 per lesson. Fixed costs would include administrative salaries, car lease payments and the rent on the office premises. These costs would not increase with the number of lessons sold (within a reasonable range) and in this example, they amount to £20,000 per month.

Exercise

Calculate LearnFast's breakeven point, the margin of safety and the monthly profit.

Solution

$$\text{Contribution per lesson} = \text{Selling price} - \text{Variable cost}$$
$$= £20 - £15$$
$$= £5 \text{ per lesson}$$

This contribution goes towards paying the monthly fixed costs. When the fixed costs are just covered, breakeven point will have been reached. Breakeven point is therefore monthly fixed costs divided by contribution per lesson:

Breakeven point (£20,000/£5)   = 4,000 lessons
Actual sales   = 12,000 lessons
Margin of safety (12,000 − 4,000)   = 8,000 lessons
Monthly profit (£5 × 8,000)   = £40,000

The managing director has suggested that, since there is little opportunity to increase sales, LearnFast should upgrade their fleet of vehicles. Fuel consumption would be lower with the new vehicles and market research suggests that pupils would be prepared to pay £22 per lesson for the improved dual-control facilities.

With the new fleet, LearnFast's cost structure would be as follows:

Variable cost per lesson   £14
Fixed cost per month   £40,000

It is not anticipated that sales can be increased above the current level of 12,000 lessons per month.

> Notice that the variable cost of each hour's lesson is reduced to £14: the result of the improved fuel consumption. However, the fixed cost has doubled to £40,000 per month: the increased car lease payments.

Exercise

Calculate the breakeven point, the margin of safety and the monthly profit after the managing director's proposed changes. Comment on whether or not you think these proposals should be adopted.

Solution

Contribution per lesson (£22 − £14) = £8 per lesson
Breakeven point (£40,000/£8)   = 5,000 lessons
Actual sales   = 12,000 lessons
Margin of safety (12,000 − 5,000)   = 7,000 lessons
Monthly profit (£8 × 7,000)   = £56,000

Summary of results:

	Present situation	Proposed situation
Breakeven point	4,000 lessons	5,000 lessons
Margin of safety	8,000 lessons	7,000 lessons
Monthly profit	£40,000	£56,000

The forecast 40 per cent increase in profit is certainly attractive but the decision to adopt the proposals would depend on a number of factors including:

◆ What is LearnFast's attitude to risk? The breakeven point is higher and the margin of safety is smaller. This means that the business as a whole will be more risky.

◆ The market appears to be stagnant: the managing director has stated that there is little opportunity to increase sales. This means that competitors will be fighting hard to attract LearnFast's customers, since this will be the only way that companies can grow. Every lesson that LearnFast loses to competitors in the future will reduce overall contribution by £8. In the present situation, each lesson lost reduces contribution by only £5. This again reflects the more risky situation with the new proposals.

◆ On the other hand, the improved contribution per lesson means that, if LearnFast could increase sales in the future, contribution and profits would grow at a much faster rate.

◆ How reliable is the market research that indicates that customers would be prepared to pay a higher rate for lessons in the improved vehicles? If the research predictions are incorrect, LearnFast could find themselves committed to a higher level of fixed costs but unable to increase the selling price in the way that they had hoped.

This exercise should have demonstrated once again how management accounting information can help managers to make better-informed decisions, but it cannot provide a definitive answer as to whether or not a particular proposal is acceptable.

10.3.5 Operational gearing

'Operational gearing' is a term used to describe the relationship of the fixed cost to the total cost of an organisation. It is similar to financial gearing that you learned about in Chapter 7.

Higher operational gearing means that, as sales increase, profits increase at a faster rate; vice versa if sales fall. In the last exercise, LearnFast was considering a change to its cost structure that would increase its operational gearing. The monthly fixed cost was expected to double and the unit variable cost was expected to reduce.

Exercise

Calculate LearnFast's monthly profits from sales of 14,400 lessons

(a) in the present situation
(b) after the managing director's proposed changes.

271

Solution

	Present situation (£)	Proposed situation (£)
Contribution per lesson	5	8
Contribution from 14,400 lessons	72,000	115,200
Fixed costs	20,000	40,000
Monthly profit	52,000	75,200

This exercise demonstrates that, with a 20 per cent increase in sales (14,400 lessons compared with 12,000 lessons), the monthly profit increases by:

	Present situation	*Proposed situation*
£40,000 profit increased to £52,000	30% increase	
£56,000 profit increased to £75,200		34% increase

In both situations the profit increased by more than 20 per cent because of the gearing effect of the spreading of fixed costs.

However, with the proposed situation the percentage increase in profit was higher because of the higher level of operational gearing.

> *Experiment for yourself, by reducing the volume of sales by 20 per cent, to prove that the percentage fall in profit will be greater in the proposed situation.*

Higher operational gearing can therefore be advantageous if sales activity is expected to increase in the future. However, management need to be aware that profit levels would fall more rapidly if activity levels began to decrease.

10.3.6 The limitations of CVP analysis

The examples in this section of the chapter have shown that CVP analysis can be a useful tool to investigate the relationship between an organisation's costs and revenues. However, it does have its limitations in terms of practical applicability. These limitations stem mostly from the assumptions which underlie the analysis:

(a) Costs are assumed to behave in a linear fashion. Unit variable costs are assumed to remain constant, and fixed costs are assumed to be unaffected by changes in activity levels. Breakeven charts can in fact be adjusted to cope with non-linear variable costs or steps in fixed costs but too many changes in behaviour patterns can make the charts very cluttered and difficult to use.

(b) Sales revenues are assumed to be constant for each unit sold. This may be unrealistic because of the necessity to reduce the selling price to achieve higher sales volumes.

(c) It is assumed that activity is the only factor affecting costs and revenues. Other factors such as inflation and technology changes are ignored. This is one of the reasons why CVP analysis is limited to being essentially a short-term decision aid.

However, much CVP analysis is carried out as the basis for forecasting future outcomes. Since a lot of the forecast data will be subject to inaccuracies, these simplifying assumptions may not lead to significant further error.

10.4 Marginal analysis

In the remainder of this chapter we will be looking at a number of common short-term decision-making situations and seeing how a choice may be made between alternative courses of action.

Generally, if alternatives are being compared there is little point in including data which are common to all courses of action. Management attention should be focused on those costs and revenues which will alter as a result of the decision. In other words, the incremental costs and revenues should be highlighted. In many cases the fixed costs will not be altered by a decision and they will not be relevant – they are not *incremental* costs and should be excluded from the analysis. However, in some situations there may be a step in the fixed cost and this extra, or incremental, fixed cost should be taken into the analysis.

We will now work through a number of examples to demonstrate how this might be done.

10.4.1 Utilising spare capacity: Example

The Perfect Plastics Company (PP) manufactures packs of plastic food containers for use in domestic freezers. They sell them to supermarket chains and to department stores, under the brand name 'Freezit'.

Sales volume is currently 80,000 packs per period, but the company has the capacity to manufacture a further 20,000 packs per period. Despite repeated attempts to seek new customers, PP's sales force has not succeeded in increasing sales above the current 80,000 packs per period.

An outline profit statement for PP's current situation is as follows:

Current profit per period

	£	£
Sales value		800,000
Variable costs	320,000	
Fixed costs	380,000	
		700,000
Profit		100,000

A large supermarket chain has recently approached PP to ask them to manufacture packs on an 'own-label' basis. The packs would be labelled with the supermarket's own brand name. They would be willing to purchase 20,000 packs per period but they are only prepared to pay 50 per cent of the normal selling price.

Unit variable costs would not be altered by the proposal but fixed costs would increase by £4,000 per period, because extra employees would be needed to help with the packing.

Is this a worthwhile proposal from a financial point of view?
We need to determine the incremental costs and incremental revenues that will arise from this proposal.

Current selling price per pack (£800,000/80,000) = £10
∴ Proposed selling price (50% × £10) = £5
Variable cost per pack (£320,000/80,000) = £4

An outline profit statement can now be prepared for the proposal.

	£	£
Incremental revenue (20,000 × £5)		100,000
Variable costs (20,000 × £4)	80,000	
Incremental fixed costs	4,000	
		84,000
Incremental profit		16,000

The proposal generates an incremental profit of £16,000 and is therefore worthwhile from a financial point of view.

Exercise

(1) How many packs must the supermarket chain purchase each period if PP is to break even on the proposal?
(2) What other factors should PP consider before making a decision?

Solution

(1) Contribution per 'own-label' pack:

Selling price £5 − Variable cost £4 = £1

Breakeven number of packs is the incremental fixed costs divided by the contribution per pack:

$$\frac{£4,000}{£1} = 4,000 \text{ packs}$$

The purchase of 4,000 packs will generate a contribution of £4,000 to exactly cover the incremental fixed costs.

(2) The sort of factors that you might have suggested include:
- ◆ Does the supermarket chain guarantee to take 20,000 packs per period? If they did not take any packs in a particular period, then profits would fall by £4,000 because of the extra wage payments.
- ◆ Would this contract affect PP's full-price business?
  - − Would other customers also demand the lower price?
  - − Would the supermarket's customers buy the own-brand pack instead of the higher priced 'Freezit' pack?
- ◆ Would the unit variable costs definitely be the same? What about any extra distribution and storage costs?
- ◆ With a unit contribution of only £1, there is not much room to accommodate any cost increases. Is the contract price fixed in the long term, or can price increases be negotiated in the future?
- ◆ Is there no likelihood of an increase in the full-price business in future? Tying up 20 per cent of capacity for low-price business could be damaging to future expansion plans.
- ◆ Can the excess capacity be sold or rented to a third party? The potential saving in fixed costs as a result of selling the capacity may be higher than the £16,000 profit generated by this proposal.

10.4.2 Closing a department: Example

Feminine Fashions (FF) is a retail ladies' clothes shop which has three departments that operate from the same premises. The results for the latest period are as follows:

	Clothes and coats £'000	Nightwear and lingerie £'000	Boots and shoes £'000	Total £'000
Sales revenue	78	120	21	219
Variable costs	48	68	16	132
Contribution	30	52	5	87
Fixed costs	23	34	9	66
Profit/(loss)	7	18	(4)	21

FF's directors are considering closing the boots and shoes department, because it makes a loss.

However, if we assume that fixed costs would be incurred even if boots and shoes were discontinued, FF's profit would fall to £16,000 per period if the boots and shoes department was closed:

	Clothes and coats £'000	Nightwear and lingerie £'000	Total £'000
Sales revenue	78	120	198
Variable costs	48	68	116
Contribution	30	52	82
Fixed costs			66
Profit			16

The £5,000 contribution from the boots and shoes department would be lost; therefore this department should not be closed unless a more profitable use can be found for the space that it occupies.

Exercise

Would your advice be altered if, as a result of the closure of the boots and shoes department, staff salaries of £2,000 per period could be saved and sales of clothes and coats could be increased by 20 per cent? Produce a revised profit statement to show this situation.

Solution

Remember that the variable costs of clothes and coats would also increase by 20 per cent.

Revised profit statement

	Clothes and coats £'000	Nightwear and lingerie £'000	Total £'000
Sales revenue (78 × 1.2)	93.6	120	213.6
Variable costs (48 × 1.2)	57.6	68	125.6
Contribution	36.0	52	88.0
Fixed costs (66 − 2)			64.0
Profit			24.0

Profit would increase to £24,000 per period therefore this is a worthwhile proposal.

This type of analysis can also be used in product range decisions, when managers are considering discontinuing a product or service because it appears to be loss making. The key performance measure must be the product's contribution, less any attributable fixed costs. In FF's case the attributable fixed costs were fixed salaries of £2,000 that could be saved by the department's closure.

> *Attributable fixed costs are those which can be identified specifically with a product or service and which would be saved if that product or service was discontinued.*

However, before we leave this example it is worth stressing again the importance of considering non-financial factors in the decision. One of the most important factors to consider in a product/service range decision, or in deciding to close a department, is the possible interdependence of the products or departments.

For example, in FF's case it might be worth keeping the boots and shoes department even if it does not generate a contribution. Customers may be attracted into the shop by the boots and shoes department and may then also buy articles from the other departments.

Likewise in a multi-product firm, if one product was discontinued customers may go elsewhere for all their requirements, because they expect a single supplier to provide a full range of related products.

10.4.3 Make or buy decisions

Managers will sometimes be faced with the decision of whether to produce internally a product or service which they sell, or to buy it from an external supplier. For example, a manufacturer of washing machines may decide to subcontract part of their product range to an external manufacturer, perhaps because they have insufficient capacity or because the supplier is able to supply the washing machines cheaper than they can be produced internally.

Alternatively, the washing machine manufacturer may decide to subcontract only a part of the manufacturing process. For example, they may purchase certain components readymade from external suppliers, but manufacture internally the remainder of their requirements.

However, make or buy decisions do not apply only to manufacturing concerns. A service organisation might also subcontract part of its services. For example, a delivery firm might subcontract overseas delivery to a company which is based in the relevant country. Furthermore, any organisation might decide to subcontract a part of its operations which is currently being performed internally. For example, the organisation's data processing or canteen operations may be subcontracted to an external specialist company.

Accounting in a Nutshell

Exercise

Multi-products (MP) Limited uses component P in its main product. It currently manufactures its own requirements of component P, but an external supplier has offered to supply all its requirements for a price of £52 each.

The cost of manufacturing component P internally is £58 as follows:

	£ per unit
Direct material	11
Direct labour	32
Variable overhead	4
Fixed overhead	11
	58

The supplier's price is lower than the internal cost of manufacture, so on purely financial grounds, should the component be purchased externally or manufactured internally? What assumptions do you need to make in order to reach a decision?

Solution

The following assumptions will be made:

◆ Fixed overheads would be incurred even if the component was not manufactured internally.
◆ None of the resources used in internal manufacture are in short supply.

The costs which would be saved by purchasing externally are the variable costs only.

	£ per unit
Direct material	11
Direct labour	32
Variable overhead	4
	47

The cost is lower than the external supplier's price; therefore MP should continue to manufacture its own requirements.

10.4.4 Opportunity costs

The Chartered Institute of Management Accountants (CIMA) defines an opportunity cost in its *Official Terminology* as follows:

> The value of the benefit sacrificed when one course of action is chosen, in preference to an alternative. The opportunity cost is represented by the forgone potential benefit from the best rejected course of action.

An opportunity cost can be demonstrated by extending the example of MP Limited from the previous exercise.

The manufacture of component P uses specialist labour skills and it is not possible to recruit any more suitably skilled employees. If the component was not manufactured internally, it would be possible to use the available specialist labour to manufacture product M.

Product M sells for £27 per unit and incurs variable cost of £22 per unit as follows:

	£ per unit
Direct material	5
Direct labour	16
Variable overhead	1
Total variable cost	22

All the labour input consists of the specially skilled employees, who are paid at the rate of £16 per hour.

We will now see whether these circumstances would alter our advice to manufacture component P internally.

Product M generates a contribution of £5 per unit (£27 − £22) and takes one hour to manufacture (£16 direct labour ÷ £16 per hour).

Each unit of component P takes two hours (£32 direct labour ÷ £16 per hour).

Every time a component P is manufactured, the company loses the opportunity to manufacture two units of M, which would each earn £5 contribution. The costs of internal manufacture of P can therefore be revised as follows:

	£ per unit
Variable cost (as before)	47
Opportunity cost: contribution forgone (2 × £5)	10
	57

This cost is higher than the external supplier's price of £52. Therefore, from a purely financial viewpoint, in this situation the component should be purchased externally.

> *You will meet opportunity costs again in the next section of this chapter, in the context of relevant costs.*

Exercise

What other factors should be considered before making the recommendation to purchase component P externally?

Solution

Other factors which you might have considered include the following:

◆ the quality and reliability of the external supply
◆ the possibility of seeking external sources of supply for product M
◆ the ability to train or recruit more personnel with suitable skills.

10.5 Relevant costs

Relevant costs are those which will be affected by the decision being taken. All relevant costs should be considered in management decision-making. If a cost will remain unaltered regardless of the decision being taken then it is called a 'non-relevant cost'.

10.5.1 Non-relevant costs

Costs which are not usually relevant in management decisions include the following:

(a) *Sunk or past costs*, which is money already spent which cannot now be recovered. An example of a sunk cost is expend-iture which has been incurred in developing a new product. The money cannot now be recovered even if a decision is taken to abandon further development of the new product. The cost is therefore not relevant to future decisions concerning the product.

(b) *Absorbed fixed overheads* which will not increase or decrease as a result of the decision being taken. We saw an example of this when we were looking at the decision criteria for deciding whether to close a department in a retail shop.

(c) *Expenditure which will be incurred in the future, but as a result of decisions taken in the past* which cannot now be changed. This can sometimes cause confusion because it is a future cost. However, it will be incurred regardless of the decision being taken and therefore it is not relevant.

An example of this type of cost could be expenditure on special packaging for a new product, where the packaging has been ordered and delivered but not yet paid for. The company is obliged to pay for the packaging even if they decide not to proceed with the product, therefore even though it is a future cash flow it is not a relevant cost of the decision to proceed.

(d) *Historical cost depreciation.* Depreciation calculations do not result in any future cash flows. They are merely the bookkeeping entries which are designed to spread the original cost of an asset over its useful life. For example, in the case of MP Limited deciding to subcontract the manufacture of component P, a manager might state: 'I disagree. Internal manufacture must be continued because we have a special machine which we purchased specifically to manufacture component P. The machine cannot be sold or used for another purpose and there is still £30,000 of the net book value to be written off.' The future cash flows of MP Limited will not be affected by the decision to discontinue the use of the machine; therefore the £30,000 net book value is not relevant.

Now you should have a good idea of how to identify relevant and non-relevant costs, so attempt the following exercise to test your understanding.

Exercise

Flexible Training (FT) Limited provides specialist in-company training courses. The company has been in negotiation for a number of months with AB Limited, attempting to secure a contract for a one-day in-company seminar. AB Limited is known to have asked other suppliers for quotations and is now requesting a final price from all potential suppliers.

It is vital that FT should secure this particular contract, as it is likely to lead to a great deal of profitable business once the quality of the course has been experienced.

You are asked to state the relevant cost of the decision to proceed and bid for the contract.

The following information may be relevant:

(1) £1,200 has been paid already to the presenter to develop the course.
(2) Fees and expenses of £1,450 will be paid to the presenter if the course goes ahead.
(3) A training film on DVD will be hired for the course at a cost of £20 for the day.
(4) Another training film has been purchased for £50, specifically for this course. The supplier has stated that £35 can be refunded for the DVD, but only if it is returned unopened.
(5) Printing of the course papers will cost £145. This consists of £110 for the incremental variable costs of printing (paper, ink and power, etc.) and £35 of apportioned fixed costs of the internal printing department.
(6) Other costs to be incurred directly as a result of this contract are £120.
(7) FT's policy is to add 50 per cent to the cost of each contract in order to recover the company's general fixed overheads. It is not expected that general overheads will increase as a result of this contract.

Solution

The relevant costs are those which will be incurred in the future as a result of a decision to proceed and place a final bid for the contract.

Relevant cost (see explanatory notes)

Item no.	£
1	–
2	1,450
3	20
4	35
5	110
6	120
7	–
Total relevant cost	1,735

(1) This is a sunk or past cost.

(2 & 3) These are relevant costs of the decision to proceed with a bid.

(4) This is the opportunity cost of using the DVD for the course. The original cost of the DVD (£50) is sunk and not relevant to the future. If the company sends the DVD back now, it can recover £35. If it uses the DVD for the course it will lose the opportunity to recover this £35, therefore this is the cost of the decision to proceed. It might be argued that this cost could be spread over a number of potential presentations of the course. However, this is anticipating something which may not occur.

(5) Only the incremental variable costs are relevant. The fixed costs would be incurred anyway.

(6) These are incremental costs which are relevant.

(7) These overheads will not increase as a result of the contract therefore a general absorption charge is not a relevant cost.

10.5.2 Minimum price quotations for special orders

This exercise determined the relevant cost of the important contract. This cost represents the minimum price which the company could afford to quote if they wish to make neither a profit nor a loss on the contract. As long as the customer pays £1,735 for the contract, FT's profits will not be affected.

Obviously this represents the absolute minimum price that could be charged. It is unlikely that FT would actually charge this amount. They would probably wish to add a profit margin to improve the company's profits.

However, this absolute minimum price does give managers a starting point for their pricing decision. They know that the company will be worse off if the price is less than £1,735. FT Limited may try to obtain some information concerning the likely prices to be tendered by their competitors. If their prices are likely to be less than or close to £1,735 then FT knows that they will not be able to offer a competitive price. On the other hand, if competitors are likely to tender a much higher price then the managers know that they are able to price competitively.

10.6 Summary

(1) Cost behaviour patterns depict the way that costs behave in relation to the level of activity.

(2) An understanding of cost behaviour patterns is necessary in order to perform cost-volume-profit (CVP) analysis.

(3) The margin of safety is the difference between the breakeven point and the projected level of activity.

(4) Operational gearing is a term used to describe the relationship of the fixed cost to the total cost of an organisation.

(5) Marginal analysis involves identifying and focusing on only those costs and revenues which will change in the short term as a result of the decision being taken.

(6) An attributable fixed cost is one which can be identified with a particular item or activity.

(7) Relevant costs are those which will be affected by the decision being taken.

Review questions

(1) Sketch a graph of the total fixed cost and the fixed cost per unit. (Sections 10.2.1 and 10.2.2)

(2) How is the breakeven point calculated? (Section 10.3.1)

(3) What is meant by high operational gearing? (Section 10.3.5)

(4) What are the limitations of CVP analysis? (Section 10.3.6)

(5) What is an opportunity cost? (Section 10.4.4)

Self-test questions

(1) A company manufactures a single product, C. Unit cost and selling price information for product C is as follows:

	£ per unit
Direct material and labour	13
Variable overhead	3
Fixed overhead	4
	20
Profit	8
Selling price	28

Budgeted output and sales of Product C amount to 6,000 units per month.

Required

Calculate the following:

(a) The monthly breakeven point, in units
(b) The monthly margin of safety
(c) The monthly profit

The company is now facing fierce competition for Product C. It has become necessary to reduce the selling price by £3 per unit and improve the product packaging. The direct material cost will increase by £1 per unit.

(d) Calculate the revised monthly breakeven point in units and the number of units which must now be sold each month in order to achieve the original budgeted monthly profit.

(2) An engineering company has been offered the opportunity to bid for a contract which requires a special component. The company has a component in its current inventory, which has a net book value of £250. This component could be used in the contract, but would require modification at a cost of £50. There is no other foreseeable use for the component held in inventory. Alternatively, the company could purchase a new specialist component for £280.

What is the relevant cost of the component required for this contract?

(3)   A manager is trying to determine the relevant cost of certain materials and labour that will be needed for a one-off contract.

    (a)   The market price of material A is £14 per kg. The contract requires 80 kg of material A. The company ordin-arily purchases 500 kg of material A each month and receives a bulk buying discount of £1 per kg on all its purchases. If this contract is undertaken the company will be able to place an order for 580 kg next month and the bulk buying discount will increase to £1.10 per kg on all material A purchased during the month. Material A is perishable and cannot be stored.

    (b)   A toxic chemical is also required for the contract. The contract requires 50 litres of the chemical, for which the current market price is £12 per litre. The company has 11 litres already in its inventory, which were originally purchased for £9 per litre. The company has no other use for the chemical and if the items already in inventory are not used on this contract the company will have to pay a total of £220 to have the 11 litres of chemical taken away and disposed of safely.

    (c)   The contract will also require 34 kg of material B which is used regularly by the company. The current inventory of 20 kg of material B was originally purchased for £2 per kg. The current market price of material B is £3.50 per kg.

    (d)   The company's 20 full-time employees will need to work for a total of 180 hours on the contract in a single week. The employees are each paid £10 per hour for a guaranteed 40-hour week. During the week in which the contract must be completed, the company already has 665 hours of work scheduled. The employees are willing to work up to 10 hours overtime per week each, at a rate of £15 per hour.

Required

Determine the relevant cost for this contract of each of the three types of material and of labour.

(4)   BSE Veterinary Services is a specialist laboratory carrying out tests on cattle to ascertain whether the cattle have any infection. At present, the laboratory carries out 12,000 tests each period but, because of current difficulties with the beef

herd, demand is expected to increase to 18,000 tests a period, which would require an additional shift to be worked.

The current cost of carrying out a full test is:

	£ per test
Materials	115
Technicians' wages	30
Variable overhead	12
Fixed overhead	50

Working the additional shift would:

    (i) Require a shift premium of 50 per cent to be paid to the technicians on the additional shift.

    (ii) Enable a quantity discount of 20 per cent to be obtained for all materials if an order was placed to cover 18,000 tests.

  (iii) Increase fixed costs by £700,000 per period.

The current fee per test is £300.

Required

  (a) Prepare a profit statement for the current 12,000 test capacity.

  (b) Prepare a profit statement if the additional shift was worked and 18,000 tests were carried out.

  (c) Comment on three other factors which should be considered before any decision is taken.

Answers to self-test questions

(1)

  (a) Fixed overhead per month = 6,000 units × £4 = £24,000

$$\text{Monthly breakeven point} = \frac{\text{Fixed overhead}}{\text{Contribution per unit}}$$

$$= \frac{£24,000}{£(28 - 13 - 3)}$$

$$= 2,000 \text{ units}$$

  (b) Margin of safety = Budgeted sales − Breakeven sales

$$= (6,000 - 2,000) \text{ units}$$

$$= 4,000 \text{ units, or } 67\% \text{ of budgeted sales}$$

(c) Monthly profit = Margin of safety units × Contribution per unit

$$= 4{,}000 \text{ units} \times £12 = £48{,}000$$

(d) Revised contribution = £(25 − 14 − 3) = £8 per unit

$$\text{Revised breakeven point} = \frac{\text{Fixed overhead}}{\text{Contribution per unit}}$$

$$= \frac{£24{,}000}{£8}$$

$$= 3{,}000 \text{ units}$$

$$\text{Number of units to be sold} = \frac{\text{Required contribution}}{\text{Contribution per unit}}$$

$$= \frac{\text{Fixed overhead + required profit}}{\text{Contribution per unit}}$$

$$= \frac{£(24{,}000 + 48{,}000)}{£8}$$

$$= 9{,}000 \text{ units}$$

(2) The relevant cost of the component to be used in appraising the contract is £50. The net book value is not relevant; it is a sunk or past cost. The company would not purchase a new component because it would be cheaper to modify the existing component held in inventory, incurring an incremental cost of £50.

(3)

(a) The relevant cost of material A is the incremental cost that will be paid to acquire an extra 80 kg next month.

	£
With the contract, purchases will be	
580 kg × £(14.00 − 1.10)	7,482
Without the contract, purchases will be	
500 kg × £(14 − 1)	6,500
Relevant cost of additional purchases of material A	982

(b) The original cost of the 11 litres already held in inventory is sunk and is not relevant to the analysis of this contract. If these 11 litres are used on the contract the company will make a saving of £220 because it will not have to pay to have the inventory disposed of.

The relevant cost of the 50 litres of chemical is therefore as follows.

	£
Saving on disposal cost of 11 litres already held in inventory	(220)
Purchase cost of additional 39 litres required (39 × £12)	468
Relevant cost of 50 litres of chemical	248

(c) Since material B is used regularly by the company the relevant cost is its replacement price. As long as the one-off contract recovers the cost of replacing any material B used, the company's everyday business will not be affected by the contract.

Relevant cost of material B = £3.50 × 34 kg = £119

(d)

Total guaranteed labour hours per week = 20 × 40 hours	800 hours
Less work already scheduled	665 hours
Available hours which are paid anyway	135 hours
The incremental cost of these 135 hours is zero.	
The relevant labour cost is the cost of the additional overtime.	
Total hours required for contract	180 hours
Less hours available in basic paid working week	135 hours
Overtime hours to be paid for	45 hours
Relevant incremental cost of labour = 45 hours × £15 per hour	£675

(4)

(a) **Profit statement for 12,000 tests**

	£ per test	£'000	£'000
Sales revenue	300		3,600
Materials	115	1,380	
Technicians' wages	30	360	
Variable overhead	12	144	
			1,884
Contribution			1,716
Fixed overhead	50		600
Profit			1,116

(b) Profit statement for 18,000 tests

	No of tests	£ per test	£'000	£'000
Sales revenue	18,000	300		5,400
Materials[1]	18,000	92	1,656	
Technicians' wages[2]	12,000	30	360	
	6,000	45	270	
Variable overhead	18,000	12	216	
				2,502
Contribution				2,898
Fixed costs[3]				1,300
Profit				1,598

[1] Material cost per test = £115 × 80% = £92
[2] Wages cost per test for second shift = £30 × 150% = £45
[3] Fixed costs for 12,000 test capacity = £600,000
Increase for extra 6,000 tests = £700,000
Fixed costs for 18,000 test capacity = £1,300,000

(c) Other factors to consider include the following.

(i) If the increased demand will continue for the foreseeable future it may be worthwhile taking on more technicians so that the extra shift, and the consequent shift premium, is not necessary.

(ii) Will the accuracy of the tests be affected by requiring the technicians to work an additional shift?

(iii) Have all costs been considered? For example, will it be necessary to rent additional storage space for the extra materials to be purchased?

(iv) Instead of accommodating the increased demand, it may be possible to earn more profit by increasing the selling price, to reduce the rise in demand.

Budgetary Planning and Control

11.1 Introduction

In this chapter you will be learning about budgets: what they are and how they are prepared and used. You will also be introduced to the importance of communication in the budgetary planning process, and the human aspects of budgeting.

11.2 The purposes of budgeting

Suppose that you and three of your friends decide to start a small business. You will be buying and selling quality handmade crafts, gifts and greetings cards, starting initially in a medium-sized highstreet shop. You will be the financial manager and your friends will take on the following roles:

◆ Chris: purchasing manager
◆ Sandy: shop manager
◆ Frankie: marketing and publicity manager

You have arranged a business bank account and each of you has paid in their savings to give the business a healthy initial cash balance. So now you need to start running the business.

Chris seeks out suitable suppliers and begins to place orders to build up an inventory of items for resale. Sandy employs a part-time sales assistant and orders some fittings for the shop. Frankie places advertisements in the local paper and orders 100 helium balloons ready for the Grand Opening.

You write out the cheques for all these expenses and carefully record the transactions on your newly purchased computerised bookkeeping system. No problem so far: you have a healthy starting cash balance. Soon the customers start to arrive and you pay the cash receipts into the bank, carefully recording the receipts on the system. Then things start to go wrong. Customers are flocking to your shop and sales are soaring. You are probably thinking, 'surely things are going right if business is booming?' But look at what is happening:

◆ Sandy has decided to take on two more staff – more help is needed to manage the bulging store room and deal with the flow of customers. Sandy has also agreed to pay regular overtime to two staff members who stay late to sort out the shop displays ready for the next day.

- ◆ Chris has agreed to pay premium rates to a supplier who guarantees next-day delivery. He argues that a new business cannot afford to turn away enthusiastic customers because of a lack of inventory to sell.
- ◆ Frankie has ordered 5,000 glossy leaflets and is recruiting a small team of temporary staff to deliver the leaflets to local houses – the idea is to reinforce the tremendous word-of-mouth praise that is spreading around the neighbourhood.

Everybody is caught up in the euphoria of booming sales and they are probably spending all of the money that is being received from customers, and more besides. Your healthy cash balance will not last long at this rate!

So how can this situation be avoided?

The answer is by using budgets. Budgets are monetary plans prepared in advance for the forthcoming period. They detail the amount of expenditure that each budget holder is authorised to incur or the income that they are expected to generate.

Each of the four people in your business would be a budget holder.

The actual income or expenditure can be compared with these budgets as the period progresses so that budget holders can tell whether their part of the business is proceeding according to budget. If it is not then they can take action to correct the deviation from plan, or they may need to get together to prepare another budget if the original is no longer representative of the current situation.

In our example, the four managers would need to get together to produce another budget once it became obvious that revenue was exceeding expectations and that the original plans for expenditure and revenue would have to be revised.

Our business consisted of just four people, yet it was still difficult to coordinate their activities without a formalised plan or budget. Imagine what it would be like in a large organisation with dozens or hundreds of managers, each incurring expenditure or generating revenue, if there was no formalised budgetary plan to coordinate their activities.

Budgets, therefore, have two main roles:

(1) They act as authorities to spend or as targets to achieve, that is they give authority to budget managers to incur expenditure in their part of the organisation or they provide targets for the revenue-generating parts of the organisation.

(2) They act as comparators for current performance, by providing a yardstick against which current activities can be monitored.

These two roles are combined in a system of budgetary planning and control.

11.2.1   Budgetary planning and control

Planning the activities of an organisation ensures that the organisation sets out in the right direction. Individuals in the organisation will have definite targets which they will aim to achieve. Without a formalised plan the organisation will lack direction, and managers will not be aware of their own targets and responsibilities. Neither will they appreciate how their activities relate to those of other managers within the organisation.

A formalised plan will help to ensure a coordinated approach and the planning process itself will force managers to continually think ahead, planning and reviewing their activities in advance.

However, the budgetary process should not stop with the plan. The organisation has started out in the right direction but to ensure that it continues on course it is management's responsibility to exercise control.

Control is best achieved by comparison of the actual results with the original plan. Appropriate action can then be taken to correct any deviations from the plan.

The two activities of planning and control must go hand in hand. Carrying out the budgetary planning exercise without using the plan for control purposes is performing only part of the task.

> *Comparison of actual results with a budgetary plan, and taking action to correct deviations, is known as feedback control.*

11.2.2 What is a budget?

A budget could be defined as 'a quantified plan of action relating to a given period of time'.

For a budget to be useful it must be quantified. For example, it would not be particularly useful for the purposes of planning and control if a budget was set as follows:

> 'We plan to spend as little as possible in running the printing department this year'; or 'We plan to produce as many units as we can possibly sell this quarter.'

These are merely vague indicators of general direction; they are not quantified plans. They will not provide much assistance in management's task of planning and controlling the organisation.

These 'budgets' could perhaps be modified as follows:

> 'Budgeted revenue expenditure for the printing department this year is £60,000'; and 'Budgeted production for the quarter is 4,700 units.'

The quantification of the budgets has provided:

◆ a definite target for planning purposes; and
◆ a yardstick for control purposes.

11.2.3 The budget period

You may have noticed that in each of these 'budgets' the time period was different. The first budget was prepared for a year and the second was for a quarter. The time period for which a budget is prepared and used is called the 'budget period'. It can be any length to suit management purposes but it is usually one year.

The length chosen for the budget period will depend on many factors, including the nature of the organisation and the type of expenditure being considered. Each budget period can be subdivided into control periods, also of varying lengths, depending on the level of control which management wishes to exercise. The usual length of a control period is one month, which means that control reports for comparison of actual results with the budget will be prepared monthly.

11.2.4 Objectives, long-term plans and budgetary plans

The first stage in planning the activities of an organisation is to set its overall objectives or mission. This is what the organisation is aiming to achieve in the long run. The most common objective of profit-making organisations is the maximisation of the organisation's wealth, but there could also be other objectives such as survival, expansion and long-term stability.

The long-term plan details how these objectives will be achieved, covering a period of, say, five years. The long-term plan would cover in broad terms aspects such as the following:

◆ Which products or services the business will offer to customers
◆ Which markets the business will operate in
◆ Whether growth will be achieved by internal growth or by acquiring other businesses
◆ The resources required, in terms of finance, personnel, equipment, etc.

The annual budget would then be set within the framework of the long-term plan (see Figure 11.1). An organisation's annual budget is an interim step towards the achievement of the long-term plan, providing more detail in terms of sales revenues, revenue expenditure, capital expenditure, etc.

> *The short term for one organisation may be the medium or long term for another, depending on the type of activity in which the organisation is involved.*

Figure 11.1 Objectives, long-term plans and budgetary plans

11.3 The preparation of budgets

The process of preparing and using budgets will differ from one organisation to another. However, there are a number of key requirements in the design of a budgetary planning and control process.

11.3.1 Coordination: the budget committee

The need for coordination in the planning process is paramount. The interrelationship among the functional budgets was demonstrated in our example at the beginning of this chapter. Frankie's activities as marketing manager affected how busy Sandy, the shop manager and Chris, the purchasing manager, would be. Chris's activities in purchasing inventory affected Sandy's need for staff to receive, check and store the items. All their activities affected you as the financial manager, for example in paying the invoices for their purchases and ensuring that the cash resources were available for the expenses that they incurred.

This means that one budget cannot be prepared in isolation, without reference to several others. The best way to achieve the necessary coordination is to set up a budget committee. In our example the four managers would comprise the necessary committee. However, in a larger organisation there should be a representative on the committee from each part of the organisation. There would be representatives from sales, marketing, personnel, etc.

The budget committee should meet regularly to review the progress of the budgetary planning process and to resolve any problems that have arisen. These meetings will effectively bring together the whole organisation in one room, to ensure that a coordinated approach is adopted in budget preparation.

11.3.2 Information: The budget manual

Effective budgetary planning and control relies on the provision of adequate information to the individuals involved in the planning process. Many of these information needs are contained in the budget manual. This is a collection of documents which contains key information for those involved in the planning process.

Typical contents could include the following:

(a) An introductory explanation of the budgetary planning and control process. Participants should be made aware of the advantage of an efficient planning and control process to them and to the organisation. This introduction should give participants an understanding of the workings of the planning process, and of the sort of information that they can expect to receive as part of the control process.

(b) A form of organisation chart to show who is responsible for the preparation of each functional budget and the way in which budgets are interrelated.

(c) A timetable for the preparation of each budget. This will prevent the formation of a 'bottleneck' with the late preparation of one budget holding up the preparation of all others.

(d) Copies of all forms to be completed by those responsible for preparing budgets, with explanations concerning their completion.

(e) A list of the organisation's account codes with full explanations of how to use them.

(f) Information concerning key assumptions to be made by managers in their budgets, to ensure consistency throughout the organisation, for example the rate of inflation, key exchange rates, etc.

(g) The name and location of the person to be contacted concerning any problems encountered in preparing the budgetary plans. This will usually be the coordinator of the budget committee (the budget officer) and will probably be a senior accountant.

11.3.3   Early identification of the principal budget factor

The principal budget factor is the factor which limits the activities of the organisation. The early identification of this factor is important in the budgetary planning process because it indicates which budget should be prepared first.

For example, if sales volume is the principal budget factor then the sales budget must be prepared first, based on the available sales forecasts. All other budgets should then be linked to this.

Alternatively, machine capacity may be limited for the forthcoming period and therefore machine capacity is the principal budget factor. In this case the production budget must be prepared first and all other budgets must be linked to this.

Failure to identify the principal budget factor at an early stage could lead to delays later on when managers realise that the targets they have been working on are not feasible (see Figure 11.2).

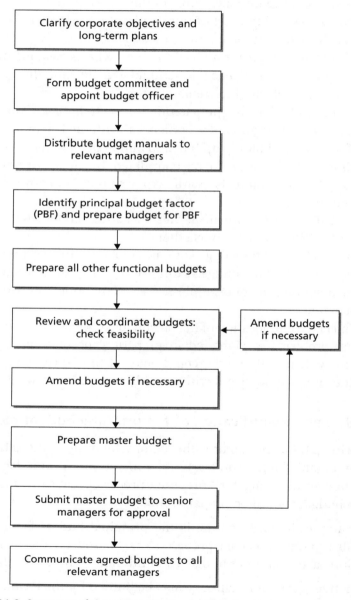

Figure 11.2 Summary of the steps in the budgetary planning process

11.3.4 The master budget: The iterative process of budgetary planning

The master budget is a summary of all the functional budgets. It may include a budgeted income statement (or income and expenditure account, in a not-for-profit organisation), a cash flow budget and a budgeted balance sheet. It is this master budget which is submitted to senior managers for approval because they should not be burdened with an excessive amount of detail. The master budget is designed to give the summarised information that they need to determine whether the budget is an acceptable plan for the forthcoming period.

The criteria used to assess the suitability of budgets may include adherence to the organisation's long-term objectives, profitability, liquidity, etc. The senior managers may require amendments to be made or they may wish to see the effect of changes in key decision variables. The budget will then be returned to the budget committee, and the budget managers will be asked to revise their budgets and resubmit them to form a new master budget. This will be presented once more to the senior management team for approval. The whole process can involve several iterations, until a cohesive plan is agreed and accepted as the organisation's target for the year.

11.4 Incremental and zero-based budgeting

In the example that we reviewed at the beginning of this chapter it was relatively straightforward to see how, once we have forecast the sales volume for the craft shop, many of the other budgets could be prepared using this as a basis.

Chris's purchasing budget would be based on the sales budget, with any adjustments necessary to allow for proposed increases or decreases in inventory. Sandy's budget for shop staff salaries would also be based on the sales budget, and on Chris's plans for the volume of inventory to be held. But what about the budget for marketing expenditure, where outputs are not so clearly linked to inputs? And how would you prepare budgets for costs such as training, and research into new product lines? Determining the level of expenditure to be included in this type of budget is not quite so straightforward.

This type of cost is called a discretionary cost, also known as policy or managed costs.

11.4.1 Incremental budgeting

Many budgets are set using an incremental approach. This means that the budget for each period is determined by reference to what was spent last period plus, perhaps, an allowance for known changes such as anticipated inflation.

Exercise

Can you identify any potential problems with using this incremental approach to budgeting?

Solution

◆ This approach is unlikely to result in the optimum allocation of resources.
◆ It tends to perpetuate inefficient and unnecessary practices and there is no incentive for managers to consider new ways of achieving the objectives for their part of the organisation.
◆ There may be an incentive to overspend if managers know that their budget allowance for the forthcoming period will be based on their expenditure during this period.

11.4.2 Zero-based budgeting

Zero-based budgeting (ZBB) was developed as an alternative to the incremental approach. It is so called because it requires each budget to be prepared and justified from zero, instead of simply using last period's budget or actual expenditure as a base. Incremental levels of expenditure on each activity are evaluated according to the resulting forecast incremental benefits. Available resources are then allocated where they can be used most effectively.

The major advantage of ZBB exercises is that managers are forced to consider alternative ways of achieving the objectives for their activity and they are required to justify the activities which they currently undertake.

Exercise

Can you identify any potential problems with using a zero-based approach to budgeting?

Solution

◆ ZBB exercises can be very time consuming.
◆ It can be difficult to identify the anticipated incremental benefit to result from incremental amounts of expenditure.
◆ Managers may feel threatened if their area of the business is subject to the level of scrutiny inherent in a ZBB exercise.

The time-consuming nature of ZBB exercises means that many organisations perform a zero-based analysis on a rolling basis. Each year a number of discretionary cost budgets are prepared from a zero base so that each one is reviewed, say, every three or four years. In the intervening years a form of the incremental approach is used for the budgets that are not subject to a ZBB exercise in that particular year.

11.5   Using budgets for control

We have already seen that the two activities of planning and control must go hand in hand. Carrying out the budgetary planning exercise without using the plan for control purposes is performing only part of the task. Budgetary planning and control activities are carried out in a continuous cycle as depicted in Figure 11.3.

The differences revealed by the comparison of the actual results with the budget are called 'variances'. An underspending is usually referred to as a favourable variance and an overspending an adverse variance.

An investigation of the variances may indicate that control action is required to attempt to bring the results back in line with budget. It may not be possible or desirable to correct all budget variances, particularly if circumstances have changed since the original budget was set. Nevertheless, managers should constantly monitor the

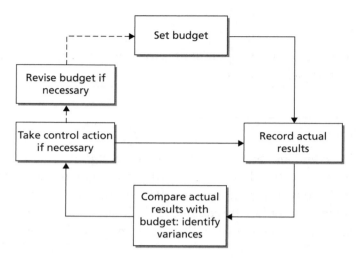

Figure 11.3 The budgetary planning and control cycle

level of budget variances, ensuring that they understand the reasons for them. This continuous monitoring will help to improve a manager's understanding of costs and their behaviour, so that the planning process can be continually refined each time it is repeated.

Towards the end of the budget period, many of the variances may be caused by the fact that the budget is no longer representative of current conditions. It may have been prepared perhaps 15 months or more ago, so that now it is rather out of date.

Accounting in a Nutshell

306

Exercise

Can you identify any problems with using an out-of-date budget?

Solution

◆ It is not possible to tell which variances are in need of management action and which are the result of the out-of-date budget. Budgetary control is compromised.

◆ Managers may be demotivated if they feel they are being blamed for adverse variances over which they have no control.

These problems may be overcome by revising the budget part way through the year. This involves updating the unexpired portion of the budget in the light of current circumstances, as shown in Figure 11.3.

This does not mean that the original budget will be discarded. It will still be necessary for managers to explain the total variance from the original budget. The difference is that part of the variance will be explained by the 'budget revision variance' so that management action can focus on the remaining variances, which are more likely to be controllable.

11.5.1 Budgetary control reports

There is no definitive layout for control reports, since they are prepared internally and may take any form that is useful to the organisation's managers. The reports will be designed to suit the purpose for which they are prepared, and certain data which is important in one context may not be important in another. However, it will be useful to review some examples so that you can get a feel for the way in which control reports might be prepared for different types of expenditure.

The control report shown in Figure 11.4 enables management to exercise control by comparison. The report is designed to compare the actual expenditure with the budgeted expenditure to date and

Cost centre no: 435

Revenue expenditure: period 3   **Date prepared:**

Cost item	Expenditure this period		Expenditure to date			Comment
	Actual	Budget	Actual	Budget	Variance	
	£	£	£	£	£	
Salaries and payroll costs	10,690	9,970	32,160	29,970	(2,190)	One extra employee
Computer services	5,988	7,900	19,632	23,450	3,818	Major part of system still manual
Stationery	245	289	765	760	(5)	
Head office costs apportioned	1,290	1,000	3,788	2,900	(888)	Central overspending

Figure 11.4 Extract from a revenue expenditure control report

show the variance to date. Overspendings or adverse variances are shown in brackets.

Notice that variances are not shown for the expenditure in the period. This implies that in this particular case the cumulative figures are more important to management, therefore the period variance is omitted to avoid cluttering the report.

Management action may now be taken to correct any adverse circumstances or perhaps to maximise any favourable variances. Not all variances are controllable and a decision must be taken on which variances are worth further management investigation.

Exercise

Can you think of factors that you would consider before beginning an investigation into the cause of a variance?

Solution

You may have thought of the following factors:

◆ *The size of the variance.*
◆ *The likelihood of the variance being controllable when the cause is found.* Some types of variance, for example those caused by the price of a purchased material, may be caused by external factors which are outside managers' control.
◆ *The likely cost of the investigation.* Managers may know from past experience that the investigation of certain types of variance can be a lengthy exercise in which the cost incurred outweighs the benefit to be gained.
◆ *The likelihood of the variance being repeated in future periods.* Even a small variance can become significant on a cumulative basis if it arises repeatedly.

In the capital expenditure control report in Figure 11.5 no variances are shown for the expenditure to date or for the individual period. In this particular case, management need to be aware of the eventual total cost of the project, and any expected overspending will then require separate authorisation.

North–east area factory: period 7					
Improvement to staff canteen and rest area			Date prepared:		
Capital expenditure authorisation code: 344					

Expenditure this period £	Expenditure to date £	Forecast total cost on completion			Comment
		Actual £	Budget £	Variance £	
2,934	6,200	8,750	8,000	(750)	Overspend: authorisation no: 348

Figure 11.5 Capital expenditure control report

Information concerning detailed variances is omitted from this particular report. This does not mean that such information is not available to managers. Following the exception principle this report has highlighted the most important variance. More detailed information on the expenditure and variances to date will probably be provided as subsidiary information.

11.5.2 Fixed and flexible budgets

309

When managers are comparing actual results with the budget for a period it is important to ensure that they are making a valid comparison. The use of flexible budgets can help to ensure that actual results are monitored against realistic targets. An example will demonstrate how flexible budgets may be used.

A company manufactures a single product and the following data show results for the month of April, compared with the budgeted figures.

Operating statement for April (Adverse variances in brackets)

	Actual	Budget	Variance
Units produced and sold	1,000	1,200	(200)
	£	£	£
Sales revenue	110,000	120,000	(10,000)
Direct material	16,490	19,200	2,710
Direct labour	12,380	13,200	820
Overheads	61,920	61,400	(520)
Total costs	90,790	93,800	3,010
Profit	19,210	26,200	(6,990)

Looking at the total costs incurred in April, a saving of £3,010 has been made, compared with the budget. However, the number of units produced and sold was 200 less than budget, so some savings in expenditure might be expected. It is not possible to tell from this comparison how much of the saving is due to efficient cost control, and how much is the result of the reduction in activity.

Similarly, it is not possible to tell how much of the fall in sales revenue was due to the fall in activity. Some of the sales revenue variance may be the result of a difference in the sales price, but this budget comparison does not show the effect of this.

The type of budget in use here is a fixed budget. A fixed budget is one which remains unchanged regardless of the actual level of activity. In situations where activity levels are likely to change, and there is a significant proportion of variable costs, it is difficult to control expenditure satisfactorily with a fixed budget.

A flexible budget can help managers to make more valid comparisons. It is designed to show the expected revenue and the allowed expenditure for the actual number of units produced and sold. Comparing this flexible budget with the actual expenditure and revenue it is possible to distinguish genuine efficiencies.

11.5.3 Preparing a flexible budget

Before a flexible budget can be produced, managers must identify which costs are fixed and which are variable. The allowed expenditure on variable costs can then be increased or decreased as the level of activity changes. Fixed costs are those costs which will not increase or decrease over a given range of activity. The allowance for these items will therefore remain constant.

Let us continue with the example. Management have identified that the following budgeted costs are fixed:

	£
Direct labour	8,400
Overheads	53,000

It is now possible to identify the expected variable cost per unit produced and sold:

	Original budget (a)	Fixed cost (b)	Variable cost (c) = (a) − (b)	Variable cost/unit $^{(c)}/_{1,200}$
Units produced and sold	1,200			
	£	£	£	£
Direct material	19,200	–	19,200	16
Direct labour	13,200	8,400	4,800	4
Overheads	61,400	53,000	8,400	7
	93,800	61,400	32,400	27

Now that managers are aware of the fixed costs and the variable costs per unit it is possible to 'flex' the original budget to produce a budget cost allowance for 1,000 units produced and sold. The budget cost allowance for each item is calculated as follows:

Cost allowance = budgeted fixed cost + (number of units produced and sold × variable cost per unit)

For the costs which are wholly fixed or wholly variable the calculation of the budget cost allowance is fairly straightforward. The remaining costs are semi-variable, which means that they are partly fixed and partly variable. For example, the budget cost allowance for direct labour is calculated as follows:

Cost allowance for direct labour = £8,400 + (1,000 units × £4)
= £12,400

The budgeted sales price per unit is £120,000/1,200 = £100 per unit. If it is assumed that sales revenues follow a linear variable pattern (because the sales price remains constant) the full flexible budget can now be produced.

> **Exercise**
>
> Following the example of the calculation of the budget cost allowance for direct labour, calculate a revised budget cost allowance for all costs for an activity of 1,000 units and produce a revised variance statement for April.

> ### Solution
>
> Cost allowance for overhead = £53,000 + (1,000 units × £7)
> = £60,000
>
> #### Flexible budget comparison for April
>
> | | Flexible budget cost/revenue allowances for 1,000 units | | | Actual cost/revenue | Variance |
> |---|---|---|---|---|---|
> | | Fixed | Variable | Total | | |
> | | £ | £ | £ | £ | £ |
> | Sales revenue | | | 100,000 | 110,000 | 10,000 |
> | Direct material | – | 16,000 | 16,000 | 16,490 | (490) |
> | Direct labour | 8,400 | 4,000 | 12,400 | 12,380 | 20 |
> | Overheads | 53,000 | 7,000 | 60,000 | 61,920 | (1,920) |
> | | 61,400 | 27,000 | 88,400 | 90,790 | (2,390) |
> | Profit | | | 11,600 | 19,210 | 7,610 |
>
> *Note*: Variances in brackets are adverse.

This revised analysis shows that in fact the profit was £7,610 higher than would have been expected from a sales volume of 1,000 units.

The largest variance is a £10,000 favourable variance on sales revenue. This has arisen because a higher price was charged than budgeted. Could the higher sales price have been the cause of the shortfall in sales volume?

Although the answer to this question is not available from this information, without a flexed budget comparison it was not possible to tell that a different selling price had been charged.

> *This is an example of variances which may be interrelated – a favourable variance on sales price may have caused an adverse variance on sales volume.*

The cost variances in the flexible budget comparison are mainly adverse. These overspendings were not revealed when a fixed budget was used and managers may have been under the false impression that costs were being adequately controlled.

You may be wondering what has happened to the remainder of the £6,990 adverse profit variance shown in our original budget comparison at the beginning of this example. This could be analysed as follows:

Difference in budgeted profit caused by volume
    shortfall (£26,200 − £11,600)   £14,600
Profit variance from flexible budget comparison   £7,610
Total profit shortfall, per original budget comparison   £6,990

This shows clearly that the adverse variance was caused by the volume shortfall, and not by differences in the expected costs and revenues from the sales that were made.

11.5.4 Using flexible budgets for planning

Although flexible budgets can be useful for control purposes they are not particularly useful for planning. The original budget must contain a single target level of activity so that managers can plan such factors as the resource requirements and the product pricing policy. This would not be possible if they were faced with a range of possible activity levels.

11.6 Behavioural aspects of budgetary planning and control

A budgetary system does not consist only of accounting, forecasting and other management techniques. The success of a budgetary planning and control system depends on the cooperation of those who are to be involved in its operation. Individuals may not always behave in the best interests of the organisation, or they may be unwilling to strive to achieve the budget as set for the period. This is known as *dysfunctional behaviour*.

A budgetary system should be designed to minimise the occurrence of dysfunctional behaviour. This can be achieved if the system's designers and operators bear in mind the behavioural aspects of such systems. The human aspects to be considered are numerous and many of them are interrelated, but the following are the most important.

11.6.1 Motivation

A budgetary system will not be successful if individuals do not want to achieve the targets which have been set for their area of responsibility. A lack of the necessary motivation can exist for many reasons, including:

◆ The targets have not taken account of the individual's *aspiration level* – the level of performance which an individual has set as a personal target. If the performance target is set too far above the aspirational level, the individual will reject the budget as unrealistic and will be demotivated. If the target is set too far below the aspirational level the individual may also be demotivated by the lack of challenge, and may then work at a level of performance below that which could otherwise have been achieved. A department or section of an organisation can also have an aspiration level, which will be the collective result of all the individuals' aspiration levels.

◆ There is inadequate provision for the recognition of achievement. When performance levels have been achieved or exceeded it is important that managers acknowledge this and reward the relevant people. The reward need not necessarily be a financial one. A good manager will be able to motivate staff with appropriate 'psychological' reward – simply acknowledging the achievement may be sufficient.

11.6.2 Communication

Targets must be communicated in clear terms to those who are expected to achieve them. People cannot be expected to perform against a target they do not know about. It is also important that targets are understood – otherwise they will be rejected. Communication of actual results is also important: this is known as *feedback*. If managers do not receive regular and prompt feedback of their actual results they will be unable to act in good time to correct any adverse trends or to build on any favourable results.

11.6.3 Participation

Participative budgetary systems are usually the most successful. If the system is dictatorial, with imposed budgets, there is more likely to be dysfunctional behaviour. Individual managers should not simply be issued with their budgets without consultation. They should be consulted about their budgets during the planning process. Managers are then more likely to accept the targets contained in the budget when it is published.

A participative budgetary system will also encourage *goal congruence*. This exists when the budgetary system motivates individuals or groups to take actions that achieve their own personal goals while at the same time achieving those of the organisation. The system is designed so that there is a relationship between the company's goals and the individuals' goals. Goals are more likely to be congruent if individuals or groups have been involved in setting their own budgets.

Exercise

Can you think of a further, non-behavioural advantage of participative budgeting?

Solution

A further advantage of a participative process is that the quality of forecasting as a basis for the budget may improve. Managers who are in direct contact with the day-to-day activities of their part of the organisation will be more aware of current conditions and better able to predict any changes in the environment which may affect the budgetary forecast.

315

11.7 Summary

(1) Budgets have two main roles: they act as authorities to spend or targets to achieve and as comparators for current performance.

(2) Budgetary planning and control must go hand in hand. Carrying out the budgetary planning exercise without using the plan for control purposes is performing only part of the task.

(3) A budget is set within the framework of an organisation's long-term plan. It is the first step towards the achievement of the long-term plan.

(4) The need for coordination in the planning process is paramount.

(5) The principal budget factor is the factor which limits the activities of the organisation. The budget for the principal budget factor must be prepared first and then all other budgets are coordinated to this.

(6) The differences revealed by the comparison of the actual results with the budget are called variances.

(7) Flexible budgets are designed to flex with changes in activity, to provide a realistic budget cost allowance for the actual level of activity achieved.

(8) A successful budgetary planning and control system is designed with full consideration of the human aspects of budgeting.

Review questions

(1) What are the two main roles of budgets? (Section 11.2)

(2) What is the role of the budget committee? (Section 11.3.1)

(3) Outline the contents of a budget manual. (Section 11.3.2)

(4) Why must the principal budget factor be identified at an early stage in the budgetary planning process? (Section 11.3.3)

(5) What is the difference between incremental budgeting and zero-based budgeting? (Section 11.4)

(6) Sketch the budgetary planning and control cycle. (Section 11.5)

(7) What is a flexible budget? (Section 11.5.2)

(8) What is dysfunctional behaviour? (Section 11.6)

Self-test questions

(1) Comment critically on the following statements:

    (a) 'A budget is a forecast of an organisation's activities for the forthcoming period.'

    (b) 'The budgetary planning process for a manufacturing and trading organisation should always begin with the preparation of the sales budget.'

    (c) 'Revising the budget part way through the period is not advisable because it leads to a lack of continuity in the planning process.'

(2) State five reasons why it might be preferable for managers **not** to be involved in setting their own budgets.

(3) The fixed budget and actual results for G Ltd for the latest period are as follows:

Production and sales	Budget 5,000 units	Actual 5,800 units
	£	£
Direct material	15,000	18,200
Direct labour	17,500	21,100
Variable overhead	10,000	11,000
Fixed overhead	14,000	15,000
Total cost	56,500	65,300
Sales revenue	80,000	93,400
Profit	23,500	28,100

Required

Prepare a flexible budget control report for the period, identifying the cost and revenue variances.

Answers to self-test questions

(1)

(a) A budget is not simply a forecast of forthcoming events. A forecast is a prediction of what might happen in the future, given a particular set of circumstances. A budget is more than this. It is a planned result which an organisation is aiming to achieve. The budget may be based on the forecast, but the forecast acts only as a starting point in preparing the quantified budgetary plan.

(b) The budgetary planning process begins with the identification of the factor that limits the organisation's activities, the principal budget factor. Often this is the sales volume, but for a manufacturing organisation it could be a factor of production such as machine capacity or labour hours. The budget for the principal budget factor should be prepared first, then all other budgets are coordinated to this.

(c) A budget is usually prepared a few weeks or months before the start of the budget period, so that towards the end of an annual budget period the original budgetary plan might be more than a year old. Therefore it is unlikely to represent a useful tool for short-term planning and control. In this situation it is common to revise the unexpired portion of the budget so that it represents a realistic yardstick for planning and control purposes.

This does not mean that the original budget is discarded. Instead, a budget revision variance is often used to highlight the difference between the original and the revised budgets. Managers can use this to guide their forecasting and planning activities in future budgeting exercises, so that the budgetary planning process is continually refined.

(2) The reasons why it might be preferable for managers not to be involved in setting their own budgets include the following:
   ◆ A participative budgeting system, where managers are involved in preparing their own budgets, can be very time consuming. Managers might not have the time to devote themselves properly to the planning task.
   ◆ Managers may be tempted to include unnecessary expenditure, known as 'budgetary slack', into their budgets in order to ensure that they have an easy target to achieve.
   ◆ Managers may not possess the necessary skills and experience to participate in the budgeting exercise.
   ◆ Training managers to understand and prepare budgets can be expensive.
   ◆ The planning exercise can distract managers from their day-to-day operational tasks.

(3) The flexible budget for 5,800 units will include extra cost allowances for all the variable costs, but not for the fixed overhead.

Production and sales	Original budget 5,000 units	Flexible budget 5,800 units	Actual results 5,800 units	Variance
	£	£	£	£
Direct material	15,000 (×5,800/5,000)	17,400	18,200	(800)
Direct labour	17,500	20,300	21,100	(800)
Variable overhead	10,000	11,600	11,000	600
Fixed overhead	14,000	14,000	15,000	(1,000)
Total cost	56,500	63,300	65,300	(2,000)
Sales revenue	80,000 (×5,800/5,000)	92,800	93,400	600
Profit	23,500	29,500	28,100	(1,400)

Note: Variances in brackets are adverse.

Making Long-term
Investment Decisions

12.1   Introduction

In Chapter 10 we saw how cost and revenue information might be used in a number of short-term decisions. In this chapter you will be learning about the main techniques that are used as a basis for making longer term capital investment decisions, such as the decision to invest in new machinery or office equipment.

12.2   The investment appraisal process

Before we begin on a more detailed look at investment appraisal techniques it will be useful to review the investment decision-making process, to help to set the investment appraisal techniques in context.

A typical investment appraisal process might consist of four stages as shown in Figure 12.1.

◆ *Identify possible investment projects.* Organisations might have formal processes for identifying possible investment projects, or the process might be less formal. In either case, it is likely that a greater number of worthwhile ideas for capital investment will be generated in organisations whose

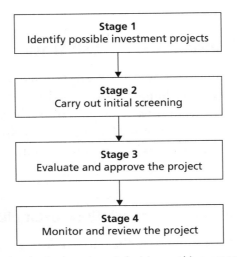

Figure 12.1 The stages in the investment decision-making process

employees are outward looking and who are encouraged to come forward with project ideas.

♦ *Carry out initial screening.* This stage involves a qualitative analysis of the project. Some investment projects might be essential, for example in order to comply with new health and safety regulations. In this case the screening process might ask questions such as whether all possible alternatives have been considered. Other projects will be discretionary and aspects to be considered will include whether the project is in line with the organisation's long-term objectives.

♦ *Evaluate and approve the project.* Once a project proposal has passed the initial screening it will be subject to more detailed financial analysis, probably using one or more of the investment appraisal techniques that we will review in this chapter. Non-financial factors will also be considered before final approval is given to proceed with the project.

♦ *Monitor and review the project.* As we saw in Chapter 11, the management tasks of planning and control must go hand in hand. Once a project has been approved as a part of the organisation's future plans, its progress must be monitored to ensure that expenditure is kept within the planned limits and that the project will be completed on time. Monitoring and review must also be continued once the investment of funds is completed, to ensure that the expected benefits, as identified in the appraisal process, are actually received.

12.3   The importance of cash flow

You should already be aware of the importance of cash flow and we have seen in earlier chapters how a business can be profitable but can still face difficulties or even failure because of a lack of cash. For this reason three of the four investment appraisal techniques that we will review in this chapter focus on cash flows.

12.3.1   The importance of cash flow: example

A company is deciding whether to invest in machine X or machine Y. Both machines will have a useful life of three years and the forecast cash flows for the two investments are as follows:

	Machine X	Machine Y
	£	£
Initial investment		
Year 0*	(30,000)	(30,000)
Cash returns		
Year 1	20,000	2,000
Year 2	10,000	12,000
Year 3	6,000	24,000
Net cash flow	6,000	8,000

*Year 0 is a convention used to indicate the very beginning of a project, effectively the beginning of Year 1.

In this case each machine requires an initial cash investment of £30,000 at the beginning of the first year. Machine X is then forecast to return cash of £20,000 in year 1, then £10,000 in year 2 and so on.

Machine Y generates the highest net cash flow over the three years therefore it might appear that machine Y is preferable. However, a closer look at the cash flows reveals that the timing of the cash flows is very different for the two proposed investments. The cash inflows from machine X occur mainly in the first year whereas it will be necessary to wait until year 3 before machine Y begins to generate larger inflows.

Exercise

Can you think of reasons why it might be preferable for an investment project to generate cash flows earlier in its life rather than in later years?

Solution

◆ Earlier cash flows help to preserve the organisation's liquidity
◆ Forecasts further into the future are likely to be less certain. Reliance on cash flows later in the project's life can therefore increase the risk associated with the investment

- Cash generated earlier from the project can be reinvested in other profitable opportunities, or simply invested to earn interest in the bank or used to repay a loan
- Forecast cash flows might lose their purchasing power due to inflation.

An investment appraisal technique that takes account of the timing of cash flows is the payback method.

12.4 The payback period

The payback period is the time taken for the project's cash inflows to equal the initial cash investment. For example, the payback period for the investment in machine X is two years because the cash inflows for years 1 and 2 sum to £30,000 (£20,000 + £10,000) which is exactly equal to the initial investment.

Exercise

Assuming that cash flows occur evenly during each year, calculate the approximate payback period for the investment in machine Y.

Solution

The cumulative cash inflow to the end of year 2 is £14,000. Another £16,000 is required during year 3 in order to equate the cash inflows to the £30,000 initial cash outflow.

Assuming that cash flows occur evenly during the year, the payback period is therefore:

2 years + [(£16,000/£24,000) × 1 year] = 2.7 years

Of course it is unlikely that we would be able to state that the payback period is exactly 2.7 years. Perhaps it would be more realistic to describe the payback period for the investment in machine Y as, 'between two and three years, probably during the second half of the third year'.

Accounting in a Nutshell

The payback period is often used as an initial screening device and a 'cut off' payback period might be set for all proposed investments. For example the organisation that is evaluating the investment in machine X or machine Y might have set a maximum payback period of three years for all projects. If a project is not forecast to pay back within this time then it is not acceptable, no matter how profitable it may be over its whole life. If the project is expected to pay back within the maximum time period then it may be further analysed using the more sophisticated appraisal techniques that we will learn about in the next section of this chapter.

The longer payback period for the investment in machine Y indicates that this machine might not after all be preferable to the investment in machine X. However we still have no way of actually quantifying the effect of the different timing of the cash flows.

Discounted cash flow techniques can be used to provide this quantification but before we proceed to study these techniques it will be useful to summarise here the advantages and disadvantages of the payback method.

12.4.1 The advantages of the payback method

◆ The method is simple to use and understand
◆ Focusing on early payback assists an organisation's liquidity
◆ Risk is reduced, since the payback method places emphasis on earlier cash flows. Reliance on cash flows later in the project can be more risky because they tend to be more difficult to forecast, particularly in a rapidly changing environment.

12.4.2 The disadvantages of the payback method

◆ Cash flows after the payback period are ignored. These may be substantial and potentially large profits may be forgone if a project is rejected because it does not pass the initial payback period screening test. For example look at the following figures for investment C and investment D, both of which are expected to generate cash flows for four years.

Year		Investment C	Investment D
		£	£
0	Initial investment	(70,000)	(70,000)
	Cash inflows		
1		30,000	55,000
2		30,000	25,000
3		45,000	5,000
4		60,000	5,000

If a maximum payback period of two years is set as an initial screening device then investment C will be rejected but investment D will be considered further. Yet the total cash inflows of £165,000 over the life of investment C are far greater than the total of £90,000 from investment D.

◆ The timing of cash flows during the payback period is ignored. For example investment J and investment K shown below have the same payback period of two years and both generate the same net cash flow over the life of the investment.

Year		Investment J	Investment K
		£	£
0	Initial investment	(10,000)	(10,000)
	Cash inflows		
1		5,000	1,000
2		2,500	2,000
3		2,500	7,000
4		3,500	6,000
5		3,500	1,000
		7,000	7,000

Due to the timing of the cash flows within the payback period these projects are clearly different but the payback method fails to distinguish between them.

◆ Establishing a maximum payback period may lead to excessive focus on shorter term projects.

12.5 Discounted cash flow

Discounted cash flow (DCF) techniques take account of the time value of money. This means that they take account of the fact that £1 received now is worth more than £1 received in the future, because £1 received now can be invested and be made to grow bigger as time passes.

The discounting process converts a future cash flow into its present value, which is the cash equivalent now of that future amount.

12.5.1 Discount factors

With DCF techniques each cash flow is converted into its present value by multiplying it by a discount factor of $1/(1 + r)^n$ where r is the rate of return and n is the number of years. It is possible to obtain present value tables of discount factors for each year at the required rate of return.

For example the discount factors for 20 per cent for the first four years would be shown on present value tables as follows:

At rate r After n years	20%
1	0.83
2	0.69
3	0.58
4	0.48

The discount factor shown for year 1 is $1/(1 + 0.20) = 0.83$. For year 2 the discount factor is $1/(1 + 0.20)^2 = 0.69$ and so on.

Exercise

Use the $1/(1 + r)^n$ formula to verify the discount factors for years 3 and 4 given above and to derive the discount factors for years 5 and 6 at a rate of return of 20 per cent.

Solution

Discount factor for year 3 $= 1/(1 + 0.20)^3 = 0.58$
Discount factor for year 4 $= 1/(1 + 0.20)^4 = 0.48$
Discount factor for year 5 $= 1/(1 + 0.20)^5 = 0.40$
Discount factor for year 6 $= 1/(1 + 0.20)^6 = 0.33$

This table of discount factors shows that, at a 20 per cent rate of interest, £1 received in one year's time has a present value of £0.83. So, if £0.83 is received now and invested at 20 per cent for one year, it will have grown to £1 by the end of year 1:

$$£0.83 + \text{interest } (£0.83 \times 0.20) = £1 \text{ approx.}$$

Therefore £1 received in a year's time has the same value as £0.83 received now.

In the same way from the table, £1 received at the end of year 2 has a present value of £0.69. This is because £0.69 received now can be invested to grow to £1 by the end of year 2.

	£
Received and invested now	0.69
Year 1 interest at 20%	0.14
Total amount now invested	0.83
Year 2 interest at 20%	0.17
Total by the end of year 2	1.00

The discount factors become smaller as the number of years increases, reflecting the fact that later cash flows have a lower present value.

The discount factors are used to calculate the present value of all of the forecast cash flows from a project. This makes it possible to compare projects or investments which have different cash flow patterns.

12.6 Net present value

We have seen that a disadvantage of the payback method is that it ignores the timing of cash flows within the payback period as well as any cash flows that occur after the payback period. The net present value (NPV) method of investment appraisal is superior because it takes account of both these factors.

The NPV of a project is the present value of cash inflows less the present value of cash outflows.

12.6.1 Net present value: example

Returning to the example in Section 12.3.1, we now have a way of quantifying the effect of the different timing of the cash flows from machine X and machine Y. The NPV of the cash flows from machine X can be calculated as follows, assuming a required rate of return of, say, 10 per cent.

	Machine X cash flows £	10% discount factor[1]	Present value £
Initial investment			
Year 0	(30,000)	1.00	(30,000)
Cash returns			
Year 1	20,000	0.91	18,200
Year 2	10,000	0.83	8,300
Year 3	6,000	0.75	4,500
Net present value			1,000

[1]You should recall that year 0 is a convention used to indicate the very beginning of a project, that is, 'now'. This means that the cash flow does not need to be discounted and the factor applied to the year 0 cash flow is 1.0. The discount factors for other years are derived using the formula: $1/(1 + 0.10)^n$. The discounting process assumes that all cash flows occur at the end of the relevant year.

When all the forecast cash flows are discounted at the required rate of return:

◆ If the NPV is positive then the project is acceptable from a financial point of view because it yields a return that is greater than the required rate.
◆ If the NPV is negative then the project is not acceptable from a financial point of view because it yields a return that is lower than the required rate.
◆ If the NPV is zero then the project is generating a return which is exactly equal to the required rate.
◆ If a choice has to be made between two or more projects that all have positive NPVs, then from a financial point of view the project with the highest NPV should be selected.

Exercise

Calculate the NPV of the cash flows from the investment in machine Y and recommend whether machine X or machine Y should be purchased. Use a 10 per cent discount factor.

Solution

Year	Machine Y cash flows £	10% discount factor	Present value £
0	(30,000)	1.00	(30,000)
1	2,000	0.91	1,820
2	12,000	0.83	9,960
3	24,000	0.75	18,000
Net present value			(220)

Machine Y generates a negative NPV and thus should not be accepted. The recommendation is to purchase machine X. Despite the fact that machine X results in a lower overall net cash flow, when the timing of the cash flows is taken into account it is revealed that machine X is the better investment.

12.6.2 Net present value: another example

Until now, the YH Company has utilised the services of a Facilities Management Company to provide all its printing requirements for headed stationery, publicity material and so on.

Consideration is now being given to carrying out these tasks in-house, using the organisation's own printing facility which will be set up for the purpose. The annual saving will be £26,200 which is paid to the Facilities Management Company under the terms of a long-term fixed price contract.

Alterations to the space which is to be used for the facility will cost £11,000 and machines costing £10,000 will be purchased. The machines will last for four years and will have no value at the end of this time.

The operating costs will amount to £17,000 in the first year, increasing by 5 per cent each year in line with the number of documents to be printed. This amount includes the rent of additional computerised equipment, staff salaries, materials, administration and so on.

The organisation uses a discount rate of 12 per cent to appraise all capital projects. Ignore inflation and taxation.

In order to calculate the NPV of the cash flows relevant to this decision the first step is to produce a table which shows the forecast cash flows for the initial investment, and for each of the four years of the machines' life. Notice that the £26,200 annual saving is not actually a cash inflow in itself but it will have an impact on the organisation's overall cash flow. Therefore it is included as an inflow in the table of relevant cash flows.

The 12 per cent discount factors are calculated using the formula: $1/(1 + 0.12)^n$

Initial investment required:

	£
Space alterations	11,000
Machine cost	10,000
Total cash flow	21,000

The relevant cash flows and the calculation of the NPV can be shown in a single table as follows:

Year	Initial investment £	Annual saving £	Operating costs £	Total cash flow £	12% discount factor	Present value £
0	(21,000)			(21,000)	1.00	(21,000)
1		26,200	(17,000)	9,200	0.89	8,188
2		26,200	(17,850)	8,350	0.80	6,680
3		26,200	(18,743)	7,457	0.71	5,294
4		26,200	(19,680)	6,520	0.64	4,173
Net present value						3,335

The proposal generates a positive NPV and thus it is worthwhile from a financial point of view. The final decision will also take account of non-financial factors such as the quality and reliability of the printing service, the effect on staff morale, the flexibility to be able to cope with higher or lower quantities of printing jobs than expected and so on.

As we saw in Chapter 10, it is always important to consider non-financial factors before making a final decision based on a financial analysis.

Exercise

Determine the payback period for the proposal. For this purpose assume that cash flows occur evenly during each year.

Solution

Using the total cash flow column in the above table the payback period can be determined as follows.

Cumulative cash flow after two years = £[(21,000) + 9,200
$$+ 8,350]$$
$$= £(3,450)$$
Payback period = 2 years + (3,450/7,457 × 1 year) = 2.5 years

---

12.7 The internal rate of return

Another investment appraisal technique that uses DCF methods is the internal rate of return (IRR). The IRR is the discount rate at which the NPV is zero and it represents the DCF rate of return for a project. If the IRR is greater than the target rate of return for a project then it is worthwhile from a financial point of view.

We can determine the IRR of a proposed investment project by a trial and error process of calculating the NPV at a number of different discount rates until a result close to zero is obtained. In practice a computer program would be used to very rapidly carry out all the iterations required.

Exercise

Calculate the NPV of the cash flows from the proposed investment in machine X (Section 12.3.1) at discount rates of 11 per cent, 12 per cent, 13 per cent and 14 per cent (we know that the NPV at 10 per cent is a positive figure therefore the IRR must be higher than 10 per cent).

Deduce an approximate IRR for the investment.

The discount factors you require are as follows:

Year	11%	12%	13%	14%
1	0.90	0.89	0.88	0.88
2	0.81	0.80	0.78	0.77
3	0.73	0.71	0.69	0.67

Solution

NPV at 11% = (£20,000 × 0.90) + (£10,000 × 0.81)
   + (£6,000 × 0.73) − £30,000
   = £480

NPV at 12% = (£20,000 × 0.89) + (£10,000 × 0.80)
   + (£6,000 × 0.71) − £30,000
   = £60

NPV at 13% = (£20,000 × 0.88) + (£10,000 × 0.78)
   + (£6,000 × 0.69) − £30,000
   = £(460)

NPV at 14% = (£20,000 × 0.88) + (£10,000 × 0.77)
   + (£6,000 × 0.67) − £30,000
   = £(680)

The NPV would be zero at a discount rate just above 12 per cent. Therefore the IRR is close to 12 per cent.

A computer program would calculate the actual IRR to a number of decimal places. If required we could also calculate a more exact figure manually by interpolation or by using a graphical approach. However for most decisions the approximate result of 12 per cent would be sufficient.

If 12 per cent exceeds the target rate of return for projects such as the investment in machine X then this project would be acceptable.

12.7.1 Advantages and disadvantages of IRR

The main advantages of the IRR as an investment appraisal tool are as follows.

◆ The calculation takes account of all cash flows, whenever they occur
◆ It makes allowance for the time value of money
◆ A percentage return is perhaps more easily understood by managers than the statement of the absolute amount of the NPV.

However the method does have some disadvantages.

◆ The IRR takes no account of the size of the investment. For example if two projects, project A and project B, both generate an IRR of 15 per cent then they will be judged as equally worthwhile using the IRR criterion. However if project A is ten times larger than project B then clearly project A generates more wealth in total than project B. This would be reflected in an NPV calculation. However in practice it is perhaps unlikely that two projects of such different magnitude would be judged against each other in a single decision.
◆ The method is difficult to apply if a project has non-conventional cash flows. All the examples we have considered in this chapter have featured conventional cash flows, which means that a single negative outflow of cash at the beginning of the project is followed by a series of positive inflows during the life of the project. However some projects might generate non-conventional cash flows whereby cash inflows and outflows occur at various points throughout the life of the project. This could result in a situation of multiple IRRs, or perhaps no IRR at all.

12.8 The accounting rate of return

It is important for you to appreciate that all of the appraisal methods we have discussed so far in this chapter are based on an analysis of cash flows. The last method that we will look at, the accounting rate of return (ARR), is the only one that is based on accounting profits.

The ARR is calculated by expressing a project's average annual accounting profit as a percentage of the average investment in the project.

$$\text{ARR} = \frac{\text{Average annual accounting profit}}{\text{Average investment in project}} \times 100\%$$

12.8.1 Calculating the accounting rate of return: example

The following costs and profits are forecast for an investment in a new packing machine.

End of year		£
0	Initial cost of machine	90,000
1	Profit before depreciation	30,000
2	Profit before depreciation	40,000
3	Profit before depreciation	30,000
4	Profit before depreciation	20,000
4	Proceeds from sale of machine	10,000

To be able to use the ARR formula above we need to calculate the average annual accounting profit and the average annual investment in the machine. The average investment over four years is calculated as follows.

$$\begin{aligned}
\text{Average investment} &= \frac{\text{Cost of machine} + \text{final sale value}}{2} \\
&= \frac{£90,000 + £10,000}{2} \\
&= £50,000
\end{aligned}$$

The next step is to calculate the average annual profit after depreciation.

	£
Total profit over life of machine:	
before depreciation (30 + 40 + 30 + 20)	120,000
depreciation (90 − 10)	(80,000)
total accounting profit	40,000
Average annual accounting profit (40/4)	10,000

ARR = (10/50) × 100% = 20%

This percentage return would then be compared with the organisation's minimum required ARR for investments of this type. If 20 per cent exceeds this required minimum then the investment in the machine would be deemed to be acceptable.

12.8.2 Advantages and disadvantages of the ARR method

The advantages of the ARR method of investment appraisal are as follows.

◆ It is easy to calculate and understand
◆ The returns over the whole life of the project are taken into account
◆ Since the ARR is very similar in concept to the return on capital employed (ROCE) and the latter is often monitored by investors, its use is consistent with the overall assessment of business performance.

However the ARR does have a number of disadvantages which seriously limit its usefulness in the investment appraisal process.

◆ It takes no account of the time value of money
◆ As with the IRR the percentage of ARR result does not distinguish between investments of different size
◆ The analysis is based on accounting profits which are subjective and affected by the choice of accounting policies. Cash flows provide a more objective basis for analysis.

12.9 Summary

(1) A typical investment appraisal process consists of four main stages.
(2) The calculation of the payback period, the net present value and the internal rate of return are all based on forecast cash flows. The accounting rate of return is based on a project's forecast accounting profits.
(3) The payback period is the time taken for a project's cash inflows to equal the initial cash investment.
(4) Discounted cash flow techniques take account of the time value of money.

(5) The present value of a cash flow is calculated as: cash flow $\times 1/(1 + r)^n$.

(6) The net present value of a project is the present value of the cash inflows less the present value of the cash outflows.

(7) The internal rate of return is the discount rate at which the net present value of a project is zero. It represents the DCF rate of return for the project.

(8) The accounting rate of return is the average annual accounting profit from a project expressed as a percentage of the average investment in the project.

Review questions

(1) What are the four main stages in a typical investment appraisal process? (Section 12.2)

(2) State two advantages of the payback method. (Section 12.4.1)

(3) State two disadvantages of the payback method. (Section 12.4.2)

(4) Calculate the discount factor for year 2 at a rate of 20 per cent. (Section 12.5.1)

(5) What are the general decision rules when assessing a project using net present value? (Section 12.6.1)

(6) State two advantages and two disadvantages of the internal rate of return method. (Section 12.7.1)

(7) In the formula for the accounting rate of return, how is the average investment calculated? (Section 12.8.1)

Self-test questions

(1) A passenger coach company is considering the purchase of a new fleet of luxury coaches. The coaches will cost £220,000 in total and will have a useful life of four years, after which time they will be sold for a total of £20,000. Forecast profits before depreciation from the operation of the coaches are as follows.

Year	£
1	90,000
2	85,000
3	70,000
4	65,000

Calculate the following for the proposed investment:
(a) The payback period
(b) The net present value of the cash flows, using a discount rate of 15 per cent
(c) The internal rate of return
(d) The accounting rate of return.

The discount factors you will need are as follows.

15%	16%	17%	18%	19%	20%
0.87	0.86	0.85	0.85	0.84	0.83
0.76	0.74	0.73	0.72	0.71	0.69
0.66	0.64	0.62	0.61	0.59	0.58
0.57	0.55	0.53	0.52	0.50	0.48

(2) The WellFit group of gymnasiums has experienced a steady decline in the number of members. The management is considering investing in updated equipment and facilities in all the gymnasiums and offering more services in an attempt to attract new members.

The management appraises investments of this type over a time period of five years, using a discount rate of 17 per cent. The initial cost of the additional equipment and refurbishments will be £100,000. At the end of year 2 a major safety check on all the equipment will cost £15,000.

Additional running costs (excluding depreciation) will amount to £13,000 each year and additional revenues as a result of the changes are forecast to be as follows.

Year	£
1	65,000
2	52,000
3	40,000
4	40,000
5	38,000

Calculate the following for the proposed investment and comment on whether it is worthwhile from a financial point of view.
(a) The payback period

(b) The net present value of the cash flows generated by the investment. The discount factors for years 1 to 4 are provided in question 1. The factor for year 5 is 0.46.

(3) A machine will cost £40,000 and will have a useful life of four years, after which time it will be sold for £12,000. Accounting profits (after depreciation) earned by the machine are forecast as follows.

Year	Accounting profit
	£
1	13,800
2	12,200
3	10,400
4	9,500

Calculate the following for the investment in the machine.
(a) The payback period
(b) The accounting rate of return
(c) The net present value at a discount rate of 19 per cent. Use the discount factors provided in question 1.

Answers to self-test questions

(1)

(a) Since the profits are stated before depreciation charges, they can be taken as cash flow figures.

Cumulative cash flow after two years = £[(220,000)
+90,000
+85,000]
= £(45,000)

Payback will occur during year 3

Payback period = 2 years + (45,000/70,000 × 1 year)
= 2.6 years

Assuming even cash flows during year 3 the payback period is 2.6 years.

(b)

Year		Cash flows £	15% discount factor	Present value £
0		(220,000)	1.00	(220,000)
1		90,000	0.87	78,300
2		85,000	0.76	64,600
3		70,000	0.66	46,200
4 (£65,000 + £20,000 resale)		85,000	0.57	48,450
Net present value				17,550

(c) The NPV at 15 per cent is a fairly large positive figure, therefore try 20 per cent first. If this is a negative result then progressively reduce the discount rate until an NPV close to zero is reached.

Year	Cash flows £'000	20% factor	Present value at 20% £'000	19% factor	Present value at 19% £'000	18% factor	Present value at 18% £'000
0	(220)	1.00	(220.0)	1.00	(220.0)	1.00	(220.0)
1	90	0.83	74.7	0.84	75.6	0.85	76.5
2	85	0.69	58.7	0.71	60.4	0.72	61.2
3	70	0.58	40.6	0.59	41.3	0.61	42.7
4	85	0.48	40.8	0.50	42.5	0.52	44.2
Net present value			(5.2)		(0.2)		4.6

The internal rate of return is approximately 19 per cent.

(d) Average investment $= \dfrac{\text{Cost of coaches + resale value}}{2}$

$= \dfrac{£220,000 + £20,000}{2}$

$= £120,000$

	£'000
Total profit over life of machine:	
before depreciation (90 + 85 + 70 + 65)	310
depreciation (220 − 20)	(200)
total accounting profit	110
Average annual accounting profit (110/4)	27.5

Accounting rate of return = (27.5/120) × 100% = 22.9%

(2) Since the running costs exclude depreciation they can be taken as cash flows for the purpose of the analysis.

Year	Initial investment	Revenue	Costs	Safety check	Total cash flow	Discount factor	Present value
	£'000	£'000	£'000	£'000	£'000		£'000
0	(100)				(100)	1.00	(100.00)
1		65	(13)		52	0.85	44.20
2		52	(13)	(15)	24	0.73	17.52
3		40	(13)		27	0.62	16.74
4		40	(13)		27	0.53	14.31
5		38	(13)		25	0.46	11.50
							4.27

Net present value

Cumulative cash flow after two years = £[(100,000)
$$+52,000$$
$$+24,000]$$
$$= £(24,000)$$

Payback will occur during year 3

Payback period = 2 years + (24,000/27,000 × 1 year)
= 2.9 years

Assuming even cash flows during year 3 the payback period is 2.9 years.

The proposed investment produces a small positive net present value and thus is worthwhile from a financial point of view. The payback period is close to three years. The acceptability of this depends on management's policy concerning a maximum payback period.

(3) Annual depreciation = £(40,000 − 12,000)/4 years = £7,000

Year	Accounting profit	Add back depreciation	Sale of machine	Cash flow	Discount factor	Present value
	£	£	£	£		£
0				(40,000)	1.00	(40,000)
1	13,800	7,000		20,800	0.84	17,472
2	12,200	7,000		19,200	0.71	13,632
3	10,400	7,000		17,400	0.59	10,266
4	9,500	7,000	12,000	28,500	0.50	14,250
						15,620

Net present value

Cumulative cash flow after two years = £[(40,000)

$$+20,800$$
$$+19,200]$$
$$= £0$$

Therefore the payback period is two years

$$\text{Average investment} = \frac{\text{Cost of machine} + \text{resale value}}{2}$$

$$= \frac{£40,000 + £12,000}{2}$$

$$= £26,000$$

	£
Total profit over life of machine	
£(13,800 + 12,200 + 10,400 + 9,500)	45,900
Average annual accounting profit (£45,900/4)	11,475

Accounting rate of return = (£11,475/£26,000)
$$\times\ 100\%$$
$$= 44\%$$

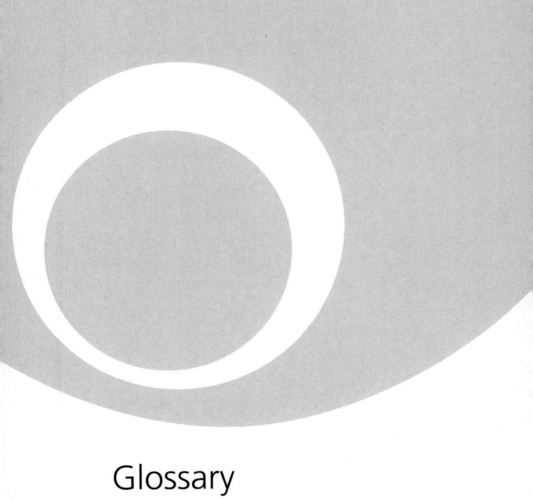

Glossary

Introduction

This glossary contains the main financial terms that might be encountered by the non-specialist. The definitions and descriptions are taken from the 2005 edition of *Official Terminology* published by the Chartered Institute of Management Accountants (CIMA), which contains a more extensive terminology. These extracts are reproduced by permission of the publishers.

Absorbed overhead Overhead attached to products or services by means of an absorption rate or rates.

Under- or over-absorbed overhead

The difference between overhead incurred and overhead absorbed, using an estimated rate, in a given period. If overhead absorbed is less than that incurred there is under-absorption. If overhead absorbed is more than that incurred there is over-absorption. Over- and under-absorption are treated as period cost adjustments.

Activity-based costing (ABC) Approach to the costing and monitoring of activities which involves tracing resource consumption and costing final outputs. Resources are assigned to activities and activities to cost objects, based on consumption estimates. The latter utilise cost drivers to attach activity costs to outputs.

Amortisation Systematic allocation of the depreciable amount of an asset over its useful life (IAS 36). Normally applied to intangible assets.

Asset Resource controlled by the entity as a result of past events and from which future economic benefits are expected to flow to the entity (IAS 38).

Audit Systematic examination of the activities and status of an entity, based primarily on investigation and analysis of its systems, controls and records.

Avoidable cost Specific cost of an activity or sector of a business that would be avoided if the activity or sector did not exist.

Breakeven chart Chart that indicates approximate profit or loss at different levels of sales volume within a limited range.

Breakeven point   Level of activity at which there is neither profit nor loss. It can be ascertained by using a breakeven chart or by calculation.

Budget   Quantitative expression of a plan for a defined period of time. It may include planned sales volumes and revenues; resource quantities, costs and expenses; assets, liabilities and cash flows.

Budget centre   Section of an entity for which control may be exercised through prepared budgets. It is often a responsibility centre where the manager has authority over, and responsibility for, defined costs and (possibly) revenues.

Budget cost allowance   Calculated after an accounting period, the cost allowance reflects the actual level of output achieved. Variable costs are flexed in proportion to volume achieved, and fixed costs are based on the annual budget.

Budget flexing   Flexing variable costs from original budgeted levels to the allowances permitted for actual volume achieved while maintaining fixed costs at original budget levels. (Variable cost allowance = Ratio of actual volume achieved to budgeted volume × original budget variable cost).

Budget period   Period for which a budget is prepared and used, which may then be subdivided into control periods.

Budget slack   Intentional overestimation of expenses and/or under-estimation of revenue during budget setting. Also known as budget padding.

Budgetary control   Master budget, devolved to responsibility centres, allows continuous monitoring of actual results versus budget either to secure by individual action the budget objectives or to provide a basis for budget revision.

Capital employed   Investment in an entity. In assessing managers it is usually calculated as total assets less current liabilities.

Capital expenditure   Costs incurred in acquiring, producing or enhancing non-current assets (both tangible and intangible). *See* Revenue expenditure.

Capitalisation   Recognising a cost as part of the cost of an asset (IAS 23). The asset will be included in the balance sheet as a non-current asset.

Carrying amount   Amount at which an asset is recognised in the balance sheet after deducting any accumulated depreciation (or amortisation) and accumulated impairment losses thereon (IAS 36).

Cash equivalents   Short-term, highly liquid investments that are readily convertible to known amounts of cash and which are subject to insignificant risk of changes in value (IAS 7).

Contribution   Sales value less variable cost of sales. Contribution may be expressed as total contribution, contribution per unit or as a percentage of sales.

Cost behaviour   Variability of input costs with activity undertaken. Cost may increase proportionately with increasing activity (the usual assumption for a variable cost), or it may not change with increased activity (a fixed cost). Some costs (semi-variable) may have both variable and fixed elements. Other behaviour is possible, for example, costs may increase more or less than in direct proportion, and there may be step changes in cost. To a large extent cost behaviour will be dependent on the timescale assumed.

Cost driver   Factor influencing the level of cost. Often used in the context of ABC to denote the factor which links activity resource consumption to product outputs, for example the number of purchase orders would be a cost driver for procurement costs.

Cost of sales   The cost of goods sold during an accounting period. For a retail business this will be the cost of goods available for sale (opening stock plus purchases) minus closing stock. For a manufacturing business it will include all direct and indirect production costs.

Cost pool   Grouping of costs relating to a particular activity in an activity-based costing system.

Cost–volume–profit analysis (CVP)   Study of the effects on future profit of changes in fixed cost, variable cost, sales price, quantity and mix.

Creditor   *See* Payables.

Current asset   Asset which satisfies any of the following criteria:

    (a)   It is expected to be realised in, or is intended for sale or consumption in, the entity's normal operating cycle.

    (b)   It is held primarily for the purpose of being traded.

    (c)   It is expected to be realised within 12 months of the balance sheet date

    (d)   It is cash or cash equivalent (IAS 1).

Current liability   Liability which satisfies any of the following criteria:

    (a)   It is expected to be settled in the entity's normal operating cycle.

    (b)   It is held primarily for the purpose of being traded.

    (c)   It is due to be settled within 12 months of the balance sheet date.

All other liabilities are classified as non-current (IAS 1).

Debtor   *See* Receivables.

Depreciation   Systematic allocation of the depreciable amount of an asset over its useful life (IAS 16). Normally applied to tangible assets. *See* Amortisation.

Differential/incremental cost   Difference in total cost between alternatives. This is calculated to assist decision making.

Direct cost   Expenditure that can be attributed to a specific cost unit, for example material that forms part of the product.

Discounted cash flow   Discounting of the projected net cash flows of a capital project to ascertain its return or present value.

Discretionary cost   Cost whose amount within a time period is determined by a decision taken by the appropriate budget holder. Marketing, research and training are generally regarded as discretionary costs. Also known as *managed* or *policy* costs.

Dividend   Distribution of profits to the holders of equity instruments in proportion to their holdings of a particular class of capital (IAS 18).

Equity Residual interest in the assets of the entity after deducting all its liabilities (IASB Framework). It is comprised of share capital, retained earnings and other reserves of a single entity, plus minority interests in a group, representing the investment made in the entity by its owners. *See* Net assets.

Exceptional items Material items which derive from events or transactions that should be disclosed in the notes to the financial statements by virtue of their size or incidence in relation to the income statement.

Fair value Amount for which an asset could be exchanged, or a liability settled, between knowledgeable and willing parties in an arm's length transaction (IAS 2).

Fair value less costs to sell Amount obtainable from the sale of an asset (or cash generating unit) in an arm's length transaction between knowledgeable and willing parties, less the direct costs of disposal (IAS 36).

Feedback control Measurement of differences between planned outputs and actual outputs achieved, and the modification of subsequent action and/or plans to achieve future required results. Feedback control is an integral part of budgetary control and standard costing systems.

Feedforward control Forecasting of differences between actual and planned outcomes, and the implementation of action, before the event, to avoid such differences.

Financial accounting Classification and recording of the monetary transactions of an entity in accordance with established concepts, principles, accounting standards and legal requirements and their presentation, by means of income statements, balance sheets and cash flow statements, during and at the end of an accounting period.

Financial gearing/leverage Amount of debt, in relation to equity, in the capital structure of an entity or debt interest in relation to profit. An entity with no gearing has no debt.

First-in, first-out (FIFO) *See* Stock (inventory) valuation.

Fixed asset *See* Non-current asset.

Fixed budget Budget set prior to the control period, and not subsequently changed in response to changes in activity, costs or revenues. It may serve as a benchmark in performance evaluation.

Fixed cost Cost incurred for an accounting period that, within certain output or turnover limits, tends to be unaffected by fluctuations in the levels of activity (output or turnover).

Flexible budget *See* Budget flexing

Gearing *See* Financial gearing and Operational gearing.

Goal congruence In a control system, the state which leads the individuals or groups to take actions which are in their self-interest and also in the best interest of the entity. Goal incongruence exists when the interests of individuals or of groups associated with an entity are not in harmony.

Goodwill

Acquired	Future economic benefits arising from assets that are not capable of being individually identified and separately recognised.
Positive goodwill	Excess of the purchase consideration over the fair value of the identifiable net assets acquired.
Negative goodwill	Excess of the fair value of the identifiable net assets acquired over the purchase consideration.
Internally generated	An entity's own view of its value above its recorded value which cannot be recognised in financial statements prepared in accordance with accounting standards.

Group A parent and all its subsidiaries (IAS 27).

Impairment Reduction in the carrying value of a non-current asset where its recoverable amount (the higher of fair value less costs to sell and value in use) is less than its existing carrying amount.

Incremental budgeting Method of budgeting based on the previous budget or actual results, adjusting for known changes and inflation, for example.

Incremental/differential cost Difference in total cost between alternatives. This is calculated to assist decision making.

Indirect cost/overhead Expenditure on labour, materials or services that cannot be economically identified with a specific saleable cost unit. The synonymous term *burden* is in common use in the US and in subsidiaries of American companies.

Intangible asset Identifiable non-monetary asset without physical substance which must be controlled by the entity as the result of past events and from which the entity expects a flow of future economic benefits (refer to IAS 38).

Internal rate of return Annual percentage return achieved by a project, at which the sum of the discounted cash inflows over the life of the project is equal to the sum of the discounted cash outflows.

Inventories Assets held for sale in the ordinary course of business in the process of production for such a sale or in the form of materials or supplies to be consumed in the production process or in the rendering of services (IAS 2). Synonym for stock.

Leverage *See* Financial gearing and Operational gearing.

Liquid assets Cash, cash equivalents and other assets readily convertible into cash, for example short-term investments.

Management accounting Management accounting is the application of the principles of accounting and financial management to create, protect, preserve and increase value for the stakeholders of for-profit and not-for-profit enterprises in the public and private sectors. Management accounting is an integral part of management. It requires the identification, generation, presentation, interpretation and use of relevant information to:

◆ inform strategic decisions and formulate business strategy;
◆ plan long-, medium- and short-run operations;
◆ determine capital structure and fund that structure;
◆ design reward strategies for executives and shareholders;

- ◆ inform operational decisions;
- ◆ control operations and ensure the efficient use of resources;
- ◆ measure and report financial and non-financial performance to management and other stakeholders;
- ◆ safeguard tangible and intangible assets;
- ◆ implement corporate governance procedures, risk management and internal controls.

Management by exception   Practice of concentrating on activities that require attention and ignoring those which appear to be conforming to expectations. Typically, standard cost variances or variances from budget are used to identify those activities that require attention.

Marginal cost   Part of the cost of one unit of product or service that would be avoided if the unit were not produced, or that would increase if one extra unit were produced.

Master budget   Consolidates all subsidiary budgets and is normally comprised of the budgeted profit and loss account, balance sheet and cash flow statement.

Minority interest   Portion of the profit or loss (income statement) and net assets (balance sheet) of a subsidiary attributable to equity interests that are not owned, directly or indirectly, by the parent (IFRS 3).

Net assets   Excess of the carrying amount of assets over liabilities. Equivalent to net worth or equity.

Net book value   *See* Carrying amount.

Net present value   Difference between the sum of the projected discounted cash inflows and outflows attributable to a capital investment or other long-term project.

Net realisable value (NRV)   *See* Fair value less costs to sell.

Net worth   *See* Net assets.

Non-current asset   Any asset that does not meet the definition of a current asset (IFRS 5). Tangible or intangible asset, acquired for retention by an entity for the purpose of providing a service to the entity and not held for resale in the normal course of trading. Previously known as a fixed asset.

Operational gearing   Relationship of fixed cost to total cost of an operating unit. The greater the proportion of total costs that are fixed (high operational gearing), the greater is the advantage to the organisation of increasing sales volume. Conversely, should sales volume drop, a highly geared organisation would find the high proportion of fixed costs to be a major problem, possibly causing a rapid swing from profitability into loss. Gearing may also be referred to as leverage.

Opportunity cost   The value of the benefit sacrificed when one course of action is chosen in preference to an alternative. The opportunity cost is represented by the forgone potential benefit from the best rejected course of action.

Overhead absorption rate   A means of attributing overhead to a product or service based, for example, on direct labour hours, direct labour cost or machine hours.

Overhead/indirect cost   Expenditure on labour, materials or services that cannot be economically identified with a specific saleable cost unit. The synonymous term *burden* is in common use in the US and in subsidiaries of American companies.

Overtrading   The condition of an entity which enters into commitments in excess of its available short-term resources. This can arise even if an entity is trading profitably and is typically caused by financing strains imposed by a lengthy operating cycle or production cycle. Undercapitalised new businesses are prone to suffer from overtrading.

Payables   Person, or an entity, to whom money is owed as a consequence of the receipt of goods or services in advance of payment, known as trade payables in International Accounting Standards.

Payback   Time required for the cash inflows from a capital investment project to equal the cash outflows.

Present value   Cash equivalent now of a sum receivable or payable at a future date.

Prime cost   Total cost of direct material, direct labour and direct expenses.

Principal budget factor Factor which limits the activities of an undertaking. Identification of the principal budget factor is often the starting point in the budget-setting process. Often the principal budget factor will be sales demand but it could be production capacity or material supply.

Product cost Cost of a finished product built up from its cost elements.

Production cost Prime cost plus absorbed production overhead.

Receivables Monetary amount owed by a person or organisation to the entity as a consequence of the sale of goods or services, known as trade receivables in International Accounting Standards.

Relevant costs/revenues Costs and revenues appropriate to a specific management decision. These are represented by future cash flows whose magnitude will vary depending upon the outcome of the management decision made. If stock is used, the relevant cost used in the determination of the profitability of the transaction would be the cost of replacing the stock, not its original purchase price, which is a sunk cost.

Relevant range Activity levels within which assumptions about cost behaviour in breakeven analysis remain valid.

Reserves Retained profits or surpluses. In a not-for-profit entity they are described as accumulated funds.

Revenue expenditure Expenditure on the manufacture of goods, the provision of services or on the general conduct of the entity which is charged to the income statement in the period the expenditure is incurred. This will include charges for depreciation and impairment of non-current assets as distinct from the cost of the assets. *See* Capital expenditure.

Semi-variable cost Cost containing both fixed and variable components and thus partly affected by a change in the level of activity.

Stock (goods) *See* Inventories.

Stock (inventory) valuation

Average cost

Used to price issues of goods or materials at the weighted average cost of all units held.

First-in, first-out (FIFO)

Used to price issues of goods or materials based on the cost of the oldest units held, irrespective of the sequence in which the actual issue of units held takes place. Closing stock is, therefore, valued at the cost of the oldest purchases.

Last-in, first-out (LIFO)

Used to price issues of goods or materials based on the cost of the most recently received units. Cost of sales in the income statement is, therefore, valued at the cost of the most recent purchases. LIFO is permitted under US GAAP but is not permitted by IAS 2.

Strategic plan Statement of long-term goals along with a definition of the strategies and policies which will ensure achievement of these goals.

Sunk cost Cost that has been irreversibly incurred or committed and cannot therefore be considered relevant to a decision. Sunk costs may also be termed *irrecoverable costs*.

Variable cost Cost that varies with a measure of activity.

Working capital Capital available for conducting the day-to-day operations of an entity, normally the excess of current assets over current liabilities.

Zero-based budgeting Method of budgeting that requires all costs to be specifically justified by the benefits expected.

Index